HUNGARY

PAUL LENDVAI

Hungary

Between Democracy and Authoritarianism

Translated by
Keith Chester

HURST & COMPANY, LONDON

First published in 2010 as *Mein verspieltes Land: Ungarn im Umbruch*
© Ecowin Verlag, Salzburg

First published in the United Kingdom in 2012 by
C. Hurst & Co. (Publishers) Ltd.,
41 Great Russell Street, London, WC1B 3PL
This translation © Keith Chester, 2012
(Chapter 14 was written in English by Paul Lendvai)
All rights reserved.
Printed in the United Kingdom.

The right of Paul Lendvai to be identified as the author of this publication is asserted by him in accordance with the Copyright, Designs and Patents Act, 1988.

A Cataloguing-in-Publication data record for this book is available from the British Library.

ISBN: 978-1849041966

This book is printed using paper from registered sustainable and managed sources.

The translation from German to English was supported by the Austrian Federal Ministry for Science and Research

www.hurstblog.co.uk
www.hurstpub.co.uk

CONTENTS

1. A Funeral as the End and the Beginning — 1
2. A Half-Hearted Change — 7
3. József Antall—A Political Phenomenon — 29
4. The Roots of Hungarian Anti-Semitism — 53
5. Gyula Horn and the Return of the Post-Communists — 67
6. The Young Comet—Viktor Orbán — 85
7. The Medgyessy Puzzle or the End of a Deception — 99
8. The Sense of Mission of an Easily Seducible Nation — 113
9. The Splendour and Decline of Ferenc Gyurcsány — 131
10. The Power of the Discreet Press Barons — 147
11. Cold War at the Top—Orbán Versus Gyurcsány — 167
12. The Roma and Jews—Targets of the Extreme Right — 179
13. The Political Suicide of the Left — 195
14. Orbán *Über Alles*—Hungary at a Dead End — 207

Notes — 233
Index — 251

1

A FUNERAL AS THE END AND THE BEGINNING

'History is the realm of the true lie'.

Antal Szerb

Heroes' Square in Budapest is not only by far the largest square in the Hungarian capital. It is also the dream of historical greatness manifested in stone, a unique monument to national glory and the romantic celebration of the nation's history. Here, on 16 June 1989, a warm early summer's day, before a gathering of 250,000 people, at a ceremony of the profoundest symbolism, a communist regime was laid to rest and the future course of the country set irrevocably on the path to democracy.

Just for its location alone, this square of the national memory is very impressive. It is situated at the entrance of the Városliget, Budapest's famous City Park, and at the end of

Andrássy Avenue, the widest street in the capital and somewhat reminiscent of the Champs-Élysées. In the middle of the square stands a 36-metre-high column erected to mark the 1896 celebrations of the thousand-year anniversary of the Magyar conquest of Hungary. The whole is topped off by an approximately five-metre-high figure of the archangel Gabriel carrying in one hand the Hungarian crown and in the other the apostolic double cross.

The Millennium Memorial itself, with its semi-circular colonnades and statues commemorating fourteen kings and heroes from Hungarian history, was however completed only in 1929. Two buildings dating from the years before the turn of the century and designed in the classical style of the *Gründerzeit* (the 19th-century 'founding years' in Germany and Austria)—to the right the Palace of Art, and to the left the Museum of Fine Arts—complete the architectural unity of Heroes' Square.

'*Temetni tudunk*' is a terse but oft-quoted Hungarian saying, which roughly translates as 'Burying people is something we know all about', or, put differently, 'We know how to hold funerals'. That held on 16 June 1989 was monumentally staged. The velvety black catafalque towered over the six Corinthian columns draped in black flags. Above, on the steps, lay five coffins with the remains of the martyrs who, at a secret trial thirty-one years previously, had been condemned to death and immediately executed: Prime Minister Imre Nagy and his four companions in misfortune. A sixth, empty coffin symbolised the 300 freedom fighters executed after the crushing of the uprising of October and November 1956 by the communist regime.

The border between remembering and forgetting is always difficult to define. In Hungary, the consolidation of the Kádár regime after the bloody suppression of the 1956 revolution by

A FUNERAL AS THE END AND THE BEGINNING

the Soviet army[1] meant a 'condemnation of memory'. Anything that recalled those days, at once triumphant and tragic, was frowned upon. But now at this memorable funeral service for Imre Nagy, after more than 30 years of collective amnesia, the falsified, marginalised and forgotten history of 1956 suddenly re-emerged as a glorious but defeated revolution; and it was under this augury that the surviving actors made their appearance on the stage of history.

It was not the nominally still ruling Communist Party that determined the celebrations on this particular day, but rather the members of the Committee on Historical Justice formed the previous year. From 9 o'clock onwards people came from all directions and streamed past the coffins near the Palace of Arts, laying their flowers and wreaths. At 1.30 church bells rang out across the country, factory whistles wailed and motorists blew their horns. The nation came to a standstill and with a minute of silence remembered the executed leaders of the revolution. After the national anthem had been sung and some lines from one of Nagy's speeches read out, five former '56ers', some of whom had been incarcerated for many years, spoke very personally, obviously moved deeply by the occasion.

But the political change that this ceremony was also supposed to represent was provided by an unknown young man, Viktor Orbán. One of the founders of Fidesz, the Alliance of Young Democrats, the bearded 26-year-old spoke last in the name of the coming generation. His anti-communist speech, formulated with extraordinary sharpness by the standards of the time, and his demands for democracy, independence and the withdrawal of Soviet troops made him famous overnight, not only in Hungary but also abroad. Even in retrospect, the epoch-making character of his courageous and politically rebellious words, which shattered the political conventions of the time, has to be acknowledged.

The entire rally on Heroes' Square was broadcast live on Hungarian TV, as was the subsequent interment of Nagy and his companions in plot 301 in the same cemetery where hitherto they had been buried in an unmarked mass grave. The Hungarian essayist Péter György has rightly hailed the 16th of June 1989 as the first example of the TV revolution in Central Europe. In a stimulating study he expresses the opinion that without the Orbán speech, which jettisoned all current taboos, 16 June would probably not have marked such an historic turning point. Orbán's star rapidly ascended and within a mere nine years he had become the now clean shaven Prime Minister of Hungary.

In spite of the somewhat risky, even aggressive, character of the speech of the representative of the younger generation, the funeral was a peaceful event. A mood of grief, but also an ominous determination never again to let hard-won freedoms go, hung over the unforgettable scene. The ambivalence of the doomed ruling party, which had already split into warring factions, was reflected in the composition of the guard of honour for the coffins. This included family and friends of the martyrs and members of the democratic opposition, as well as those party officials who, though all too recently on the opposite side of the political divide, had managed to make a timely switch: Miklós Németh had evolved from a conventional *apparatchik* into an increasingly independent Prime Minister and later, in September 1989, would be one of those responsible for the historic opening of the border for the refugees from East Germany; Péter Medgyessy, Deputy Prime Minister and member of the Central Committee of the Communist Party, would 13 years

A FUNERAL AS THE END AND THE BEGINNING

later be appointed head of government as the victorious 'independent' candidate of the Socialists; and Mátyás Szűrös had, as secretary of the Central Committee, been a top-ranking party official but had shortly before been shunted off into the politically meaningless post of president of the Parliament.

The sole exception amongst these people was represented by the Minister of State Imre Pozsgay. As a member of the Politburo of the Communist Party he had been the first politician in the Kádár administration to have the courage to publicly describe (in January 1989) the events of the autumn of 1956 not as a 'counterrevolution' but as a 'popular uprising'. Unlike many who had turned their backs on the old regime as it headed for oblivion, Pozsgay, at that time the Hungarian politician best known in the West, acted early out of inner conviction. As we shall see, in the following months and years the varied and occasionally turbulent history of this man and others who contributed to the collapse of the communist system reflected the precipitous about-turns of domestic politics.

And what of János Kádár, the man who had been, between his adroit changing of sides in November 1956 and his loss of power in May 1988, the all-powerful intermediary of the Kremlin? Seriously ill and now reduced to honorary party president, he had appeared unexpectedly and without prior notice at a meeting of the Central Committee in April 1989 where he delivered an utterly confused speech in which he made indirect reference to his responsibility for the execution of Nagy. Dramatists and authors, biographers and psychologists have all since picked over the words and hints of this disturbed old man, the stuff of a Shakespearean drama.

On the day of the funeral, the 77-year-old Kádár sat in his house on the Rózsadomb, home to Budapest's political and

5

business elite, and without mentioning by name Imre Nagy, the comrade he had betrayed and delivered to the gallows, asked his wife and the nurses present 'Is that man being buried today?' Three weeks later, on 6 July 1989, János Kádár died. It was to be a deeply symbolic day, for that very morning the Supreme Court had officially rehabilitated Imre Nagy and his companions.

And yet, despite the historic burden that weighed heavily on Kádár, more than 60,000 people filed past his coffin in just 24 hours when he was laid out in the entrance hall of the then party headquarters. Moreover, in poll after poll taken in Hungary since 1989 the betrayer and murderer of Imre Nagy is remembered as a jovial father of the nation and the 'hallmark of a golden era'. At the end of the 1990s 42 per cent of those polled deemed Kádár to be 'the most likeable [Hungarian] politician of the twentieth century', and to this day he remains at the top of any ranking of historical personalities of the century.

This subsequent romanticising of the Kádár regime may in part be a reaction to the huge new problems that have emerged since 1989. But the 'system change lite' in Hungary is inseparable from the style with which the Communist Party wielded power and ruled, from the policy of 'little freedoms' and the concessions in day-to-day life which were part and parcel of the Kádár line, and which, taken together, gave rise to the description, popular in the Western media at the time, of Hungary as the 'the happiest barrack in the Socialist camp'. The ambivalence in the judgement on the former dictator is the key to an understanding of the tendency, so pronounced in Hungary, of seeking refuge in the past.

2

A HALF-HEARTED CHANGE

Initially as a foreign correspondent and subsequently as a television commentator for the Austrian Broadcasting Corporation I was in the unique position of being able to observe from Vienna—both as an outsider and, thanks to my knowledge of the language, as an insider—the fascinating process of the change to the political system in Hungary. It was at best a half-hearted change, and has remained so. In the witty but ironical observation of my friend and colleague Adam Michnik in Warsaw, the East Europeans were trying to convert an East German Wartburg car into a Mercedes, and, as if this weren't enough, we were doing it while actually driving the new car. How was it possible to rebuild everything within a system with people who had lived for two generations under a dictatorship? Only by seeing it that way can we begin to understand the apparent contradiction of what the Hungarian political scientist Ferenc Mislivetz observed in 2007, that as far as the institutions and the political system of Hungary were concerned, Hungary might well be a democracy—but a democracy without democrats.

What actually happened in the much-lauded *annus mirabilis* of 1989 in Hungary, in the country that had witnessed the greatest popular uprising in post-war Europe? Unlike what happened in the other Eastern Bloc countries, the system change did not emerge from a political coup or dramatic revolutionary events. In stark contrast to the first heady days of the apparently victorious uprising in the autumn of 1956, there was no feeling among the people of a moral renewal or a strong desire for a reckoning with the dignitaries of the old regime. Not a single top official or head of the various secret services was ever held to account.

The character and the significance of events in the course of the increasing polarisation of domestic politics of the last two decades have all become fiercely disputed. The vocabulary and the battle lines between the respective protagonists have over time become confusing to foreign observers because of the abrupt changes of position by the individual political groups. Indeed if, like Rip Van Winkle, somebody had slept through the twenty years of radical change after 1989, he would hardly be able to recognise any of the main political actors or organisations of today.

The once bearded young revolutionary Viktor Orbán is today the leader of a large clerical, staunchly nationalistic and right-wing conservative party, which after its decisive election victory in April 2010 claims that, as the dominant political force, it can govern Hungary as it wishes and without any strong opposition for the next 15 to 20 years. The totally crushed Socialists, in their time the political heirs of the Leninist ruling party, were and indeed still are accused of opening

A HALF-HEARTED CHANGE

the floodgates to foreign capital and selling out the country to global capitalism without any consideration of the working people. The liberal Alliance of Free Democrats (Szabad Demokraták Szövetsége or SzDSz), once one of the noisiest anti-communist parties and in 1990 the second strongest in the land, formed on several occasions over a 12-year period government coalitions with both the ex-communists themselves and the very Socialists who had fought the SzDSz spokespersons tooth and nail in 1989–90. Following internal splits the Liberals practically disintegrated in 2009 and even the centre-right Hungarian Democratic Forum (Magyar Demokrata Fórum or MDF), once the most powerful middle class party in the country, has shrunk to a minuscule size. The rightwing extremist Jobbik group, which has risen meteorically, seems to be a completely new force, but its origins are firmly rooted in Hungarian twentieth-century history.

Everything that took place before and after the radical change of the system in 1989 was in a deeper sense a reflection of the historic experience of 1956.[1] Despite it being the strongest challenge yet to the Soviet empire in Eastern Europe, the decisive meaning of that spontaneous and unexpected popular uprising (23 October to 4 November 1956) was its demonstration of the reality that the peoples of Central Europe could not fundamentally alter the status quo (that is, Soviet hegemony) without outside help.

From the 1960s, however, Hungary was considered a touchstone for how much freedom a communist system could grant and tolerate without dramatic and radical changes, and without provoking a Soviet intervention. The merciless crushing of the opposition and the for long total Soviet backing of the Kádár regime, the profound disappointment at the West

9

which—just as in 1849 and 1945—had abandoned the small country to its fate, and the general widespread apathy conspired together to provide the Communists with both the time and opportunity, as well as the necessary room for manoeuvre, first to neutralise and later to win over important elite groups with material concessions.

The refined tactic of carrot and stick bore fruit relatively quickly. In the decade after the October uprising real wages per capita rose by 47 per cent. The peripheral concessions that were granted (the chance of pursuing a career without party membership, greater permissiveness in cultural life and the reduction of daily harassments to a minimum) eased life for the average citizen considerably. Satisfying the desire for greater prosperity and for somewhat more freedom gradually led to a process of consolidation and normalisation, one that nobody could have dared to expect in 1956. The opportunity to travel to the West, repeatedly extended and psychologically of enormous importance, contributed much—in marked contrast to the other Eastern Bloc countries—to the acceptance and growing popularity of the regime.

In the 1970s and 1980s there emerged a new type of Hungarian, the successful petty bourgeois whom the political scientist László Lengyel has called 'Homo Kádáricus' by comparison with 'Homo Sovieticus'. In his analysis this new man lived in the state economy, but at the same time also in the private parallel economy, profiting in both town and country from this ancillary income. In the 'heyday of mature Kádárism' public and private life were divided by the maxim 'We up here play politics—you down there, live'. This tacit *modus vivendi*, in which both the Communist Party and the people were equally

A HALF-HEARTED CHANGE

aware of what was possible and what was not, permitted a Hungarian variety of communism.

The most important event of the 1980s—economically, psychologically and politically—was the move of the regime to allow the establishment of small firms with up to 30 employees; this was followed by economic co-operatives within enterprises (accounting for approximately 10 per cent of all industrial workers), which after normal working hours could work on their own account. Including the private plots within the collective farms, an estimated 17 to 19 per cent of national income was being produced in this so-called second economy as early as 1985.

This great change in society sparked off a passionate debate about the rich and the poor. A literary magazine described the secret of the Hungarian 'economic miracle' as follows: 'In the first shift, your main job, you save your energy for the second shift, your extra job, which is when you earn the money with which, in your third shift, you can build your house'. A sociologist formulated it thus: 'You can't live from your wages, but you can make a lot of money from your second job'. And as always in Hungary the contradiction was quickly summed up in a joke: 'What is communism? The longest route from capitalism to capitalism'.

It should however be remembered that, despite all the clichés about a 'communist wonderland' common in much of the Western media at the time (the phrase is taken from the title of a book on Hungary published by the German news magazine *Der Spiegel* in the summer of 1983), these changes for the better took place within what remained a communist system. Throughout Kádár's rule there were three fundamental taboos which nobody was allowed to question: the one-party system

HUNGARY

(the dictatorship of the Party); the loyalty of the alliance with the Soviet Union (foreign rule); and the appraisal of the uprising of 1956 as a counterrevolution (the legitimacy of the reprisals, including the Nagy trial). The long and twisted journey of János Kádár (1912–89) took him from executioner and gaoler to 'father of the nation' and 'good monarch' during the 32 years of the regime inextricably associated with his name. With hindsight, and irrespective of his now well-documented evil role behind the scenes in the judicial murders of his former comrades-in-arms László Rajk (1949) and Imre Nagy (1958), we cannot ignore the enormous political significance of his personality. In his public appearances the former typewriter mechanic and lifelong *apparatchik* always distinguished himself from other top communist politicians. Thanks to the intervention of Bruno Kreisky, first as foreign minister and later as Chancellor of Austria, I was able to experience this at first hand on two separate occasions, once in 1964 and then in 1981.

At a Congress of the Patriotic People's Front in Budapest in 1964, I witnessed Kádár giving an impromptu speech, full of ordinary, everyday language. He swore, conjured up the breach with the Stalinist past, chatted with and admonished his audience, poked fun at them and recounted anecdotes. With his own almost puritanical lifestyle, his personal modesty and sense of humour, he was able to win over broad swathes of the population to be favourably disposed towards the regime. The highly respected national poet Gyula Illyés told me in an television interview in the spring of 1981 that Kádár had succeeded in gaining the trust of the people by his 'matter-of-factness, his modesty and his achievements'. Unlike other Eastern Bloc leaders, Kádár tolerated no personality cult. There were never any pictures of him hanging in public buildings, nor were images of him ever carried, as a type of monstrance, in ceremonial parades. He was, as a Hungarian political scientist has noted, 'a dictator without personal dictatorial tendencies'.

For 32 years, with inimitable tactical skill, subtly, cynically and when necessary brutally, Kádár removed his potential rivals; he satisfied the Kremlin's Hungarian 'moles' in order then to oust them all the quicker; he promoted and defended the most important reformers in order to expose them, without a moment's hesitation and under pressure from Moscow, as pawns. Yet, through his political successes, Kádár managed to keep his merciless side concealed and forgotten. Through Chancellor Kreisky, I met him in November 1981 for a TV interview for an Austrian TV documentary on Hungary. Kádár was then at the height of his popularity and could easily afford to grant a lengthy exclusive interview to an exiled Hungarian journalist. Something similar would have been unthinkable in any other communist country at that time.

At the end of the interview, after a number of questions on politics, I made an allusion to the slight difference in age between him and Kreisky, who was also visiting Budapest then. Kádár was pensive and animated in equal measure. He had never given much thought to the question of age. 'When I work, then I have no time, and if I don't work, then I don't want to think about it ... People tell me, "Stay healthy, we need you" ... That's all I can say about the question of age. There's a lot of work to be done and I am far more concerned about work than with the passing of time'. That he still pushed aside the question of age at the 1985 party congress, and even later as a 75-year-old, undoubtedly contributed to the memorable circumstances of his fall. For what Paul Valéry once wrote about the exercise of power was also valid for the venerable and increasingly ailing

Kádár: every ruler knows how fragile the authority of rulers is, except when it comes to his own authority.

What then were the reasons for the fall of Kádár and ultimately for the peaceful collapse of Kádárism, of the system upon which he indelibly stamped his mark? The domestic political crisis that triggered off the collapse arose from the severe economic crisis and the rapidly mounting massive foreign debts. As early as 1982 the economy was, as the secretary for economic affairs on the Central Committee, Ferenc Havasi, freely confessed, in a 'clinically dead condition'; insolvency could only be staved off by loans from the IMF. As a consequence of the increase in both output and wages (in a small country largely devoid of natural resources) forced through by Kádár despite the warnings of economic experts, the net convertible debt soared between 1984 and 1987 from $8.8 billion to $17.7 billion. The acute economic crisis increasingly undermined faith in the system, the basis of the legitimacy of the settlement between the ruling party and the people: the consumer-oriented policies and the freedom of travel to the West had awoken expectations which the regime could not satisfy.

The standard of living was compared more and more with that in the West and less and less with that pertaining before the 1956 uprising. Between 1978 and 1988 real wages fell by 17 per cent. This in turn led to dissatisfaction among large sections of the population and to resentment at the widening gap between pensioners, those on low incomes and the *nouveaux riches*. On the dark side of the last decade of Kádárism also lay alcoholism (Hungary had the highest consumption of spirits in the world), the highest suicide rate in the world, growing crime rates and drug addiction, as well as declining life expectancy. It is against this background that the slow and then rapidly accelerating erosion of the consensus between the circles around Kádár and the public at large, between the Communist Party and the people, which was also a consequence of a generational change (40 per cent of Hungarians were under 30 years old), must be understood.

With this mixture of miscalculation, hesitation and passivity, Kádár, who considered himself to be both unassailable and indispensable, lost at one and the same time the trust of the people and the backing of the Kremlin. *Beszélő*, a magazine printed and distributed underground to the active, though numerically small democratic opposition since the late 1970s, pronounced the bitter truth as early as June 1987: 'Just as the country had once identified the successes of the era with János Kádár, so now it does the fiasco that marks the end of that era. The popularity of the party leader is falling faster than the forint. There is one thing everybody, from worker to party cadre, is agreed upon: Kádár must go!' Once again the people of Budapest reacted to the deteriorating economic situation with a joke: 'Why doesn't Kádár retire from politics?' 'I also can't understand it'. 'It's quite simple. He wants to wait so long until he can hand over the country in same condition as when he took it over in November 1956'.

Mikhail Gorbachev's accession to power in Moscow in 1985 was crucial. That very autumn he advised Kádár, twenty years his senior, to find a 'worthy successor'. In view of the changes in the political landscape in the Kremlin, well understood by the Hungarian public, Kádár no longer appeared to be the guarantor of stability, but rather a brake on progress. The waning of his authority, obvious to all through his catastrophic appearances on television, opened the way to the settling of internal party conflicts by a putsch of the apparatus against János Kádár and his closest supporters. Yet the changing of the guard at an extraordinary party conference in May 1988 only took place after a direct intervention from Moscow. The head of the KGB, Vladimir Kryuchkov, who spoke fluent Hungarian and had been Third Secretary at the Soviet embassy in Hungary in 1956 during the October uprising, was sent secretly to Budapest two days before the decisive party meeting in order to persuade Kádár, whom he knew well, to retire 'with dignity' before it was too late.[2]

The man of the moment was the professional functionary Károly Grósz (1930–96), whom Kádár had promoted to Prime Minister in June 1987. Skilful mobilisation of the party apparatus set in motion a political earthquake at the party conference. Kádár, it is true, became party president, but the members of his immediate circle were purged; a third of the Central Committee was removed and the Politburo almost completely renewed. However, the advent of the reformers, among them Imre Pozsgay and Miklós Németh, merely marked the prelude to the struggle for the top leadership and, ultimately, for the political survival of Kádár's heirs. As general secretary of the Communist Party, which at that time still had more than 830,000 members, and as a very active prime minister, Grósz appeared to have concentrated extraordinary power in his hands. Just four weeks after his election as party leader I had a three-hour interview ranging over his career and political priorities with the new strong man who shortly before had been a barely known party secretary.[3]

The day before our meeting in his magnificent prime minister's office I witnessed in the centre of Budapest an unauthorised demonstration of civil rights activists commemorating the

A HALF-HEARTED CHANGE

30th anniversary of the execution of Imre Nagy. I saw how special police units with raised batons drove off the approximately 400 peaceful demonstrators. This scene served as an unexpected and at the same time deeply symbolic start to my interview with Kádár's successor. When I related to him what I had seen, Grósz, whose manner had initially been very amicable, reacted very sharply, brusquely rejecting any criticism of the police. His reply to my direct question as to whether he could imagine the rehabilitation of Imre Nagy or a radical reevaluation of 1956 came like a bullet out of a gun. 'No! We reject any rehabilitation of Nagy. And as far as 1956 is concerned, if we should accept it as something like a revolution, then we would be the counterrevolutionaries. No, there is absolutely no question of these things'.

Again and again Grósz emphasised his readiness for a political opening up, but also warned that things would not be allowed to slip out of control. The refulgent showman, who exuded unbridled energy and native cunning, rarely evaded a direct answer. But he left no doubt that the party, under his leadership, only intended to rescue and renew the one-party system by concessions, but not in any way to undermine or destroy it.

Károly Grósz was a sly old fox, an intriguer, but he lacked vision and was not a strong leader. At our subsequent meetings (in the late autumn of 1988 and in May 1989) he no longer seemed to be in the driving seat but a passenger. Not mincing his words, the embattled leader of a party now clearly in irreversible decline conceded that he had underestimated the three most important factors: the extent of the problems which had accumulated over the previous decade, the intensification of the economic crisis, and what he called the 'subjective side', the

17

lack of 'personal and political unity in the uppermost reaches of the leadership'.

Grósz squandered his authority and power in barely a year, a momentous time during which the government led since November 1988 by the young economic expert Miklós Németh threw off the shackles of party control, new political groups were formed and 'real existing Socialism' collapsed throughout the Eastern Bloc. With bad grace he was forced to accept the advance of the reformers in the party, the approval of the multi-party system, the public appearance of opposition groups and the calling of an extraordinary party conference as stations on the road to the peaceful change of regime.

That the national question, a strict taboo during the communist dictatorship, would have a central political meaning for the future of the country was shown in a huge demonstration of 80,000 to 100,000 people at Heroes' Square on 27 June 1988. Though organised by opposition groups, it was officially authorised and was intended as a protest against the plans of the Ceauşescu regime to raze villages to the ground and the implied suppression of the large Hungarian minority in Romania. There were already almost 30,000 refugees from Transylvania in Hungary. Incidentally, the fact that Károly Grósz as party chief and head of the government first actually accepted, at the height of tensions in the middle of August, Nicolae Ceauşescu's invitation to a meeting in Arad and then cut a poor figure there proved in retrospect to be the beginning of the end of his relatively short leadership role. His dramatic warnings made during a TV appearance (and subsequently withdrawn) of an 'economic state of emergency' and his demagogic evocation of the dangers of a 'White Terror'[4] fell flat. His tumble from grace was as quick as his rise. After a glitter-

A HALF-HEARTED CHANGE

ing start, which owed much to his manipulation, Grósz turned out to be a transitional figure, quickly and even more quickly forgotten.

In the process of the Party's disintegration, and the transition from late-Kádárism to the soft system change, in the decisive period between 1987 and 1989, the main role was without doubt played by Imre Pozsgay, who was three years younger than Grósz. After a long career in the party machine in the provinces, this talented man was promoted to government in 1975, first as secretary of state and a year later as a minister for Culture and Education. Both in this function and after his demotion to the politically meaningless post of general secretary of the Patriotic People's Front in 1982 Pozsgay forged close contacts primarily with nationalistic writers and intellectuals.

Pozsgay's moment came in September 1987. In his capacity as general secretary of the Front he gave the welcoming address at a meeting of 181 predominantly nationalistic intellectuals in Lakitelek near the town of Kecskemét. His appearance there and his subsequent arranging of the publication of a communiqué in the daily newspaper of the People's Front, together with an interview in which he hailed the gathering as a constructive contribution to the dialogue with the Party, were a challenge to Kádár and his line. Pozsgay was admonished by the leadership because of the publication of the manifesto, but not removed from office. After the successful putsch in May 1988, he was promoted to the Politburo and later became a minister of state in the Németh government.

Imre Pozsgay, with whom I conducted several extensive interviews during this period, was at that time the first leading Communist Party official who would openly speak with Western correspondents about the fate of the almost three million Hun-

19

ans in the 'fraternal countries' of Romania and Czechoslovakia, as well as in the Yugoslav province of Vojvodina and in Soviet Ukraine.[5] He never made any secret of his conviction that the ruling party would have to find a consensus with the public on the great questions of the past and present. His audacious leap into the unknown in acknowledging the Hungarian October as a popular uprising, and the rehabilitation of Imre Nagy and his executed comrades (see Chapter 1), not only won him recognition at home and abroad. Pozsgay was also instrumental, together with the already independent Prime Minister Miklós Németh and the new foreign minister Gyula Horn, in the decisions on the removal of the 243km-long Hungarian Iron Curtain and the opening of the border with Austria for tens of thousands of East German citizens on 11 September 1989.

In this phase of the gradual dissolution of communism, Pozsgay had several irons in the fire. His ever closer contacts with the nationalist intellectuals who had in the meantime organised themselves into the Hungarian Democratic Forum (Magyar Demokrata Fórum or MDF) did not prevent him from continuing his efforts to conquer the power base of the Communist Party primarily from within, but also from without by founding so-called reform circles. In addition he was the patron and president of a newly formed Movement for a Democratic Hungary. In a radio interview given on 28 January 1989 when the party leader Grósz was out of the country attending the annual World Economic Forum meeting at Davos, Pozsgay openly attacked the edifice of lies that had been constructed around the 'counterrevolution' of 1956. His move to destroy the very ideological basis of the regime and to acknowledge the events of that year as an uprising appeared to many as foolhardy but was in fact a courageous challenge to the majority in the party leadership. This camp consisted initially of the silent orthodox party functionaries who proclaimed their loyalty to 'Kádárism without Kádár' and were open to the idea of reform only from within the system.

The fourth and ultimately decisive group comprised the reform economists and those original supporters of 'socialist pluralism' (subsequently renamed 'democratic socialism') who were prepared to push the boundaries of the institutional framework of the system. The minutes of the Central Committee meetings of 1989 (over 1,950 pages long and first published in two volumes in 1993) provide us with a graphic picture of the initially rather cautious but then ever more open war of words.

Additionally, we have the minutes and interviews cited by two of the best authorities on the collapse of the communist regime in Hungary, the left-wing political scientist Zoltán Ripp and the American contemporary historian Rudolf L. Tőkés, who is Hungarian by birth.[6] These are supplemented by the impressions I gained during numerous discussions and interviews with the leading figures during this exciting transitional period. As all my talks both then and in the course of the following two decades were conducted in Hungarian, without the filter of a translator or a minder, I was able to observe very closely the choice of words and reactions of my interlocutors.

In Hungary, just as before in Poland, developments led to the formation of a round table to inaugurate the negotiations between the opposition and the ruling party. Despite the apparent parallels there were, however, enormous differences. In Hungary the Catholic Church was not a self-confident, let alone a mediating force between the Party and a strong independent trade union leadership advised by outstanding intellectuals. The struggle for change was thus played out in Budapest primarily within the communist power elite. The times were totally bizarre. In February the Central Committee in all seriousness voted, for example, on whether a new party badge should be introduced (only one in four was in favour ...), a vote that took precedence over the historic decision on the establishment of a multi-party system. And when it came to the struggle for jobs, there was no question of principles, just of power and sinecures. After Gorbachev had frankly told Prime Minister Németh in March 1989 that the Kremlin would oppose neither the multi-party system nor the introduction of private property in Hungary, there began an all-out struggle for power in the Communist Party without even a modicum of solidarity.

The unstoppable strengthening of the opposition was primarily due to the increasingly evident disintegration of the ruling party and the upheavals shattering the Eastern Bloc, from the success of the round table and the opposition victory in Poland to the collapse of the dictatorships in East Germany and Czechoslovakia, in Bulgaria and Romania. In contrast to the violent clashes and mass protests elsewhere in the Soviet empire, the relationship between those in power and the opposition in Hungary was characterised on both sides by self-restraint and a willingness to communicate.

Against the background of the indelible memory of the October tragedy and the hopes of the 1956 uprising that had been crushed by Soviet tanks, the monopoly power of the ruling party was not questioned. To the very end everybody in politics strove for gradual reform and an orderly change of power. The right-wing extremists of today and the left-wing critics of the soft transition to parliamentary democracy all forget the fact that at the time 70,000 Soviet troops with almost 1,000 tanks, 1,500 armoured vehicles, 622 pieces of artillery and 196 rocket batteries were 'provisionally' stationed on Hungarian soil (and would remain so until the winding-up of the Warsaw Pact in 1991); also easily overlooked is the reality that the party controlled, in addition to the intact, immense apparatus of the secret service, the armed units of the so-called Workers' Guards.

New political parties and groupings sprang up like mushrooms. By the end of 1988 there were already 21 diverse groups in existence, and 12 months later this number had tripled to 60. The strongest party by far, and nationwide the best organised, was the MDF. The nationalist-populist intellectuals who had founded it were, despite previous occasional bans on the publications of their figureheads (for example the poet Sándor Csoóri and the playwright István Csurka), considered by Pozsgay and later by other influential Communist Party functionaries to be people with whom they could do business; in time they become close partners. For this reason they were, unlike other opposition groups, financially supported.

In contrast to the ever cautious nationalist-conservative groups, the activists of the democratic opposition courageously and openly stood up for human rights, for the rehabilitation of the victims of the post-1956 repression, and for radical reforms. Among their ranks were protagonists of the October uprising (for example Imre Mécs, an engineer whose death sentence had been commuted to life imprisonment) and intellectuals who had served long prison sentences such as Miklós Vásárhelyi, the poet István Eörsi and Árpád Göncz, who was to be twice elected State President. Their magazine *Beszélő* (first published as a badly printed *samizdat* in 1981 with only a tiny circulation) and their petitions of solidarity with the Czechoslovak and Polish opposition reached, thanks to the Hungarian language programmes broadcast on various shortwave radio stations (above all Radio Free Europe in Munich),[7] wide circles of the intellectual and government elite, and slowly mobilised them. This was also true of the statements of the partly nationalistic group opposed (partly on ecological grounds) to the Hungarian-Czechoslovak joint project for a hydro-electric power station at Gabčíkovo on the river Danube. And it was even more valid for their response to the anti-minority resettlement plans of the Romanian dictator.

The Alliance of Free Democrats (SzDSz), founded in November 1988 with the philosopher János Kis as its intellectual mastermind, maintained the tradition of the democratic opposition. The SzDSz was, together with the Alliance of Young Democrats (Fidesz), which set a maximum age of 35 for its members, the spearhead of the anti-communist opposition. Of all the groups and organisations which emerged in this period only two re-founded pre-war parties survived the momentous year of 1989: the Smallholders' Party and the Christian-Democratic Peoples' Party. The revived Social Democratic Party vanished after a few months on account of irreconcilable disputes.

The split leadership of the ruling party wanted to slow down and control the now seemingly inevitable transition to free elections, playing off the still weak and inexperienced opposition groups against each other. In spite of their jealousies, their political and personal differences of opinion, the new parties and alternative groups established an opposition round table on 23 March 1989 to commence negotiations on the modalities of the change of system with the ruling communists (officially known as the Hungarian Socialist Workers' Party,

A HALF-HEARTED CHANGE

Magyar Szocialista Munkáspárt or MSzMP). This round table was merely a short-term marriage of convenience. Unlike that in Poland, the Hungarian opposition never had an umbrella organisation such as Solidarność.

After wearisome preliminary talks the official negotiations within the framework of a national roundtable were formally opened in parliament on 13 June. As a face-saving concession to the ruling party the opposition previously accepted the participation in the round table of the loyal associations and institutions which had served to legitimise the one-party rule of the MSzMP as a 'third side'; they were not, however, granted any right of veto.

In all, 1,302 delegates and consultants, divided into 15 commissions and working groups, took part in no fewer than 238 separate meetings. The basic document was to be ceremonially signed in parliament on 18 September 1989 in front of TV cameras. The delegates agreed on constitutional changes and the creation of a constitutional court, as well as modifications to the penal code; additionally, they regulated the position of parties and the election of MPs. But then a political bomb exploded: the radical parties, the SzDSz and Fidesz, as well as the League of Free Trade Unionists—albeit without exercising a veto—refused to sign the document. Their spokespersons announced that the two parties wanted to hold a referendum on those questions still unresolved: the ban on party posts in the workplace, the dissolution of the workers' militia combat groups, the disclosure of the assets of the ruling party, and the postponement of the presidential election until after the parliamentary elections.

The reform communists were in disagreement on the first three points, above all on the proposed ban on party organisa-

25

tion in the workplace, but the real question of political power concerned the function and person of a directly elected head of state. Imre Pozsgay was the undisputed candidate of the ruling party and in view of his standing and his high profile seemed almost assured of victory. Therefore he, and indirectly his party, would be able to shape the new political landscape before the first democratic elections due to be held in March 1990.

An open row broke out in the camp of the opposition, which in public remained united but in reality was already deeply split. Although the self-liquidation of the ruling party was becoming all too apparent, the relationship between the opposition and those in power, even at this phase, constituted the main fault line. It was widely assumed (and, as we shall see, not without reason) that there was a secret agreement on the future distribution of power between Pozsgay and the MDF leadership—that is, with its new party boss József Antall. The SzDSz and Fidesz quickly gathered and presented to the election commission more than 100,000 signatures, thereby forcing a referendum for the end of November.

The actual burial of the Communist Party took place on 7 October 1989 in the middle of the campaign for the referendum; on the same day its direct successor, the Hungarian Socialist Party (Magyar Szocialista Párt or MSzP), was founded. Nyers, Pozsgay, Németh and Horn formed the leadership core in the newly elected Presidium. Rezső Nyers was the president, Németh remained Prime Minister and Pozsgay the presidential candidate. (Grósz had opposed the founding of a new party.) The hopes of the reform communists, who had triggered the dissolution of the old organisation, were nonetheless very soon dashed. At the time of its demise in October, the

A HALF-HEARTED CHANGE

MSzMP still had 725,000 members, of whom, after the congress, only a mere 5 per cent were prepared to join the new Socialist Party.

To the disappointment of his supporters Pozsgay had missed the right moment for the break with the old party. He seemed exhausted and disoriented. Perhaps he had secretly realised that his time was rapidly running out. In his book about the 'negotiated revolution' in Hungary Tőkés writes: 'If Pozsgay had split the party at the congress and pulled out with his supporters, then he would have won the referendum by a large majority'.

In the referendum 95 per cent of voters approved the first three proposals (a ban on party cells in the workplace, dissolution of the armed workers' militias, and disclosure of party assets). However, on the fourth point, the timing of the presidential election (that is, before or after the parliamentary election) only a paper-thin majority (50.07 per cent, or a mere 6,101 votes more than required) backed the initiative of the SzDSz and Fidesz. Foreign observers were disappointed that only 58 per cent of the electorate actually bothered to turn out. The referendum was, however, valid and it was without doubt a politically significant defeat for the Socialists, who had called upon voters to cast a 'no' vote in all four cases. The MDF, very much on the defensive and suspected of having made a deal with the communists, also suffered a setback, particularly since the speakers of the Forum had called for a boycott of the referendum.

The real loser was, however, Imre Pozsgay, who at a press conference the day after the vote abandoned any hope of his becoming the first Hungarian head of state freely elected by the people. In the subsequent March elections a crushing defeat in the constituency of Sopron swept him off the political stage.

After quitting the party in the autumn of 1990 and after a vain attempt to form a political splinter group, Pozsgay, briefly Hungary's most popular politician in the crucial years of change, faded into oblivion.

3

JÓZSEF ANTALL—A POLITICAL PHENOMENON

In the autumn of 1989 a new star shot into Hungary's political firmament. On 28 October at the national conference of delegates of the MDF (Hungarian Democratic Forum) József Antall, a virtually unknown museum director, won 97 per cent of the votes and was elected chairman of a party (and hence its top candidate in the forthcoming elections) which he had only joined a mere six months previously. Then a miracle took place. The 57-year-old medical historian, whose name was then known only to one Hungarian in three, won a landslide election victory in the spring of 1990. Until his premature death in December 1993, Antall presided over the country as an internationally respected prime minister at the head of coalition with an absolute majority during the transition to democracy, a market economy and independence.

Who was Antall? How did he achieve this political miracle? How is his term in office judged today and what remains of his legacy?

I had no inkling of his future when in the spring of 1989 I met him in Budapest for the first time on the fringes of a meeting of the Colorado-based Aspen Institute, at a reception in the residence of the indefatigable American Ambassador, Mark Palmer. We had a short but intensive exchange about the turmoil in Hungarian politics and the possibilities for Western influence. He was, as always, elegantly but not conspicuously dressed. He gave me his visiting card, beautifully embossed with all his titles in Latin, English and Hungarian; it was undoubtedly the most distinguished of any circulating in Budapest at the time. But then, everything about the general director of the Semmelweis Museum of the History of Medicine in Budapest and the vice-president of the International Society for the History of Medicine was distinguished. Not only did Antall come from the pre-communist upper class, but he also embodied it in his entire behaviour, in his clothes and manners, and, when all is said and done, in his attitudes towards his opponents, partners, favourites and public opinion.

His father was government commissioner for refugees during the Second World War and in this capacity assisted tens of thousands of Polish, Jewish and other refugees. For this he was imprisoned by the Gestapo for several months after the German occupation of Hungary in March 1944. After the war, Antall's father received many distinguished foreign honours for his anti-fascist activities. He was a minister in the coalition government formed in 1945 representing the Smallholders' Party, and even after the communist seizure of power remained until 1953 (formally) a member of the parliament which had already been brought strictly into line. During the October 1956 uprising and for some time after its crushing by the Soviets, Antall's spacious apartment in the heart of Budapest was an important meeting place for the politically active anti-communists from the middle classes and petty nobility.

As a student the young Antall took part in the 1956 uprising; the following March he was arrested. Through his contacts with various senior party officials, his father was able to secure his quick release after five days. When, some years later, József Antall was banned from working as a secondary school teacher of history on account of his upright bearing and his 'damaging influence' on the pupils, Antall senior was able to find a place for his son in the Museum of the History of Medicine. Here, thanks not least to his close friendship with Emil Schultheisz, the museum's director (and later Minister of Health), József Antall rapidly rose to the rank of a deputy director. Despite the fact he was not a member of the Party, on his 50th birthday he was awarded one of the highest honours of the regime, the Golden Order of Merit for Labour. In 1984 József Antall was promoted to general director of the museum.

Since the age of 16 Antall had prepared himself for a political career; as he grew older, he even began to groom himself for the office of prime minister. In his personal library he assembled a collection of three to four thousand books on history and politics. Before his friends and relatives, sometimes alone in front of his wife, he gave impromptu short presentations on foreign policy. After 1974 Antall was allowed to travel to the West where he was able to cultivate contacts with influential friends and acquaintances from his student days who had emigrated. He spoke fluent German and could express himself on specialist topics in French.

HUNGARY

As chair of the Hungarian and vice-president of the International Society for the History of Medicine, as well as editor-in-chief of its journal, József Antall, like so many other members of the petty nobility and middle-class elite, was certainly no longer being persecuted; on the contrary, he was a beneficiary of the soft line approach of the Kádár regime. Even if they had declared themselves prepared to accept the immutable realities, Antall and his friends were convinced anti-communists. Not for a moment would they have any truck with the vision of a socialist society, however much it might change its character.

Yet the appearance of the smooth professional success was deceptive. It was no accident that Antall kept himself politically inconspicuous, even during the inexorable disintegration of late Kádárism.[1] From the reports of no fewer than 24 agents over the years (amongst them two of his friends), the reader gains the impression of a profoundly cautious man, deeply mistrustful of the opposition critical of the regime. At the time of the Prague Spring, he protested in identically worded personal letters addressed to Kádár himself, to the Prime Minister and to the Minister of the Interior about the secret police's blatant tailing of his person. He received no reply but the irksome tailing ceased. In subsequent years Antall never signed any of the protest letters of civil rights activists, and even in the last two years of the communist regime, by which time the risk was minimal, he never took part in any meetings or demonstrations. He was not invited by the nationalist writers and intellectuals to the legendary conference with Imre Pozsgay held at Lakitelek in September 1987. His name was not even mentioned in the first Political Yearbook issued in the spring of 1989.

Antall initially had contacts with groups which at the turn of 1988 wanted to relaunch the pre-war parties such as the

JÓZSEF ANTALL—A POLITICAL PHENOMENON

Smallholders or the Christian Democrats. However, in February 1989 he became a member of the Hungarian Democratic Forum (MDF) although, according to his closest friends, he still remained extremely cautious and uncertain. At the first national congress of the MDF in March, Antall gave a poor speech and was not even elected to the party Presidium. At the opening of the national round table between the opposition and the ruling party, he was still only sitting in the second row.

The leading personalities of the MDF remained aloof from the seemingly long-winded consultations. But Antall immediately understood the growing importance of this political workshop for the change of regime. With his extensive knowledge of history and foreign policy, his evident tactical skills, his great intelligence and brilliant interventions, he began to dominate its deliberations. In his biography of Antall, József Debreczeni tellingly observes that *'the system change would have happened without him. But it would have been very different. In the ranks of the opposition there was not one single comparable personality'* (italics in the original).

It was against this background of opaque intrigues swirling around the ultimately failed presidential candidature of Pozsgay, the representative of the post-communists, that on 21 October Antall, a man barely known to the members of the Presidium and who hitherto had had no close contact with the nationalistic-minded intellectuals, was elected chair of the MDF with 97 per cent of the vote, thereby becoming the top candidate for the first free parliamentary elections.

In the late autumn of 1989, after his first great political success, I was able to persuade Antall to grant me an exclusive interview. The French quarterly magazine *Politique Internationale*, which mainly published extensive interviews with lead-

33

ing personalities from world politics, accepted my proposal and requested me to interview Antall, who was already being regarded as the most promising candidate for the post of the first democratically elected prime minister. In order to ensure absolute privacy, we met in my hotel room in Budapest's Castle District. Our discussion lasted several hours. His profound knowledge of contemporary history and international developments, as well as his great intelligence, impressed me very much that evening.

Antall spoke freely and at ease with himself. In polished sentences, larded with quotations taken from memory, he explained to me at length his view of the world and above all the political line of his party, the MDF, which comprised a mixture of Christian, traditional national and liberal elements. The recorded interview, conducted in Hungarian, was first transcribed, translated into French and corrected by my French colleagues at Radio Österreich International. It was then printed, albeit in a much shortened version, in the next edition of *Politique Internationale*. Antall thanked me in a personal letter for this first extended account of his political philosophy in a respected foreign publication.

In our talk, just as in almost all his interviews at this time, Antall emphasised the importance of the ideas of the German economist Wilhelm Röpke (1899–1966) on the social market economy (which Röpke also called 'the third way') for his own intellectual and political development. The Hungarian politician greatly admired this system as well as the post-war achievements of Chancellor Konrad Adenauer and the father of the German economic miracle, Ludwig Erhard. He described himself thus: 'I am a nationally committed, liberal Christian Democrat who believes in a unified Europe. If we omit just one of these elements, then the whole definition becomes incorrect'.

JÓZSEF ANTALL—A POLITICAL PHENOMENON

In spite of, or perhaps just simply because of the election campaign, which was already under way, Antall undertook an ambitious programme of foreign visits and established personal contacts with US President George Bush Senior, France's President Jacques Chirac, Britain's Prime Minister Margaret Thatcher, and above all the German Chancellor, Helmut Kohl. On a number of occasions he came to Vienna where he met in particular the Austrian Deputy Chancellor and head of the Austrian People's Party (ÖVP), Alois Mock. It is not an exaggeration to state that no other Central or Eastern European politician, except for the special case of Václav Havel, was so quickly and so widely recognised in the West as József Antall. In this turbulent period of political upheaval, he also participated in an international conference aboard a ship on the Danube organised by the ÖVP in Vienna, together with other leading Christian Democrat and conservative politicians from Czechoslovakia, Slovenia, Croatia, the GDR and Romania. In conjunction with this, I chaired a discussion on Club 2, a late-night talk show on Austrian television, on 11 January 1990. Here too, Antall came over supremely well, exuding self confidence.

It was, naturally, almost entirely due to him that the MDF as a conservative-nationalist-Christian 'force of inspiring confidence' was able to convincingly defeat its main opponents, the liberal Free Democrats (SzDSz), in the ensuing elections. Three factors determined the rather surprising results.

The post-communists had been badly damaged by the failed Pozsgay candidature as had, to a lesser degree, the MDF. Then a bombshell exploded on the political scene in the first week of January. A high-ranking secret service officer revealed that the internal counter-espionage service of the Ministry of the Interior had continued unhindered to bug and carry out surveillance on opposition politicians. The long-serving minister, a close friend of Pozsgay, together with two deputies, was forced out. The scandal was quickly dubbed Dunagate in Budapest. Almost at the same time, however, Pozsgay, a man under considerable pressure, succeeded in suddenly replacing Endre Aczél, the highly respected chief editor on Hungarian television responsible for the most important news and news magazine programmes, with a close nationalist ally. Of this, Antall's biographer, Debreczeni, wrote: 'I am convinced that without this manoeuvre, the SzDSz would have won the election'.

Twelve of the then 65 registered parties were permitted to take part in the elections, but only six were able to jump over the required 4 per cent hurdle in the first round. Nationwide the MDF led with 25 per cent, followed by the SzDSz with 21 per cent. The Smallholders won 12 per cent of the votes, the post-communist MSzP 11 per cent, Fidesz 9 per cent and the Christian Democratic People's Party (KDNP) just under 6 per cent. Two weeks later, in the second decisive round in 176 individual constituencies, the MDF picked up support from the two other right-wing parties. In the final result, of the 386 seats contested, the MDF gained 164 (42 per cent), the SzDSz 94 (22.4 per cent), the Smallholders 44 (11 per cent), the MSzP 33 (9 per cent), Fidesz 22 (5 per cent) and the Christian Democrats 21 (5 per cent).

Nonetheless, the turnout in the first truly free elections was disappointing: in the first round only 65 per cent and in the second a meagre 45.5 per cent. In the struggle for power the fault line lay not—as might have been expected—between the opposition and the post-communist MSsP, but more and more between the MDF with its conservative, nationalist roots and the sharply anti-communist and apparently radical moderniser, the SzDSz. The coalition government with the Smallholders and the Christian Democrats which Antall sought to form would have a comfortable, working majority of 60 per cent in the new parliament. But even before the new government could be put together, the prime minister designate was endeavouring in secret negotiations to conclude a pact with the largest opposition party, the SzDSz. This was intended to strengthen his own position in exchange for political concessions.

If we assume that, in the words of the German sociologist Ronald Hitzler, there are 'in politics, in this game for power, no rules, save that of you and your ideas prevailing', then it can be safely said that József Antall will go down as one of the most talented politicians and accomplished tacticians in Hungarian history. The pact with the SzDSz, concluded in the greatest of secrecy in only three weeks, was according to his biographer Antall's 'supreme achievement'. What had happened?

The two parties agreed on strengthening the position of the head of government. Following the German pattern, he could only be toppled by means of a 'constructive vote of no confidence', that is, only when his opponents could muster the support of more than 50 per cent of MPs for their proposal; and even in this case they would have to simultaneously nominate the next prime minister. Moreover, parliament should only vote on the head of government; the members of the cabinet would be nominated by the president on the basis of a list of names proposed by the prime minister. Furthermore, the number of those laws requiring a two-thirds majority was to be drastically reduced in order to guarantee the government a reasonable scope for manoeuvre.

Finally, the head of state, contrary to a law passed by the old (communist dominated) parliament, should be elected by MPs (as was the wish of the Free Democrats) and not directly by the people. In addition, Antall declared himself, in the name of the MDF, to be willing to concede the presidency to the SzDSz and to accept as a common candidate for this post the opposition's nominee, the writer and translator Árpád Göncz.

Antall did not inform the Presidium of his own party, the MDF, about these negotiations, nor did he seek its approval. In this politically crucial question Antall acted entirely on his own, presenting his colleagues in the party leadership with a *fait accompli*. 'It was as if an international grand master was playing chess with a lacklustre amateur; he had absolutely no need to make any recourse to deception, but just relied on his own knowledge and superiority' (Debreczeni). Of course the two future coalition partners of the MDF were not let in on the secret negotiations either.

The anger of the partly nationalistic founding fathers of the MDF was immense. But the cool newcomer gave the inner leadership of his party an ultimatum: the agreement with the Free Democrats would have to be approved, or else there would be no coalition, no functioning politics in parliament, in other words, no government. 'He behaved incorrectly and blackmailed us over and over again: "If you don't like what I'm doing, then I'll resign"' was how Zoltán Biró, the former acting head of the MDF, summed it up. Shortly afterwards he and Pozsgay founded their own new party, which quickly failed.[2] The consequences in the subsequent struggles for power in the MDF confirmed the sardonic conclusion of the German critic Ludwig Börne (1786–1837): 'The secret of power lies in the knowledge that others are more cowardly than we are'.

In accordance with the MDF-SzDSz pact, Árpád Göncz, then 68 years old, was elected in May 1990 first as leader of the

Parliament, then as provisional Head of State and finally in August (by 295 votes to 13 against) as State President for a period of five years. Yet within a few months, Antall's idea of having Göncz elected president proved to be, from his point of view, a grave blunder. Antall had known Göncz, 11 years his senior, from the time of the 1945–48 coalition as a committed middle-class politician from the Smallholders' Party and had not reckoned on the jovial man of letters turning out to be an independently minded president. Antall had miscalculated, and within two months the estrangement between the two was evident to all and sundry.

From the very beginning there was a yawning gap between the international reputation of the government (and above all of Prime Minister Antall), on the one hand, and the rapidly deteriorating mood among the people and the fall in the government's popularity on the other. The dissolution of the Warsaw Pact and COMECON, as well as the withdrawal of Soviet troops, inaugurated for Hungarian foreign policy a historic epoch of full sovereignty and freedom of action. Antall's government laid down three basic objectives: joining as quickly as possible the European and Atlantic organisations, active participation in the regional organisations now freed of Soviet influence, and support and promotion for Hungarian minorities in the neighbouring countries.

It was in connection with the latter that Antall, who had otherwise acted rather cautiously on the global stage, uttered at the third national congress of the MDF on 3 June 1990 his most famous and internationally most controversial words. 'As Prime Minister of this country of 10 million, I would like to be in my heart and soul Prime Minister of 15 million Hungarians'. This declaration, which was much criticised and discussed at the time, outraged government circles in Romania, Slovakia and Serbia. Among the representatives of the Hungarian minorities in those countries it provoked mixed reactions, whilst in Hungary itself it led to passionate debate. That the Magyars in the successor states of the Habsburg Monarchy require political and cultural support both for the promotion and protection of their interests against the nationalists of their host states was and is indisputable. However, I am also in retrospect convinced that under the conditions of the general opening up in Central and Eastern Europe at that juncture the Hungarian Prime Minister committed a serious political error and unintentionally gave a boost to anti-Hungarian chauvinistic forces in some neighbouring countries.

Shortly afterwards in October, under dramatic circumstances, the inexorable decline of the Antall government began. People had expected a rapid economic upturn and naïvely had hoped only for benefits from the change of regime and the first freely elected government. Antall undoubtedly contributed to this economically unjustified optimism. One week after the elections he remarked that Hungary could be a member of the European Union within two to five years and could achieve average European levels of development within ten years. In the meantime the realities of mass redundancies and price increases were contributing to the deterioration of public sentiment and the unpopularity of the governing coalition.

In the two rounds of local elections held in October 1990, the coalition suffered an unexpectedly large defeat. Two weeks later an overnight 65 per cent hike in petrol prices, which had been preceded by repeated government denials, precipitated a strike and street blockades by taxi drivers and private haulage companies. Transport throughout the country ground to a halt. As a result of the failure of the Minister of the Interior, who was clearly out of his depth in coping with the situation, events threatened to slip out of control. It only added to the drama of the confrontation that the SzDSz supported the taxi drivers whilst the State President pleaded for negotiations, rejecting any use of force and unmistakably distancing himself from the government's position. Eventually the government retreated and reduced the price increase.

At the height of tensions the Prime Minister was, following a difficult operation, in a deep sleep and was only able to defuse the situation at the very end of the negotiations in a television interview he was forced to give in his pyjamas in hospital. Only then did the public learn that Antall had been fighting cancer for some months. It is not known when he himself first became aware of his illness. It was incurable and the necessary treatment was begun too late by the doctors. Antall now began to spend frequent and increasingly lengthy stays in hospital, followed by periods of convalescence (especially from 1992). The question remains open of how far life lived at the limits, often against medical advice, influenced his political decisions.

At any rate it is clear that for a long time Antall continued to look prime ministerial: dressed in a discreet elegance, with well-proportioned features, a clear look, silver-grey hair neatly parted, and an assured demeanour. His dominant position in the government was unassailable. He exploited the head start his parents' home and education had endowed upon him over the political newcomers in his government. The ambitious and elitist Antall brought to his office the talents, experience and attributes which virtually recommended him to the tasks of a prime minister.

Antall's Interior Minister of many years and successor as head of government, Péter Boross, characterised him thus:

I saw an utterly self-confident man who became so naturally Hungary's prime minister that it almost seemed to be a miracle ... He had no doubt that he was holding the office of prime minister, and that he could and would fulfil this role. His beginning had been very impressive, and he influenced the members of the cabinet to an extraordinary extent ... He enjoyed an enormous advantage over them. He appeared out of nowhere as a genuine prime minister and acted as one.[3]

Even such harsh critics as the political analyst and economist László Lengyel conceded that 'he was fully suited to the role of prime minister of the system change ... When he entered a room, there was no question that he was the head of government of Hungary'. Nevertheless, he adds: 'Nothing could be decided without Antall, but there was no professional state apparatus to prepare and execute decisions. Antall did not have a team'. Secretary of State József Kajdi, an admirer and loyal employee in the prime minister's office, who witnessed everything at close quarters, spoke of 'overwhelming concepts' in foreign and educational policy. But Antall was 'almost indifferent about economic, financial and similar issues', not daring 'to decide anything nor to entrust decisions to anybody else'.

It seems reasonable to assume that no government could have managed the change of system without fundamentally undermining full employment, as well as excessive wages and salaries, both artificially maintained by enormous foreign debts. It is of course very easy in retrospect to reproach Antall for not first having declared insolvency on account of the ruin of the inherited system, and for not having promised his people 'blood, sweat and tears' until some sort of stabilisation had been achieved.

Hungarian society was simply not prepared for the unexpected and enormous burdens thrust upon it. To give just a few

JÓZSEF ANTALL—A POLITICAL PHENOMENON

examples: GDP shrank by 20 per cent between 1988 and 1993, falling by 12 per cent in 1991 alone; real wages declined by 4 per cent in 1990 and 8 per cent in 1991; the rate of inflation was 35 per cent in 1991, 23 per cent in 1992, and only in 1993 did it drop under 20 per cent; consumption decreased by 11 per cent; unemployment, hitherto unknown in the country, reached at times 12 per cent; thousands of enterprises were closed and half-a-million jobs disappeared.

All too soon a bitter joke was making the rounds in Budapest. 'Antall did in two years what Kádár couldn't in 30: he made socialism popular!'

Polls showed the popularity of the Prime Minister plummeting from 67 per cent in 1990 to 47 per cent in 1991; it fell further to 41 per cent in 1992 and finally to 36 per cent in 1993. In contrast to President Árpád Göncz, who remained popular until the end of his two terms in office, public opinion held Antall, who was so revered in the West, to be overbearing, aloof and elitist. For his part, the Prime Minister complained bitterly in his family circle (according to his son György Antall) that

> the people regarded the withdrawal of the Russians, the restoration of independence and national sovereignty, political freedom, democracy with indifference ... He knew that the 'socialist petty bourgeois' who did not care about anything apart from his immediate material interests had been born in the decades of the Kádár regime and had become the determining factor in society ... He knew that, but nevertheless it saddened him, the moral condition of his country, of his people.[4]

It was not the incompetence of Antall's government in itself but the fallout from the bursting of the balloon inherited from the Kádár regime that precipitated the difficult transition crisis. Nevertheless, some details from József Debreczeni's extraordinarily positive 1998 biography, and even more Eszter Rádai's interviews with Antall's three finance ministers, give rise to justified doubts about his suitability either as his country's supreme crisis manager or as a resolute head of government.[5] Apart from those few cabinet ministers who belonged to his network of family and friends, Antall had appointed important ministers, both from within his own party and from among the ranks of his two coalition partners, without administrative experience and without his knowing much about them.

The Finance Minister Ferenc Rabár related that there was no relationship of trust between Antall and his ministers, and that he (Rabár) perhaps had only once ever had a lengthier discussion with his boss, although he was responsible for the crucial financial portfolio. In his time cabinet meetings began at midday on Thursday and lasted until two or three in the early morning of Friday. He had himself never read the MDF programme, nor had he ever fostered contacts with other colleagues responsible for economic questions. Rabár was an advocate of a 'shock therapy', with the complete liberalisation of prices, wages, import and exchange rates in conjunction with a strictly controlled budgetary policy.

It speaks volumes that there was never an agenda for cabinet meetings. Once the ministers, who incidentally had for the most part not previously known each other personally, discussed for hours whether the mayor of a community should again, as in the past, be called 'judge'. One day during a meeting, Rabár received an urgent phone call from the vice-president of the National Bank to the effect that the foreign exchange reserves were exhausted and that Rabár should therefore propose a ban on imports to the cabinet. When Rabár returned to the meeting a discussion was in full swing as to whether the old title should be restored for the leader of a county. (It was not.)

Rabár decided to keep the matter about the reserves to himself and forego discussing it with anybody. In the end the crisis somehow resolved itself. In cabinet Rabár was repeatedly outvoted, and on account of the intrigues by another politician (the man then responsible for the coordination of government policy and today the Minister of Economic Affairs in Orbán's administration) he was not able to push through his draft budget. Rabár then led the crucial and ultimately successful negotiations about the price of petrol with the striking taxi drivers, although he had already resigned weeks before.

In these turbulent years Antall reshuffled his cabinet several times and 'consumed' a total of three finance ministers. The last one, Iván Szabó, was previously Minister of Industry and the acting chair of the MDF. He belonged to its moderate wing and in his interview with Rádai mercilessly exposed the frail condition of the coalition government: 'In reality there was nothing to Antall save his extraordinarily charismatic appearance!'

The tensions between the Prime Minister and the chauvinistic, anti-Semitic founding fathers of the MDF came to a climax in August 1992 when the extreme right-wing spokesman, the playwright István Csurka, maintained in an article published in the party newspaper that Hungary's independence was being endangered by a Jewish conspiracy with connections to a New York-Tel Aviv axis, and this at a time when the country was in the hands of a dying man. This 'completely and fundamentally Nazi ideology' unfortunately had the 'support of the great majority of party members' (Debreczeni). The media had in the meantime revealed that Csurka, under the codename 'Rasputin', had been active as a secret service informant for some years after the suppression of the 1956 uprising.

Nevertheless, the fate of Antall's government hung by a thin thread. The Smallholders quit the coalition at the beginning of 1992 following an internal split. Now the coalition government comprised just two parties and about two dozen former MPs of the Smallholders' Party. On the eve of the vital national congress everything was still open. With a brilliant speech, and some manipulation of the agenda, Antall succeeded in forcing Csurka's supporters into a minority of the Presidium. Some months later the radical right-wing politician, who had gained an international notoriety, was barred from the governing party.

Antall categorically refused to have any former Communist Party members in his government. This excluded (on paper at least) 860,000 (and with their family members two or three million) Hungarians. Yet he also opposed resolving once and for all the question of dealing with the agents and informers of the secret police during the Kádár regime. Why was this so? His closest colleague in both the government and the party, the Finance Minister Iván Szábo, was quite frank about this in the above-quoted interview. The very stability of the government would have been endangered by any witch-hunt because many (perhaps 30 to 35) MPs in the coalition had been informants or agents. Indeed, some sources suggest there were almost 50 such cases. The same was also true of the Socialists. And, as we shall see, even 15 years later the still unresolved issue of the agents had, together with rampant corruption, become a cancer within the Hungarian body politic.

It was in this period too that the media war broke out. The majority of the radio and TV programmes broadcast by left-leaning and liberal editors and producers incurred the displeasure of the conservative-nationalist coalition government.

JÓZSEF ANTALL—A POLITICAL PHENOMENON

The dispute climaxed when President Göncz rejected the Prime Minister's proposal to dismiss the heads of the state radio and television and to appoint deputy heads loyal to the government. The open dispute between the two former friends continued until Antall's death. Polls revealed that 79 per cent of those questioned deemed Antall responsible for the conflict.

Additionally, in an internal paper the leader of the MDF parliamentary party had already suggested in August 1991 a 'radical change of the political and intellectual position of the public broadcasting services in Hungary'. The struggle over press freedom split the political and intellectual elite of the country into two and led, in a sideshow, to the breach of my personal relationship with Antall. In the autumn of 1991 he received a delegation of the International Press Institute (IPI), to which more than 2,000 publishers and editors-in-chief from all parts of the world belonged. They were concerned about the growing pressure on the electronic media in Hungary to toe a more pro-government line. There was also the question of whether *Magyar Nemzet*, a Hungarian newspaper steeped in tradition, should be sold, as desired by the majority of its editors, to the liberal Swedish newspaper *Dagens Nyheter* or, as contrived by the government, to the right-wing Hersant newspaper group in France.

The Prime Minister, who was very sensitive to all questions concerning the cultivation of international contacts and above all the image of his government, became increasingly irritated and nervous during a discussion with a group of us: the director of the IPI, Peter Galliner, the chief editors of the *Neue Zürcher Zeitung*, the BBC and the *Guardian*, and myself, the representative of the Austrian Broadcasting Corporation

(ORF). It is more than possible that he was already feeling the effects of a new, more intensive phase of his debilitating illness. Whatever the case, Antall suddenly threw his press card over the table to me and bade me inform the other journalists assembled there that he himself had been a member of the Hungarian Association of Journalists for many years. All the accusations of the *Magyar Nemzet* editors were curtly dismissed as unfounded, all the embarrassing questions were rejected with a simple reference to the strict impartiality of the government. The atmosphere was decidedly cool when we went our separate ways.

During our stay in Budapest our delegation also met István Csurka and the nationalist poet Sándor Csoóri, who a few weeks previously in a much discussed essay had asserted that 'the liberal Hungarian Jewry wished to subsume the Magyars in style and thought'. The reaction of many writers was fierce. Imre Kertész (later, in 2002, winner of the Nobel Prize for Literature) publicly quit the Writers' Union in an open letter and 99 intellectuals protested, also in an open letter, to the President about the marginalisation of people on arbitrary racial or confessions grounds.

The demons which had once led to Auschwitz had been awoken by the 'national fuse'.[6] They were also to be seen in the subsequent crude attacks that Csurka and an MDF MP made on George Soros. The accusation against the investor and philanthropist was that his foundation, in collaboration with Hungarian and international Jewry, was part of an anti-Hungarian conspiracy. Even during the Kádár era, Soros had assisted innumerable civil rights activists and intellectuals with grants and scholarships. Later he founded, at enormous cost, the Central European University (CEU) in Budapest. Antall's

JÓZSEF ANTALL—A POLITICAL PHENOMENON

evasive statements in his exchange of letters with Soros are not among the most dazzling from his pen.

The summer 1992 annual congress of the IPI in Budapest was the first to take place in a post-communist state. What the people in London (only later did the IPI move its headquarters to Vienna) intended as worldwide recognition for the pioneering role of Hungarian journalists both under communism and during the critical years of the change of regime appeared in the eyes of the Antall government, which was already locked in a bitter struggle with the media, as a conspiracy of 'external and cunning foes'. Political scientists such as László Lengyel were even at the time pointing to the conspiracy complex of Antall, an ailing man profoundly disappointed by domestic political setbacks. In the magnificent chamber of the Hungarian parliament I had my last exchange of words with Antall after his opening speech at the IPI congress. 'You are not the conductor here, just the first violinist', he remarked cryptically as we passed one another.

The final year of the Antall government, despite or perhaps because of the break with Csurka's extreme right-wing group, took place against the background of a further demonstrative lurch to the right, not only regarding current and future policy but also with a throwback to the past. The reburial of the remains of the Regent Miklós Horthy, who had died in exile in Portugal in February 1957, in the presence of 50,000 mourners including seven members of the government, was not an official act of state but nevertheless a deeply symbolic move.

Weighed down by the pressure of both the opposition and the far right in his own party, the dangerously ill head of government was not able to push through the policy of compromise which was closer to his own personal and political instincts. As the contemporary historian Zoltán Ripp has pertinently noted: 'The bitter truth is that Antall's death preceded what would have become an ignominious fall'.[7]

After a short interlude with the Minister of the Interior, Péter Boross, as his successor, the MDF suffered a crushing electoral defeat and lost almost three quarters of its seats.

Antall justifiably considered himself to be wiser and better than everybody else in his party, in the coalition government and also in the opposition, which he cleverly outplayed initially. His arrogance, however, increasingly blocked his access to the intellectuals and the people. In contrast to his great international reputation, amongst his fellow countrymen he was always rated in the middle to lower ranks on the popularity lists for politicians. Yet, almost a quarter of a million people paid their last respects to the dead man laid out in state in the parliament building whilst heads of states and governments from around the world attended his funeral on 18 December 1993.

Antall had actually already accomplished his greatest service to the nation before he even entered the political arena as Prime Minister: the epochal election victory after decades of dictatorship and the historic pact he concluded with the SzDSz on his own initiative. As a man he was, in contrast to most leading politicians after 1989, beyond reproach, honest and in every respect personally incorruptible. In the sense of Jakob Burkhardt's reflections on history, Antall was rather a 'momentary great man', in whom a short phase of history is condensed, and at the same time a 'relatively great man' owing to the weaknesses of others.

József Antall, however, cannot be ranked as a 'historically great man', for which the criterion is not just a shift of power but a fundamental transformation of social structures and consciousness. His relatively short era could not really vindicate the exuberant hopes of the Hungarians after 1989, but at least it opened up a peaceful transition to a successful consolidation of a democratic and independent Hungary.

4

THE ROOTS OF HUNGARIAN ANTI-SEMITISM

'In reality the Hungarians are like the Jews, a scattered people, a people who have been subjugated and deprived of their rights, but who like the Jews have not given up ... They have practiced the art of survival'. The German writer Horst Krüger (1919–99) compared the Hungarians with the Jews in a subtle essay on the impressions he had garnered during a number of journeys to Hungary in the 1970s.[1] Today hardly anybody in Hungary would even dare to make such a comparison. Perception of the self and perception of the other are trapped on both sides in an irresolvable dialectical relationship. The policy of collective amnesia pursued during the decades of communism, which eroded every ethical and moral standard, created an apparently even balance of suffering. Mixed into this are political considerations, concrete economic interests and profound ignorance spreading over generations.

In the years immediately following the quiet collapse of the Kádár regime many observers, myself included, were seduced by the illusion that, with the disappearance of the one-party dictatorship, the 'age of the intellectual organisation of political hatreds'[2] together with the web of lies inherent within the system could be replaced by normal democratic relations. Yet even in its first months and years the Antall government provided one piece of evidence after another that history was still casting a long shadow. Initially, the writer Imre Kertész belonged to the 'childlike and gullible' who had not anticipated this phantom. But soon he fell 'from one surprise to another; lies, hatred, racism, stupidity were erupting all around me; it was just as if a boil which had been festering for 40 years was suddenly lanced by the surgeon's knife.'[3]

After Kertész, an Auschwitz survivor, was awarded the 2002 Nobel Prize for Literature, principally for his book *Fateless*, which had been published in Hungary in 1975 and barely noticed at the time, he became the target of anti-Semitic attacks and innuendoes, the more so as he has been living in Berlin since 2000. In an outspoken interview given on the occasion of his 80th birthday the Nobel laureate, not for the first time, stirred up the hornet's nest that is Hungarian anti-Semitism. 'Right-wing extremists and anti-Semites rule the roost. The old vices of the Hungarians, their hypocrisy and their tendency to repress bad memories, are flourishing just as they always have. Hungary in the war, Hungary and Fascism, Hungary and Socialism. The past is never dealt with. Everything is whitewashed.'[4] Kertész' sarcastic words sparked off a storm of indignation among the right in his native land and even led many liberals to shake their heads. In an article entitled 'The Insulted' the noted literary critic Sándor Radnóti came to the conclusion that, with his merciless satire, Kertész was painfully, unmistakably and characteristically a Hungarian.

What Kertész says, and of course he is not alone in this, about the failure of Hungarians to confront their own past is sadly all too true, as are his findings that the situation has consistently deteriorated in the last ten years. In order to be able to understand the alarming radicalisation of the political atmosphere and the ascent of the extreme right, we have to examine the roots of Hungarian nationalism and, above all, the path which led from the extraordinary (apparent) symbiosis between Jewish Hungarians and gentile Hungarians at the beginning of the 20th century to the perplexing about-turn to political anti-Semitism and ultimately to the Hungarian variant of the Final Solution.[5]

With a unique language and history the Hungarians are, with the exception of the Albanians, perhaps the loneliest people in Europe. The author Arthur Koestler, who dreamed in Hungarian but wrote his books first in German and later in English, once said, 'Perhaps their exceptional loneliness can explain the strange intensity of their existence. To be a Hungarian is a collective neurosis'. Since the conquest of the territory in 896 CE loneliness has been the determining factor in Hungarian history. To this we may add the fear of a slow death of the nation: one ethnic Hungarian in three lives outside the country.

There has always been an ever changing relationship between a resident population and conquerors, between newcomers and the excluded. King St Stephen, the Christian founder of the Hungarian state, reminded his son in 1030: 'A country that only has one language and one kind of custom is weak and fragile. Therefore, my son, go out and meet the settlers. Treat them decently so that they prefer to stay with you than elsewhere ...' From the 11th century Germans and Slovaks, Romanians and Croats, Serbs and Jews came to Hungary and were subsequently absorbed into Magyardom. Many of the celebrated great heroes, the political and military leaders of the wars of liberation against the Turks and Habsburgs, the outstanding figures of literature and science were often completely, or at least partially, of foreign origin.

During the reign of the Emperor Joseph II (1765–90) the Hungarians comprised only a third of the population in Hungary. The idea of a Hungarian state was, despite Magyarisation campaigns in Slovakia, in Transylvania or Croatia, not racially but exclusively culturally determined. Each and every person who professed their acceptance of the Hungarian nation had the same career chances in society. Thus, following the Compromise[6] of 1867 between Austria and Hungary, the government in Budapest, by pursuing a dynamic policy of linguistic and political assimilation, was able to claim 600,000 Germans, half a million Slovaks and 700,000 Jews as Hungarians in its official statistics. The number of 'Hungarians' as a proportion of the population in the Hungarian half of the Habsburg Monarchy had been raised to 48 per cent by 1910.

It was this 'golden era' of Jews willing to assimilate that the historians John Lukacs and Robert A. Kann have described as 'unique' and as the 'most successful example of a successful assimilation and equality of treatment under the law'. There were 16 Jewish MPs in the parliament in Budapest. Convert Jews could reach the highest positions: Baron Samu Hazai became Minister of War, whilst Theodor Herzl's nephew Ferenc Heltai was the Mayor of Budapest. The appointment of Vilmos Vázsonyi, a practicing Jew, as Minister of Justice in 1917 completed the symbolic breakthrough for the Jews who had become patriotic Hungarians.

THE ROOTS OF HUNGARIAN ANTI-SEMITISM

The thousand-year history of the Apostolic Kingdom of Hungary came to an abrupt end in the summer palace of Trianon in the park of Versailles on 4 June 1920. Hungary lost more than two-thirds of its territory and three-fifths of its population. More than three million Hungarians now lived under foreign suzerainty, half of these in self-contained areas of settlements along the borders of the successor states (Czechoslovakia, Romania and Yugoslavia).

To this day, the word Trianon symbolises for all Hungarians the greatest tragedy in their history. Approximately 350,000 to 400,000 civil servants, officers and members of the middle classes quit the ceded territories between 1918 and 1920. These politically alert people, who had been degraded from the ruling classes to the homeless, formed a fertile recruiting ground for extremists of all kinds, from populist rat catchers and the death squads of radical nationalists to anti-Semitic army officers. The idea of the restoration of the lost territories was kept alive in the inter-war years in kindergartens and schools, at church services and in the press.

The breakup of Austria-Hungary and the resulting 133 days of the communist Hungarian Soviet Republic, which on 21 March 1919 followed the democratic government, destroyed the pact between the ruling political class and Hungarian Jewry. The fact that the leaders of the communist regime were overwhelmingly of Jewish origin, such as Béla Kun, the strong man in the Revolutionary Governing Council, provided a convenient pretext for equating Jews and communism, even though most Jews had rejected Bolshevism. When in November 1919 Admiral Miklós Horthy entered Budapest on a white stallion at the head of the White National Army, he called the Hungarian capital in his speech 'the sinful city'. That was the signal for vehement anti-Semitism. The Red Terror of the Soviet dictatorship was quickly superseded by the even more relentless White Terror of the right-wing officer detachments and paramilitary organisations.

The bottled-up dissatisfaction of the newly impoverished middle classes and the refugees from the successor states finally had a lightning conductor. Thanks to Hungary's own stab-in-the-back legend about internal foes, the Jews became—even though 10,000 Hungarian Jews had fallen at the front in the Great War—the deadly enemy par excellence of the Hungarian nation. But it was not only the relatively high proportion of Jews active in the radical revolutionary events of 1919 that destroyed the historical accord between them and the Magyars. The historian Oszkár Jászi in his great work on the fall of the Habsburg Monarchy revealed the true reasons behind this: Magyarisation and with it the cooperation of the Jews in the struggle against the nationalities was no longer necessary or desirable, and it was for this reason that public opinion changed so radically. As Jászi put it, a nationalist bogey was replaced by a Jewish one.

All this was of tremendous importance for the dynamic of Hungarian anti-Semitism in the interwar years. Having risen to unique heights in the Monarchy, the Hungarian Jewish community now found itself the first anywhere in Europe after the First World War to be subjected to anti-Jewish legislation. In 1920 parliament passed a law restricting the entry of Jewish students to university. As far as the Horthy regime is concerned, the great thinker István Bibó summed up the new programme in his essay 'On the Jewish Question'. With the dissolving of the settlement between the Hungarian body politic and Jewry there 'arose the counterrevolutionary construction which henceforth stood fully for nationalism, anti-democracy and anti-Semitism on the one hand and for the connection between democracy, homelessness and Jewry on the other'. In any case Trianon proved to be a fatal stumbling block on the road to democratisation in the Western European mould. Revisionist politics shaped daily life throughout the interwar years. The young generation was brought up in the spirit of 'No, no, never!' and the rallying cry 'Rump Hungary is no kingdom, Greater Hungary is a paradise'. Reckless nationalism and the mythology of a revisionist campaign propagated without any sense of proportion formed the basis for the disastrous path which ultimately led Hungary into the even greater catastrophe of the Second World War as a loyal satellite of Hitler's Germany.

The revisionist course towards the successor states and the strengthening of the extreme right saw Hungary falling ever deeper into the grip of the Third Reich. In just two and a half years (1938–41) the Horthy regime, to the accompaniment of Hungarians' indescribable jubilation, succeeded in regaining almost half of all the lost lands from Czechoslovakia, Romania and Yugoslavia on the nod of the Axis Powers. The national territory was enlarged by 85 per cent and the population by 58 per cent to 15 million. But whilst two million Hungarians had been 'brought back home', three million non-Magyars (Romanians, Slovaks, Serbs etc.) were now also living under Hungarian rule. This fact did nothing to disturb the euphoria of Hungarian public opinion, of the officer class and of civil servants, who were with few exceptions blinded by a virulent nationalism and who now assumed the administration of the restored territories (all of which would be lost in 1945). The proportion of non-Magyar nationalities in Hungary rose from 7.9 per cent in 1939 to 22.5 per cent in 1941. Hungary was once again a multi-ethnic rather than a homogeneous nation.

The number of Jews increased by 80 per cent to 725,000. For them the expansion of the national territory brought with it especially tragic consequences. The Jews in Transylvania, southern Slovakia and Vojvodina, men and women such as my grandparents, my uncles and aunts in Transylvania or the doctor Oszkár Lendvai, a former first lieutenant in Bratislava, had identified themselves with the cause of Hungary, often at great risk to their careers, their property and sometimes their freedom. They had all hoped for a return to the 'good old days of peace'. Instead they were confronted with the full severity of the three Jewish laws (1938–41). The number of converts designated as Jews tripled to 100,000. The destruction of their livelihoods and in due course the Final Solution thus threatened 825,000 people in total.

Nowhere in Central and Eastern Europe had the Jews been able to live so long in relative safety as in Hungary. But nowhere were they so quickly and so brutally driven to their deaths as in the land of the Magyars. István Bibó's assessment of the situation after Aryanisation, the exclusion of the Jews from economic life, and finally the deportation (in seven weeks in 147 trains) of the 437,000 Jews living outside Budapest is a grim one. What took place was 'a dreadful picture of avarice, of uninhibited hypocrisy and, in the best case, the calculated scrabble for the newly vacant jobs by a substantial section of this society. This was an unforgettable shock not only for the Jews, but also for all Hungarians with any decency'.[7]

It must of course be immediately added that the majority of Hungarians do not share this unerringly honest opinion at all. Quite apart from the ramifications of the wartime economy, the long-term consequences of the 'changing of the guard' and the rise of a new 'Christian middle class' in business and industry, as well as in the professions, should not be underestimated. The historian Gyula Juhász has concluded that for the majority of the educated in Hungary the racist ideology was primarily a vehicle to obtain the jobs and positions the 'assimilated' had been compelled to give up.[8]

The German invasion of 19 March 1944 met neither military nor civilian resistance. Indeed, on the contrary, there was widespread collaboration not only in the lightning deportations but also in the mass robberies and murders. Using recently discovered documents, in their sober standard work Christian Gerlach and Götz Aly describe the 'national enrichment', the means whereby

> the majority of the population and the state apparatus became corrupted and acquiescent in favour of the German course of action. The Hungarians and their authorities had to carry out the dirty part of the robbery ... Almost unnoticed they [the Germans] made the Hungarians into a nation of fences, middlemen who in the end were only able to retain a small portion of the loot for themselves, but had to deliver the greatest part to the Germans in a manner that was completely clean (at least to the outside world) and aroused the least suspicion.[9]

The two German academics point both to certain parallels in the deportation of the ethnic Germans in Hungary and the subsequent redistribution of their property after the Second World War and to 'the iron silence of the majority of the population as well of those governing in post-war Hungary, a silence that has survived every change of system and regime'. They emphasise that radical and utterly humiliated Hungarian nationalism is the link between revisionist Hungarian expansion, the policy of ethnic homogenisation and the deportation of the Jews; it was the crucial precondition for the murder of the Jews. In the final phase before the collapse, the Arrow Cross Party seized power with German assistance. The hit squads of the fascist movement are estimated to have killed 50,000 Jews in Budapest alone. In all, it is estimated that the number of Jewish victims totalled 564,000, of whom 297,000 were in Trianon-Hungary (rump Hungary without the territories regained between 1939 and 1941) and roughly 100,000 in Budapest.

Hungary paid a high price for its alliance with Hitler's Germany and for the failure of the belated and dilettante attempt to jump ship made by the aged Regent Horthy in October 1944. The eight months of fighting on Hungarian territory and the confiscations of property by Soviet, Romanian and German troops destroyed 40 per cent of national wealth. Including the Jews, 6.2 per cent of the 14.5 million inhabitants of Greater Hungary (1941), approximately 900,000 people, are estimated to have died. The flight westwards of the military and administrative apparatus, roughly a million civilians, should also not be forgotten. Most of the refugees later returned but about 100,000 remained in the West.[10]

The Hungarian historian György Ránki has pointed out that nowhere in Eastern Europe had the Jews so identified with a nation as in Hungary. For this reason the tragedy of the Jews was the tragedy of the Hungarians. And this is what makes the recently published findings of the sociologist Mária Vásárhelyi on the ignorance of the young people so astounding. How is it possible that in the generation of those aged between 18 and 30 only 4 per cent know what the word Holocaust means? That only 13 per cent can give a figure for the number of victims? This is in fact no wonder when we consider that the history atlas prescribed for use in the 2009 school-leaving exams does not once mention the Jewish laws, the Holocaust and the

THE ROOTS OF HUNGARIAN ANTI-SEMITISM

deportations. Meanwhile, those books which in 1944 propagated hatred against the Jews continue to appear unhindered. Since the early 1990s anti-Semitic banners ('The Holocaust is a lie') and racist chanting are to be seen and heard at football matches. A selection of racist, anti-Jewish and anti-Roma outbursts in daily newspapers and on radio and TV was already published in 2000 and 2001.

The results of the Hungarian and international opinion polls published in February 2009 are shattering. Two-thirds of the adult population in Hungary believe that the Jews are too powerful in the business world, 7 per cent more than two years previously. In comparison, in seven EU states, 15 per cent of those asked in Great Britain agreed with the same question, whilst in France and Germany 33 per cent did; only in Spain was the percentage higher than in Hungary. Thus it is not surprising that almost 50 per cent of respondents in Hungary believe that Jewish financiers are responsible for the current world economic crisis, by far the highest percentage in the survey.

Approximately 40 per cent of adults in Hungary believe that for the Jews living in the country the interests of Israel are more important than those of their 'mother country'. Among younger people this figure falls to 27 per cent. Nevertheless, Vásárhelyi finds the infection of the younger generation with anti-Semitic prejudices disturbing: 30 per cent of the young people polled were openly anti-Semitic while a further 29 per cent were sympathetic to anti-Semitic stereotypes. The extraordinarily high percentage of 'don't knows' only reflects the tendency to conceal prejudices. If the even more virulent anti-Roma sentiment is also taken into account, then the conclusion is horrifying: just one young Hungarian in ten is open minded and tolerant whilst only about 20 per cent, even if they

63

are not free of prejudice, do not identify themselves with openly racist opinions.

Polls on recent Hungarian history reveal a rejection of any attempt to come to terms with the past and a strong tendency to embrace nationalistic and xenophobic stereotypes. Everything in Hungarian history that was a failure or 'unpleasant' is blamed on the neighbouring countries, on minorities or on foreigners living in Hungary. Vásárhelyi believes that the historical lies and the self-deception are today stronger than at the time of the change of the system in 1989. Finally, the trivialisation of the Holocaust in Hungary is the most common stereotype. Between 2005 and 2009 the percentage of Hungarians saying that 'The Jews speak far too much about what happened to them' rose by 10 per cent to 46 per cent. Approximately two-thirds of those polled accept the standpoint of the right that the victims of the Holocaust can only be spoken of in conjunction with the victims of communism.

There is no comparison between the feelings of the great majority of Hungarians and those of the approximately 80,000 to 100,000 Jews living in Hungary, exclusively the children and grandchildren of Holocaust survivors. The studies of Mária Vásárhelyi and her colleagues reveal that 58 per cent of those polled believe that the Germans were responsible for the Holocaust whereas the Hungarians protected the Jews for as long as possible. Equally disturbing is the fact that this figure rises to 68 per cent among university graduates.[11] Without doubt the shroud pulled over the guilt of the beneficiaries among the older generation, and their suppression of that guilt, play here just as important a role as (after the first post-war years) the silence and accommodation during the four decades of communist dictatorship.

THE ROOTS OF HUNGARIAN ANTI-SEMITISM

In spite of the ostensible and hypocritical anti-fascist propaganda spread by the communist regime, which was mostly directed against Germany, everything possible was done in the schools and media until the very end to pull a mantle of silence over the past. And this historical legacy, never once reassessed, has now been passed on to the next generation. We shall be returning to this stance of forgetting and forgiving with regard to the inheritance of the red dictatorship. But only now has it become evident that Hungary is paying a very high price for this policy of silence on its history.

This chapter has dealt with the roots of the old anti-Semitism and the present degree of ignorance. All governments after the 1989 change of the regime have been responsible for the failure of the entire educational system. It is, however, clear that the political discourse in Hungary has played a crucial role in the strengthening and mobilisation of prejudices: much of the responsibility for this can be assigned to the emergence of a right-wing and extreme right-wing empire of daily, weekly and monthly print media, as well as electronic media and internet portals in recent years. The question of how far the link between politics, the media and the economy stretches will be considered in subsequent chapters, as will the rise of the most faithful disciples of the erstwhile Arrow Cross Party in Hungarian politics.

5

GYULA HORN AND THE RETURN OF THE POST-COMMUNISTS

In June 1994, six months after the death of József Antall, the Hungarian electorate rebuffed his inheritance. The coalition government had been weakened by internal power struggles. Led by the former Minister of the Interior Péter Boross, it suffered a humiliating defeat whose true extent nobody had anticipated. Its humbling was primarily due to its dilettante economic policy and the political zigzags of the previous four years.

The number of MPs of the Hungarian Democratic Forum (MDF) shrank dramatically from 164 to 38, and of the Smallholders' Party, which had split, from 44 to 28. Against this, the Socialists (MSzP) succeeded in quintupling their representation from 33 to 164. The Liberals (SzDSz) declined from 93 to 69 whilst the small parties, Fidesz under Viktor Orbán and the Christian Democrats (KDNP), remained practically the same with 20 and 22 seats respectively.

The many opinion polls and sociological studies published since 1989 confirm that the system change that had been so eagerly awaited had left large sections of the population discouraged and disappointed, largely on account of the deterioration in living conditions and the growing gap in standards of living between winners and losers of the transition. As early as 1991 40 per cent of respondents believed that the new system was worse than the old; this had risen to 51 per cent by the beginning of 1994 and 54 per cent one year later; on the same dates only 31 per cent, 26 per cent and 27 per cent respectively thought things were better than under Kádár. The degree of disappointment expressed in these polls was higher than was to be found in similar polls conducted in the former German Democratic Republic, Poland, the Czech Republic and Slovakia. Unskilled and semi-skilled workers, as well as those employed in the agricultural sector, were the most embittered: 65 per cent considered the old regime better than the new. Entrepreneurs and the well educated expressed the greatest satisfaction: only 29 per cent preferred the Kádár regime. The mixture of dissatisfaction and fear of the future created a strong nostalgia for the Kádár era among many people.

The swing in mood to a deeply rooted pessimism and feelings of isolation superseded relatively quickly the national disposition to a trait that Hungarians call '*délibáb*', which literally means *fata morgana*, a mirage. People were no longer prepared to see the place of Hungary in a rapidly changing Europe through rose-tinted spectacles. All this prepared the ground for the return to power of that party whose predecessors had for four decades been responsible for the 'little freedoms' but also for the infamous deeds of the communist dictators.

Gyula Horn, the 62-year-old chairman of the victorious post-communists and future Prime Minister, was in every respect the diametrical opposite of his predecessor. Antall was a member of the nobility, of the highly educated, multilingual and self-assured elite. Horn, on the other hand, was literally a proletarian, a man who in his memoirs wrote that he 'had grown up in absolute squalor, in conditions that today are barely imaginable'. His father, a convinced communist, spent four months in prison after the collapse of the short-lived Soviet Republic of Hungary in 1919; he worked as a furniture remover, was repeatedly arrested and shortly before the end of the war was shot by Nazis near the Austrian border. Horn's mother was forced to raise her seven sons alone; as an 11-year-old, the young Gyula was working as a messenger boy in a factory making cardboard boxes.

By attending night school the talented youngster, now 16 years old, very quickly caught up on the missing four years of elementary school and completed his school-leaving exams at a special boarding school. In 1950, with his first suit packed in his suitcase, he set off for Rostov-on-Don in the Soviet Union. He spent four years there at the College of Economics and Finance and then, armed with a diploma and a good knowledge of Russian, began his career as a lowly tax expert in the Ministry of Finance in Budapest. The popular uprising in October 1956 marked a break in his life too. After the defeat of the revolution by the Soviet army the reliable young communist served for about six months in a special unit of the militia and was rewarded with a posting in the diplomatic service.

Horn worked for three years in Sofia and six in the Hungarian embassy in Belgrade, where he achieved the rank of counsellor. He next moved to the hub of power, to the international department of the Central Committee in Budapest. Here he rose to be head of department and finally, in 1985, was appointed secretary of state in the Foreign Ministry. It was in this period, during the opening to the West, that I first met him. At our first meeting, aware of my books and articles on the countries of the Balkans, he revealed to me that in the 1970s he had published two books on Yugoslavia under the pen-name of Gyula Várady.

Horn subsequently received the degree of doctoral candidate (under the then system of academic distinctions) for his dissertation, 'An Analysis of the Yugoslav Economic System'. Our mutual interest in the fascinating but ultimately failed experiments of the Tito system in Yugoslavia was the first topic of our discussions. Later, with the radio turned up and standing next to an open window, he whispered his critical observations about Soviet foreign policy.

His hour as a politician of European renown struck in the summer of 1989. As foreign minister in Miklós Németh's government Horn, together with the Austrian foreign minister Alois Mock, had cut the barbed wire fence, that symbol of the Iron Curtain, between the two countries in the presence of a large number of journalists. Three months later, on Sunday 10 September, the Hungarian reform government, ignoring the noisy protests of the regime in East Berlin, opened the border to all citizens of the GDR then on Hungarian soil. This internationally crucial decision, which allowed thousands of East German refugees legally and without hindrance to leave the country, was announced at 7 pm simultaneously by Gyula Horn on Hungarian TV and worldwide by the Hungarian news agency MTI. By the time the Berlin Wall fell two months later, approximately 60,000 East German citizens had fled to the Federal Republic of Germany via Hungary.

'Hungary broke the first stone in the Wall'. This was how in December 1989 the German Chancellor Helmut Kohl, standing before the Hungarian parliament, described the Hungarian leadership's contribution to the total collapse of the GDR regime, paving the way to German reunification. Horn's portrayal in his memoirs and in subsequent interviews of his own role in this act of liberation is contested by the then head of government, Miklós Németh, and by some contemporary historians. Nonetheless, the fact remains that, ever since his television announcement, which has subsequently been broadcast repeatedly throughout the world, the historic opening of the borders has been irrevocably and primarily linked, in Germany at least, with the name of Gyula Horn. For this reason Horn received the prestigious Charlemagne Prize from the city of Aachen, as well as many other German and Austrian awards and accolades. In the town of Wertheim am Main in Baden-Württemberg there is even a street named after him.

Horn first became known to a wider public in Hungary at the end of May 1990 when he was elected party chairman by two-thirds of the delegates at the Socialists' party conference in the wake of their electoral defeat. Some years later, during the election campaign of 1994, questions were asked about his role as a member of the disreputable special militia active after the crushing of the 1956 uprising. A Hungarian refugee living in Sweden maintained in a television interview that in 1957 Horn had physically mistreated him in a prison hospital. According to Horn, the man was a criminal who allegedly received several thousand dollars for his statement. Whatever the truth of the matter, there was no solid evidence of Horn having been involved in the reprisals against the rebels, even if he had never made a secret of the fact that his older, Moscow-educated brother had been killed by unknown resistance fighters several weeks after the Soviet invasion.[1]

On 5 May 1994 Horn held his final speech of the election campaign at a mass rally in the large provincial town of Miskolc. But just before nine o'clock in the evening the car in which he was travelling back to Budapest rammed at high speed into an unlit lorry parked at the side of the road. Horn was badly injured. His second vertebra and his right-hand wrist were broken, and he also suffered slight concussion. Released from hospital in Miskolc one week later, the future head of government had to wear day and night for two months a type of metal crown and a collar to enable his broken vertebra to heal. The complicated appliance, attached to the upper part of his body, weighed more than seven kilos and was for Horn both painful and at times barely tolerable in the heat of the summer. However, despite persistent rumours to the contrary, there was never any evidence of foul play.

Although they had won an absolute majority in the elections, the Socialists immediately began negotiations with the Liberals (SzDSz) on the formation of a coalition government. This, it should be recalled, was the party that had been the most virulently anti-communist in 1989–90. Before the election the Liberals had announced that they would only consider entering a coalition with the Socialists if the latter failed to secure a majority. Bálint Magyar, the most influential spokesman in the party, even said that they would not join a government led by Horn. Of course, all this was hastily forgotten after the election. At their party conference and with the approval of an overwhelming majority, the Socialists invited the Liberals to form a coalition with them, an offer quickly endorsed at an SzDSz party meeting where 80 per cent of the delegates were in favour. After three weeks of negotiations, a 144-page coalition agreement was signed.

Why did these once irreconcilable opponents choose the path of cooperation? In view of the catastrophic economic situation and the inevitable budgetary cuts that would have to be made, and because of the anticipated opposition of many Socialist MPs, a broad-based government, one with over 72 per cent of seats in parliament, would be in a stronger position to act; it could also modify those laws requiring a two-thirds majority. In addition it should not be forgotten that the election result, totally unexpected in the West, could all too easily have shaken the confidence of Western investors. It was this closing of ranks with the SzDSz, the very party which in the eyes of influential political and financial circles in the USA and the EU was regarded as the standard bearer of Western values—the market economy and human rights—that made the former reform communists politically acceptable in their new social-democratic garb a mere four years after the disappearance of the communist system.

As Prime Minister of a coalition government Horn proved to be a shrewd political operator. Taking Kádár's oft-cited words 'Who is not against us is with us' as his maxim, the political scientist Laszlo Lengyel aptly concluded that Horn sought compromises with everybody: with the West, with Hungary's Central and Eastern European neighbours, with Western investors, with domestic big business, with the trade unions, with the man on the street and, not least, with the SzDSz. Accordingly Horn was from the very beginning walking a tightrope between the various groups, trends and individuals, often representing contradictory positions. Wily, choleric, prepared if necessary to make U-turns to retain power, he could drop even friends such as Tamás Suchman, the Minister of Privatisation, as a hot potato.

Western observers were as bemused by the fact that a reform communist of the old guard was now acting as midwife to the introduction of capitalism and seeking to attract foreign capital as they were by the decision, despite a comfortable majority, to form a coalition with the Liberals, who had previously been violently anti-communist. After many exploratory talks, including one with Horn himself (still visibly labouring under the consequences of his accident), I succeeded in having the first full-length TV interview of a foreign broadcaster with the future prime minister. The Austrian Broadcasting Corporation broadcast a portrait of Horn, followed by a half-hour interview, on 8 July 1994.

Horn was willing to speak frankly about his past, including his membership of the special militia unit in 1956, as well as his personal weaknesses in his dealings with those in positions of responsibility. In particular he stressed the unusual fact that in this corner of Europe capitalism had to be established top-down. The goal was the social market economy, albeit one bound by social partnerships. Repeatedly Horn emphasised the importance of budget reform, the reduction of the deficit and state debts. He added that if no agreement could be reached with the trade unions within a few months, then there would be social unrest in the transition period.

It seemed remarkable to me at the time how openly Horn acknowledged the existence of various strands of opinion within the pluralistic Socialist Party; but he also firmly believed that it was unacceptable, once somebody had assumed a political position, to constantly complain and threaten resignation. Personal sensitivities and taking offence had no place in politics. This was a slightly veiled hint to certain grumblers within his party. László Békesi, the Minister of Finance, who was nine years his junior, was one of Horn's harshest critics and, for a long time, a secret rival within the Socialist Party leadership. In the eyes of the ever mistrustful SzDSz coalition partner, the highly talented Békesi was by far the most important guarantee that the post-communists in their new guise as social democrats would not only profess their belief in the principles of the market economy but also take them seriously in practice.

The first eight months of the new government were overshadowed by constant feuding between Horn and his Finance Minister, sometimes in public but mostly in private. All observers agree that because of this political infighting eight crucial months were lost.

Békesi knew that without radical budgetary cuts Hungary was threatened with economic and financial bankruptcy. He demanded tax cuts for business and a 9 per cent devaluation of the forint (he had initially wanted one of 16 per cent); moreover, he called for a salary freeze for teachers and doctors employed in the public sector, and even for MPs. Like his failed successor, he demanded in vain the closure of unviable schools, hospitals and self-governing territorial institutions, as well as the use of the proceeds from privatisation mainly for reduction of Hungary's substantial foreign debts.

Respect for Békesi as an economic policymaker went well beyond party boundaries. But he believed Horn was ill-suited for the position of prime minister. In one bitter interview Békesi claimed he was like a cuckolded husband, always the last to learn of the truth. After seven and a half months Békesi, who in the words of one of his successors (Péter Medgyessy) made his politics too emotionally, without any finesse or ability to adapt, threw in the towel and resigned on 28 January 1995.[2]

His departure was a setback for the Liberals (the SzDSz), who had supported the Békesi line by all possible means both within the coalition and in the media. In general the Liberals were increasingly disappointed by the policies of Gyula Horn and his comrades who nostalgically hankered after the past. Those liberal politicians and intellectuals who from the beginning had had reservations about the coalition with the post-communists, or even rejected it, saw in retrospect the resignation of Békesi at the end of January 1995, or at the very latest the explosion of the so called Tocsik scandal in November 1996, as the last chance to quit a coalition increasingly discredited owing to rampant corruption.[3] According to the first chairman and mastermind of the Liberals, János Kis, it was this failure to act, rather than the joining of the coalition government in itself, that laid the foundations of the subsequent electoral defeat of the SzDSz in 1998 and ultimately their final collapse ten years later.

Here it should be noted that in an interview after his resignation Békesi also said the Liberals had made a mistake in not leaving the government; this he attributed to their weakness, their uncertainty and the seductions of power. Although Horn threw every agreement completely overboard, the Liberals stuck to the coalition and were compelled to bear a share of the responsibility for its failings. And thus began the steady erosion of the Liberals as a political force in Hungary. But it should also be recognised that without the SzDSz the next and very last attempt at reform would not have succeeded. It was only with the very negative response to Békesi's resignation, both at home and abroad, that the Prime Minister finally comprehended that the country was on the brink of collapse. At the end of 1994 one third of all government expenditure was being devoted solely to interest payments on foreign debt.

Gyula Horn, the symbolic and convinced representative of the 'little man from the Kádár era', had initially believed that the German Chancellor Helmut Kohl would, out of gratitude for the opening of the border, grant Hungary generous credits, thereby enabling him to avoid having to make deep cuts. What the Germans were prepared to offer, however, fell far short of his expectations. Thus Horn had to accept the most radical reforms to date, which included sweeping privatisations. He then had, very grudgingly, to push the measures through his Socialist Party.

On 12 March 1995, quite out of the blue, the new Finance Minister Lajos Bokros, in close agreement with the president of the National Bank György Surányi, announced together with Horn what the public called 'the Bokros package'. The resulting abolition of social benefits, reductions in wages and pensions, the introduction of student fees, the sliding devaluation of the forint with an estimated annual exchange rate loss of 26–27 per cent, as well as other changes in taxes and customs duties, taken together made deep inroads into the standard of living of the average Hungarian. Real wages fell by 18 per cent in 1995–96 (as against a fall of 20 per cent between 1990 and 1994) and the purchasing power of pensions by 25 per cent. Two cabinet ministers resigned immediately in protest.

Almost overnight the Bokros package won back for Hungary the confidence of foreign capital and international financial institutions such as the IMF and the World Bank. By the beginning of 1998 the budget deficit had been reduced from 10 per cent to 4.2 per cent of GDP and net indebtedness from $21 billion to $8.7 billion. Hand in hand with this financial stabilisation, the Socialist-Liberal government carried out an ambitious privatisation of state property. The former reform communist Horn, for whom the very idea of selling off state assets had been an anathema, bragged in parliament and at party meetings that his government had raised 1,007 billion forints through its programme of privatisation between 1995 and 1997. The level of foreign investment in Hungary reached approximately $18 billion (more than in every other transition country in Eastern Europe), and the private sector was responsible for 80 per cent of GDP, compared with only 20 per cent at the beginning of the government's period in office.

However, behind the facade of this success story a bitter struggle was raging between the determined reformer Bokros and trade union representatives, who were greedy for both power and money and were acting in alliance with diverse populist young party officials in the Socialist leadership. Just like his predecessor László Békesi, Bokros, increasingly unpopular on account of his rather informal style, had to fight for every individual reform measure in the teeth of massive resistance from within his own party. In this he could not rely on the wily old fox at the head of the government manoeuvring between the different interest groups.

Publicly or in private Bokros threatened to resign six times. But Horn was a crafty political realist. He accepted Bokros' seventh attempt at resignation without turning a hair in order to pursue shortly afterwards a different political line, which had the agreement of the trade union wing of his party. Nothing was (and, to date, nothing has been) changed in the hugely expensive and confused systems of social insurance and healthcare. More than a fair share of the blame for the failure of the Bokros concept for the restructuring of these dilapidated structures can be laid at the door of Horn's capitulation to the powerful bosses of the two big banks: Sándor Csányi of the national savings bank (OTP), who is today the wealthiest man in Hungary, and Gábor Princz of the post office bank, which has since gone bankrupt. Moreover, the rather dubious vetoes of the Constitutional Court presided over by László Sólyom have also contributed, in the opinion of independent observers, to the grave dilution of important reform proposals.

With his winning style and remarkable deftness, Péter Medgyessy,[4] Horn's third Finance Minister, succeeded in establishing a normal and human relationship in his contacts and dealings with his Prime Minister, a man with a marked inferiority complex, profoundly mistrustful of others. Medgyessy established the routine of the two men holding a one-hour meeting early every Tuesday morning. He was able to rescue the substance of the Bokros reforms and even introduced a system of private pensions, without of course taking any of the tough decisions needed on the expensive system of self-governing territorial authorities, healthcare, health insurance and education. Nevertheless, compared with that of the Antall government, the macroeconomic performance of the Socialist-Liberal coalition was considerably more positive.

During these years I met Horn on a number of occasions: at the World Economic Forum at Davos, on his visits to Vienna, and also in his imposing office in the parliament building in Budapest. He never made any secret of his irritation with certain ministers from his junior coalition partner or his reservations about his reform minded finance ministers, Békesi and Bokros. He admired the German Chancellor Kohl and foreign minister Hans-Dietrich Genscher, as well as the leading Social-Democrat politicians in Austria, particularly Chancellor Franz Vranitzky and the president of the parliament, Heinz Fischer.

Horn's foreign policy priorities were accession to the EU (supported in a referendum by more than 85 per cent of Hungarians) and improvement in relations with the neighbouring countries with large Hungarian minorities. The conclusion of a basic agreement with Slovakia and Romania renouncing any alterations to the borders established by the Treaty of Trianon (1920), together with an affirmation of minority rights, paved the way for the participation of parties representing the Hungarian minorities in future coalition governments in both countries.

One of the more interesting and promising initiatives of Horn's government was the organisation in Budapest at the beginning of 1996 of a conference of roughly one hundred 'successful Hungarians' from around the world. Three specialist groups discussed the future of the country. Speaking in perfect Hungarian at this unusual event Otto Habsburg (the eldest son of Karl I, the last Emperor of Austria and King of Hungary) called for the overcoming of Hungaro-pessimism. At the plenary meeting in the parliament, both the Hungarian-born American political scientist Charles Gati from Washington and I demanded a clear break with the practices of the past and the opening of the archives of the secret police to their victims and for academic research. We also criticised the unbroken hold of the intelligence services over the archives.

Subsequently, I confronted Horn during one of his visits to Vienna and asked him why, despite our submission of a written request, Gati and I still had not received any documents from the archives. 'I have been assured that there no documents whatsoever about you in the archives', he replied with a friendly smile. In response to my question whether he seriously believed that there was not a file on me, one of the foreign journalists who had frequently visited Hungary before the change of system, Horn promised that his office would take up the matter with the 'competent authorities'. As to the infamous agent question,[5] it was not until the end of 2005 that I finally received 395 pages of operational material and reports from the historical archive of the state security service.[6]

Yet it was the numerous bribery scandals, large and small, that weighed far heavier on the Horn's debit side than any failings on the agent question. These were of course closely linked with the overbearing hubris of the Socialists, who, according to Békesi, bore even less resemblance to a modern social-democratic party in 1998 than they had four years previously. Instead of moving forward the Socialists had slipped back, behind the level of 1989. In an unpredictable and impenetrable struggle for power among the various factions, a struggle that had everything to do with the spoils of power and little or nothing with principles and the common weal, corruption won the upper hand. With the first successes in financial stabilisation the almost traditional arrogance of office holders returned.

The public was outraged when it learned that a construction company within the orbit of the Postbank, whose collapse the government could only prevent in the spring of 1997 with a massive injection of financial aid, was responsible for the building of a large villa for the Horn family. The claim that the construction costs had been covered by the proceeds from the sale of two flats owned by Horn and the royalties from the German edition of his memoirs did little to dispel doubts. The huge severance payment of 15 million forints paid out to Lajos Bokros when he left the chairmanship of the Budapest Bank to become the Minister of Finance also caused a lot of bad blood. Although this had all been completely legal, it had coincided with a massive fall in the living standards of the average Hungarian.

Even more questionable was what was known as the Tocsik scandal. This revolved around the distribution of 'proceeds' from dubious real estate deals with local authorities to the two coalition partners and shady transactions concerning the covering of Russia's $900 million trading debts with Hungary. Certain senior office-holders in several parties became rich, as did individual savvy managers of state-run concerns, key figures who not only procured money for party finances but also, in many cases, obtained substantial sums for themselves.

The fact that in the Tocsik scandal some of Horn's personal friends (for instance, the minister responsible and the chair of the supervisory authority) were sacrificed must be placed on the plus side of the first Socialist-Liberal government. The Liberals also criticised Horn for the agreement signed with the Vatican guaranteeing full state funding for church schools and hospitals, as well as other privileges for the Catholic Church. Yet, despite these concessions, the church threw its not inconsiderable weight behind the opposition party Fidesz in the 1998 elections.

However, it should be emphasised that the first Socialist-Liberal coalition did not abuse its overwhelming majority between 1994 and 1998. The government had a number of achievements to its credit: its economic reforms, media policy, its foreign policy initiatives and the separation of the administration of the courts from the executive, placing it under the prerogative of a National Council of Justice. The well-known liberal economist and ex-SzDSz MP Tamás Bauer even maintains that the Horn government, which was led by a member of the former special militia, was paradoxically the most successful post-communist reform government.

Yet none of this prevented the Socialists from losing the 1998 election, even if only by a narrow margin. The defeat was due not only to the Tocsik affair but also to Horn's squabbles with the SzDSz and his unsuccessful dealings with the authoritarian Slovak Prime Minister, Vladimír Mečiar, over the construction of the hydroelectric power plant on the Danube at Nagymaros, a project fiercely opposed by Hungarian public opinion. To this sad list may be added the arrogance of the Socialists, who failed to come up with any convincing programme and conducted a miserable election campaign. After his defeat, and probably much too late, Horn resigned the leadership of the party. He left behind a party rattled by infighting and corruption affairs. His successor László Kovács was a reliable and respectable man, but he lacked charisma and his experience lay primarily in foreign affairs. The political stage would, however, from now on be dominated by Viktor Orbán, the most talented and most controversial politician in Hungary, and by his Fidesz party.

6

THE YOUNG COMET—VIKTOR ORBÁN

The real sensation of the May 1998 elections in Hungary, the third free poll after the downfall of the communist regime, was not the relatively narrow defeat (at least in percentage terms) of the Socialists (MSzP) but rather the triumph of Fidesz, something which even shortly beforehand had seemed totally inconceivable. The party, which in 1990 and 1994 had been the weakest in parliament, now became the dominant force in Hungarian politics.

In the first round of voting for the party lists the Socialists came out on top with 32.5 per cent ahead of Fidesz on 28.8 per cent, but the total poll showed a clear majority of 54.5 per cent in favour of the right. Thanks to the support of other right-wing parties, in the second round of voting in the individual constituencies Fidesz was able to increase its number of seats sevenfold to 148. Together with the revived Smallholders' Party (48 seats) and the rump MDF (19 seats), Viktor Orbán formed a right-wing conservative coalition government with a strong absolute majority. He was therefore not dependent on the support of the 14 MPs of the extreme right-wing and anti-Semitic Hungarian Justice and Life Party (MÍEP) founded by István Csurka in 1993.

At the age of 35, Viktor Orbán was the youngest democratic prime minister in Hungarian history.[1] Driven by an overwhelming lust for power, the youthful politician succeeded, through his own extraordinary efforts and with great tactical skill, in conjuring up a new victorious party out of the ruins of the Democratic Forum (MDF) following its collapse. Who could have predicted such a career when on 30 March 1988, just before midnight, Orbán and 36 other students founded the Alliance of Young Democrats (Fiatal Demokraták Szövetsége or Fidesz) as an independent youth organisation in the large lecture hall of a law college in Budapest? What has happened in the subsequent two decades with Orbán and his party has repeatedly recalled the timeless relevance of the warnings of Hans Kohn, the historian of nationalism, about history being an 'open process in which the unpredictable, the unexpected can happen at any time'.[2]

The systematic and masterly swing to the right, made without the slightest scruple, was undoubtedly the single most important factor in the unprecedented rise to power of the hitherto weakest party in parliament, one that had suffered two crushing defeats. After 1994, Orbán and a handful of his closest friends began to transform the original grass-roots movement of young revolutionaries step by step and ever more successfully into a charismatic 'Führer' party. The carefully cultivated radical-liberal rhetoric and anti-bourgeois stance was replaced in both style and substance by a smooth and subsequently accelerating transition towards the conservative values that the young Orbán and his friends had once so mocked. Standing shoulder to shoulder with the Catholic and Protestant churches and against its left-wing and liberal political rivals, Fidesz now consciously played the card of the myth of the Hungarian nation.[3]

After the weak liberal wing, led by his popular rival Gábor Fodor, split off and then joined the SzDSz in October 1993, Orbán strengthened his control over Fidesz and exploited his one realistic opportunity for any future success: right-wing conservative, nationalist option. Hence, in April 1995, just after the sudden shock of the drastic budget cuts presented by the then Finance Minister Lajos Bokros, he accused the Socialist-Liberal government of having misled the people and of representing not the interests of Hungarian voters but those of international finance. Two years later, on 12 June 1997, he went further and in a major speech accused the Hungarian government of being, despite constitutional law, 'alien' and not subject to national influence.

After the Tocsik scandal the Fidesz offensive against the 'most corrupt government of the century' was running at full steam. On the eve of the election, with the unconditional support of the churches, Fidesz promised an annual economic growth rate of 7 per cent and cleansing of the Augean stables of corruption. Following an energetic election campaign Fidesz and the other right-wing parties won power in Budapest. On 6 July 1998 Orbán was elected Prime Minister.

The details of the personal and political career of Viktor Orbán, this 'meteor in the sky of Hungarian politics' (Debreczeni), and the consequences of his first term in office (1998–2002) are well known. Equally familiar are the many details of the sophisticated system he conceived to win, consolidate and retain power during the subsequent eight years in opposition. For this we may thank above all the two comprehensive biographies on Orbán (totalling 1,020 pages) that the political scientist and journalist József Debreczeni wrote within the space of seven years. The author's past lends a particular authenticity and also a personal touch to these thoroughly researched and objective works: even before the change of system Debreczeni was one of the first four freely elected MDF MPs, and between 1994 and 1996 he even worked as Orbán's personal political adviser.[4]

What has moulded the image of Viktor Orbán both as a student leader and during his entire career is his absolute will to power, even though he has been able, thanks to an increasingly compliant media, to convey primarily the image of a purposeful politician with character, modesty and a clean pair of hands. He has understood how to dissociate himself in a timely manner, when necessary, from maladroit and unacceptable officials within his own party, and never to allow himself to be held responsible for any slip-ups. As Gábor Fodor, his onetime close friend (and subsequent rival) from the law faculty, has observed: 'Even as a young man in the 1980s Viktor Orbán was already possessed of those domineering, intolerant ways of thinking and behaving that are all too evident in him today. There was also an expediency about him, one without any principles. But not only that. He was, in addition to all of this, open, sincere and likeable'.[5] The evaluation of Orbán as a man admired by his supporters and feared by his opponents, a man with widely acknowledged strong leadership qualities, remains ambivalent. His authoritarian style of leadership is considered by most independent observers as being, at the very least, problematic and potentially dangerous for the young Hungarian democracy. After the parliamentary elections of 1998, the political scientist László Lengyel characterised the victor as follows: 'Orbán trusts nobody. He is a tiger by nature, striking down his victims mercilessly ... he knows no inner barriers'. In his introduction to Orbán's ever mutating political tactics and strategies, Debreczeni comes to the following conclusion: 'Viktor Orbán is a man who almost automatically believes in the *veracity* of whatever he considers to be politically *useful* to him'.

What marked out the leadership style of Prime Minister Orbán and his shaping of the central processes of political decision-making in that first period? Orbán was from the very beginning an unconditional advocate of the primacy of politics over economics. Particularly in the second half of his first premiership, he started to listen more to those advisers who wanted to put a brake on further austerity measures and instead to promote welfare benefits, above all family support and subventions for house construction. Protecting and fostering the domestic economy rather than the 'unbridled expansion' of foreign capital should help legitimise the dominance of politics over economics, especially in view of the approaching parliamentary elections. At the time Orbán casually observed in an interview that there was also a life outside the EU. In a similar chilling vein, and much to the surprise of his audience, he was also distinctly reserved at an event organised by the Austrian Chamber of Commerce during a public discussion (which I was conducting) on the accession of Central and Eastern European candidate countries to the EU.

Orbán's first government was marked by the power-oriented political elements of the decision-making process: the consolidation of the prime minister's office as the key centre of that very process and the simultaneous weakening of the parliamentary control mechanisms. These four years witnessed the development of a rhetorical leadership, a concept originating in the USA whereby the person of the head of government stands at the centre of government communications. József Debreczeni gives an array of pertinent details in his description of a government style dominated by a one-man leadership.

Orbán, for example, took his oath of office as Prime Minister two days before all the other ministers. Whenever the 35-year-old head of government entered the room before the beginning of a meeting of the cabinet, all ministers rose in greeting. Normally, there was no discussion on those proposals previously discussed and decided upon in the small circle around Orbán. The fact that no minutes were ever taken and no tape recordings made of the proceedings of a cabinet meeting was the subject of particular criticism. Mere summaries were later compiled. This practice was without precedent, all the more so because during both the Dual Monarchy and the Horthy era, and even during the four decades of communist rule, minutes of cabinet meetings were always taken.

Quite correctly, political scientists emphasise the importance of parliamentary control mechanisms. 'Parliamentary control of the government is the most important form of democratic control in a representative democracy during a legislative period'.[6] For this very reason the government's decision to alter the order of business in parliament sparked off widespread criticism. Instead of weekly meetings during ordinary or extraordinary parliamentary sessions, meetings were henceforth to be called every three weeks, thereby restricting the right of an immediate interpellation. In their articles, the authors of the German study quoted above point out that it is precisely this policing of government by the majority parliamentary party that is effective, because it permits not only a retroactive, but also a concomitant and even an anticipatory control. However, during the Orbán government no pertinent information could be collected because the sessions of the party factions in parliament also, were not recorded on tape.

Orban's relationship to the capture and exercise of power, and similarly his understanding of political communication and media management, can only be really understood if we recall his off-the-record thoughts on this, taped by Debreczeni in the summer of 1994 while collecting material for his biography on the recently deceased Prime Minister József Antall. Only seven years later did the biographer make these important comments available to the public in his first book on Orbán.

After the worst electoral defeat of Fidesz in 1994 (it won just 5 per cent of the seats), Orbán reproached Antall with extraordinary acerbity for what the young politician deemed to be the late Prime Minister's greatest mistake: his failure to create and leave an inheritance of either a communications framework or an economic basis for any future conservative government:

Antall bears the personal responsibility. Not because we are in opposition but because we stand completely naked, with bare bottom in opposition ... There isn't a single newspaper. Some of the newspapers were stolen, and he allowed others to be robbed from under his nose and the rest he kept in state ownership ... there is no radio, no TV station. There's nothing. And for this there is no excuse.

Orbán saw as Antall's other great mistake that he

neglected to cultivate personal contacts with the eight to ten big capitalists ... What should have been done? To make it clear in front of the bankers that these eight to ten people are our people ... And then let big business arrange everything else according to its own logic. These people could have perhaps have been helped in the investment funds, in the calls for tenders ... After an international negotiation he [Antall] was asked in a small group of people why he had not proposed a possible joint economic venture. To this Antall replied that he had not come to do business but to improve the position of the country. In his view, business had no part in politics although it is very substance of politics ... He had no feeling for anything like this. Absolutely no feeling.

For Orbán these experiences of his predecessor's alleged omissions were instructive, and from the beginning the Fidesz leader pursued three main goals:

(a) the maximum exploitation of the communications media and the mobilisation potential of the government apparatus to build up his political power, together with the direct and indirect takeover of leadership positions in public service broadcasting, and the founding of new daily and weekly newspapers by personalities loyal to him;
(b) filling important public positions, above all the offices of the head of the state, chief public prosecutors and the president of the National Bank, with people owing absolute allegiance to him;
(c) establishing particularly intensive and, for all concerned, lucrative relationships with the conservative right-wing and nationalist-minded bankers and industrialists.

One of the most pertinent descriptions in the public domain of the first Orbán government's style comes from László Békesi, the former Minister of Finance in the first eight months of the Socialist-Liberal coalition, who later broke with Horn and his party for reasons of principle. Békesi's analysis, made at the end of 1999—that is, in the middle of the legislature period—can be considered the opinion of an incorruptible and qualified observer:

Orbán is an extraordinarily talented, unbelievably resolute and determined politician. But these virtues are at one and the same time the source of his mistakes. He is driven by such a ruthless lust for power that this from time to time prevents him from either considering matters or making decisions realistically. He is vain and can therefore neither bear criticism nor work in a team. The manner in which he has established the structure of government shows precisely that he regards himself not as a prime minister but as a 'Führer'. His style of governing is stamped upon the entire state apparatus of power: he centralises, re-nationalises in statist-populist ways, interferes in trials ... With such traits he is not suited to leading a country. Viktor Orbán must learn that even at the top of the ladder there are rules that have to be followed, such as the principles of live and let live, thinking as a team, being fair to opponents ... Unfortunately his bad traits have become stronger ... Viktor Orbán will never recognise that he should push through his personal ambitions in his party, in his government, in parliament, in the wider domestic political audience, in a non-aggressive way ... To the outside world he will of course, albeit grudgingly, show his European face.[7]

In the first years the young and energetic head of government enjoyed positive coverage in the foreign media. However, domestically the coalition government, and in particular the Smallholders' Party, was, according to newspaper reports, increasingly mired in corruption and nepotism. Even critics of the corrupt practices of the Horn government were left speechless. Orbán was compelled to finally dispense with those ministers of his coalition partners accused of taking bribes. Then the public outrage at the dubious transactions in connection with the sale of the Fidesz party headquarters forced the resignation of a close political ally of the Prime Minister from a prominent position. On the margins of this curious affair, there were also dubious dealings in some credit and share transactions connected with the acquisition of a quarry, with ramifications in high places.

At the time József Debreczeni drew the conclusion that 'In the West a similar scandal would have led to the fall of a head of government. He would have to resign. Not in Hungary. Here it is not necessary to stand down'. In his second biography of Orbán, published in 2009, Debreczeni devotes a long and detailed chapter (the facts of which have never been denied) to extensive business interests of the Prime Minister and his family; he also unequivocally hints at the abuse of the powers of the position of prime minister.[8]

In 2001, with a very clear eye on the 2002 parliamentary elections, the restrictive budgetary policy was radically reversed to an expansive one. The minimum wage for 750,000 employees was raised first by 50 per cent in 2001 and then by 25 per cent the following year; real incomes rose in the first half of 2001 by 4.5 per cent, but almost doubled in the second two quarters to 8.4 per cent. In the course of the year pensions were increased twice, a nominal increase of 16 per cent and a 5.8 per cent increase in real terms. When the special allowances for 120,000 civil servants, the 70 per cent increase in the salaries of professional soldiers, the augmented state interest rate credits for private loans for house building and the increased family allowances, as well as the special allowances for railway workers, doctors and nurses and others, are all taken into account, it is hardly surprising that for the first time since 1994 the 5.2 per cent growth in consumption was considerably higher than that of GDP, which stood at 4.3 per cent.

In the first quarter of the election year of 2002 the growth rate of real earnings was three times that of GDP. Industrial production stagnated whilst the balance-of-payments deficit and turnover in the retail trade doubled. Yet, apart from a 9 per cent increase in private consumption, every other economic indicator indicated a deteriorating situation. A report by Zita Mária Petschnig, an independent and respected political economist, published in January 2006 reveals that the foundations for the subsequent and even more dangerous economic crisis in Hungary, for which the successor Socialist-Liberal coalition was primarily responsible, were laid in the final phase of the Orbán government.[9]

Meanwhile, in the right-wing daily and weekly press, even on one of the most popular programmes on public service radio, the trivialisation, defence and glorification of the Horthy regime were keenly pursued. The international media, NGOs and civil rights groups were ever more frequently concerned with the anti-Semitic and anti-Roma gaffes in public life.[10] The calculated breaking of taboos, which was by no means restricted to the publications of István Csurka's Justice and Life Party (MIÉP) and which influenced broad swathes of the student youth, provoked a very negative echo in the publications of Jewish organisations abroad, especially in the USA. The fact that after the 9/11 terrorist attacks Prime Minister Orbán did not immediately and resolutely distance himself from Csurka's outrageous anti-Semitic and anti-American statements was, according to press reports, the reason why President Bush was not prepared to meet Orbán while the latter was in the USA in February 2002 for the award ceremony of an honorary degree from Boston University.

The inflammatory talk of Fidesz politicians on the right and the desire for autonomy among the Hungarian minorities in the neighbouring countries won the enthusiastic favour of most of their representatives. At the same time, however, it also provided political ammunition to the nationalist voices in those countries. That the Socialists were equally willing to engage in populist sloganeering to the detriment of the minorities when it suited their purposes was shown by their exploitation of an agreement that Orbán signed with the Romanian Prime Minister Adrian Năstase at the end of 2001. This was ambiguously worded and could be interpreted as granting a three-month work permit and social insurance to every Romanian citizen, not just to the Hungarians living in Romania. Although it was evident that in practice this would involve a maximum of 81,000 people, the Socialists launched a massive campaign of intimidation claiming that '23 million Romanians were at our door'.

For their part the Socialists, as was their wont before an election, were rocked by a power struggle, primarily revolving around the candidate for the post of prime minister. László Kovács, the long-serving foreign minister and Horn's successor as party chief after 1998, negotiated first with the former Prime Minister Miklós Németh, who was working as a highly paid vice-president at the EBRD in London. Németh, however, presented such far-reaching, personal demands that the party leadership chose in the end Péter Medgyessy, the Minister of Finance and Vice-Premier before and after the changes of 1989. He had not joined the MSzP when it was refounded, but the reappearance of this elegant and moderate politician was approved in opinion polls.

As an advocate of the 'national centre' and of political accommodation, Medgyessy seemed a more reassuring figure to the floating and undecided voters than the aggressive, overweening Orbán. Although the outgoing Prime Minister succeeded in winning over voters from the extreme right and thereby keeping Csurka's party out of the new parliament, his confrontational election campaign mobilised potential Liberal and Socialist voters. In the television debate between the two candidates, Medgyessy came across as more personable and cultivated than Orbán, twenty years his junior.

At the elections in 2002, 72 per cent of the electorate went to the polls, the highest number since 1989. The centre-left won a narrow victory, achieved not least because the Liberals (SzDSz) were able to jump over the 5 per cent hurdle. The result, 198 seats for Fidesz, 188 for the MSzP and 20 for the SzDSz, was without doubt a huge shock to Orbán and his team. Both in Budapest and as a participant in TV discussion programmes, I experienced those tense days myself, dominated as they were by the doubts and threats of the defeated right alleging election fraud. Thirsting for revenge, Orbán's media ringleaders demanded retaliation for the 'stolen victory'. After the election, in a last extended interview with Jozsef Debreczeni held on 4 May 2002 to conclude the first biography, Orbán brusquely rejected any accusations of excessively confrontational tactics. On the contrary, he maintained he had not been sufficiently adept in the campaign and had been nowhere near tough enough in his directing of the government; more channels of information in new newspapers and the electronic media should have been created.

The glamour and misery of the first Orbán era proved to be the prelude to a politically and morally, economically and culturally disastrous polarisation in Hungarian society.

7

THE MEDGYESSY PUZZLE OR THE END OF A DECEPTION

The news, just three weeks after the Socialist-Liberal government under Péter Medgyessy had assumed office, came like a bolt out of the blue. Under the sensational banner headline 'A secret agent at the head of the government' the opposition newspaper *Magyar Nemzet* printed on its front page a facsimile of an order dated 2 March 1978. Issued by the communist Interior Minister, this appointed Péter Medgyessy, at the time deputy head of the central department in the Ministry of Finance, as a 'top secret' counterintelligence officer with the rank of first lieutenant under the codename 'Comrade D-209'.

Before the Hungarian parliament the Prime Minister justified this hitherto concealed detail from his glittering CV as follows: 'Between 1977 and 1982, as a counterintelligence officer active in the field of the transactions of the Ministry of Finance, I rendered assistance preventing foreign spies from acquiring any state secrets and from their hindering Hungarian access to the IMF'. Medgyessy emphasised that this work had 'nothing to do with spying but rather he was working in the interests of defending the homeland'. Later he added he had also written analyses on financial questions for the Ministry of the Interior.

Neither then nor in the interview I conducted with him in the course of the preparation of this book did Medgyessy ever display any embarrassment or misgivings, let alone any sense of shame. He claimed that the tasks of intelligence or counterintelligence should not be confused with the repressive operations of an interior ministry or a secret service. He had done nothing illegal and after his appointment to the post of Deputy Minister of Finance in 1982 he was removed from active service with the rank of captain in the reserve. As a counterintelligence officer he had only received a small bonus or, to be more precise, some gifts; moreover, the then Minister of Finance had been informed about his activities.

While we were chatting about his career in his tastefully appointed consultant's office in a villa in the fashionable Gellert hill district in Buda, I asked him whether he had not been blackmailed. Shortly before our meeting one of his former colleagues, a cabinet minister, had told me that in the 1970s, as a young civil servant in the Ministry of Finance on a trip abroad, Medgyessy had been caught smuggling foreign exchange during the border check in the train. He had hidden two or three hundred dollars in his trouser turn-ups. This odd little story was confirmed by another ex-minister. Medgyessy's response to what he called a 'ludicrous invention' was a roar of laughter. Moreover, he said, everybody in communist Hungary who had had anything to do with foreign countries had been involved in similar intelligence activities; in this connection he mentioned the names of some past and present Fidesz ministers.[1]

Whatever the truth of the matter members of the Socialists' coalition partner, the SzDSz, were deeply shocked at the revelations about the Prime Minister's hidden past. Medgyessy immediately called for a vote of confidence, but at a party meeting the same evening SzDSz MPs rejected this by 17 votes to three. They wanted to begin negotiations with the Socialists straight away in order to heave a new prime minister in the saddle by means of a 'constructive motion of no confidence'. But within 24 hours the situation had been completely turned around. The previous day the Socialist MPs had overwhelmingly supported Medgyessy and rejected any idea of a constructive motion of no confidence; he SzDSZ could therefore only negotiate with the opposition on the matter. So the question was: Medgyessy or Orbán?

Of the two, the SzDSz opted for 'the lesser of two evils' (as the party chairman put it) and remained in the coalition. In a second round of voting Liberal MPs supported Medgyessy in a vote of confidence by 11 votes to seven. In stark contrast to the top leadership of the Socialists, which long before the election had been informed about their candidate's past, the Liberals had had no prior knowledge of this explosive revelation. This was confirmed to me by Iván Pető, the party's chief whip at the time. The vote of his junior coalition partner gave Medgyessy some breathing space but was far from being any expression of confidence in the Prime Minister.

Unlike the politicians and intellectuals, ordinary voters were barely bothered by the D-209 affair. An opinion survey conducted some days after the scandal broke found that two-thirds of those questioned were completely indifferent about the

Prime Minister's past; he therefore had no need to resign. Two months later Medgyessy was even the most popular politician in Hungary and 62 per cent of those polled believed the country was heading in the right direction ...

As we shall see, working for the Ministry of the Interior and the secret service always was and always has been regarded as little more than a peccadillo. But in a devastating analysis the mentor and former leader of the Liberals, the philosopher János Kis, promptly lamented the moral bankruptcy of his party, condemned the deception of the voters and predicted serious, long-term political consequences. The reservations of the Liberal MPs of the SzDSz, driven by purely tactical considerations, ultimately contributed to their subsequent sharp conflict with Medgyessy and led to his unexpected fall. In retrospect the reaction to the Liberals' opportunistic stance during the following years also accelerated the inexorable demise of these relics of the former democratic opposition.

Who exactly was Péter Medgyessy, a man who gave every appearance of being an independent technocrat and who in April 2002 led the Socialists to a narrow win in the polls against Viktor Orbán's party, which had for so long seemed assured of victory? In contrast to both his predecessor and his successor as prime minister, Medgyessy came from a bourgeois family of intellectuals, with links to the petty nobility, originating in Transylvania (now in Romania). Born in Budapest in 1942, he joined the Communist Party in 1965 as a university student of economics and then made a smooth and rapid career in the Ministry of Finance. A high flier in the civil service, the adaptable and talented Medgyessy was just 40 when he was named Vice-Minister. His confidential side job as a top secret counterespionage officer had no doubt eased his rise.

THE MEDGYESSY PUZZLE OR THE END OF A DECEPTION

In 1987 Medgyessy was appointed Minister of Finance. Once again he demonstrated his total loyalty to the communist regime by dissolving, as was desired, the Institute for Financial Research, a theoretical workshop of economic reformers that was much criticised by party hardliners. In the last reform communist government of Miklós Németh, Medgyessy held the post of Deputy Prime Minister responsible for Economic Affairs. In the same period (1987–89) he was promoted to the Central Committee of the Communist Party.

After the collapse of the Communist regime in 1989 this sociable and very well connected man bided his time. As the CEO of the French-owned Paribas Bank in Hungary, Medgyessy, who spoke excellent French, was leading a very comfortable life. Following the victory of the MSzP, Horn wanted to appoint him Minister of Industry, but at the last minute a party stalwart got the job. Instead Medgyessy took over the post of CEO of the state-owned Investment Bank and, as mentioned in the previous chapter, ultimately became Horn's third Minister of Finance in the Socialist-Liberal government.

During the Orbán era he returned to the world of finance, this time as president of the Inter-Europa Bank and vice-president of an insurance company. It is not quite clear what actually was the decisive factor in his election on 9 June 2001 as the Socialists' front runner for the post of prime minister. The leader of the MSzP, László Kovács, successfully blocked the attempted return of Miklós Németh to Hungarian politics. Saying he would 'rather be the second or fifth man in a successful party than the first man in a defeated one', Kovács left the door open to former comrade Medgyessy, who was by then a personality without any party affiliations. Party insiders maintain that it was the struggle between Miklós Németh and

László Kovács for nomination as the Socialists' top candidate that paved the way to Medgyessy's premiership.

Most sources agree on the pivotal role of Piroska Apró in Medgyessy's unexpected political comeback. A former top civil servant and deputy minister in the Ministry of Trade, Apró had been a close friend of Medgyessy ever since they had studied together at the Economics University. Among the many jobs held after 1989 by this highly talented and spectacularly well connected daughter of the long-serving Communist Party Politburo member Antal Apró, she had been chief of the personal staff of Prime Minister Horn and later president of the Export-Import Bank; she was also an extremely successful businesswoman. She not only set the course for the unexpected rise of Péter Medgyessy but later even arranged for her own equally talented, multilingual daughter, Klára Dobrev, to be his chief of personal staff. Dobrev was married to the one-time young Communist Party official, Ferenc Gyurcsány, who had after 1989 become a wealthy businessman. The couple were among Medgyessy's closest advisers during the election campaign (see chapter 9).

The controversial and impenetrable D-209 affair was just one of the reasons for the new Prime Minister's place in recent Hungarian history. Given his previous career, his financial and economic policies have also remained a riddle to most observers. For Péter Medgyessy very much owed his slim victory over Viktor Orbán to his image of a self-confident, imperturbable, experienced and very professional technocrat, an internationally accomplished expert with a veneer of statesmanship. He had worked for almost 28 years in the Ministry of Finance, had been Minister of Finance himself for years both before and after the collapse of the communist regime, and had also held many top positions in the world of private banking. However, as head of government he immediately began to start throwing money around in his much quoted '100-day programme'. Or, as the internationally respected economist András Inotai has put it: 'His unforgivable crime was that, as a gentleman, he insisted on fulfilling his election promises'.

Perhaps never before had a Hungarian prime minister distributed so many electoral goodies in such a short time as Medgyessy did in the summer of 2002. The salaries of public sector employees (about 800,000 people) were raised by 50 per cent, scholarships and grants by 30 per cent, taxes on the minimum wage (already raised by Orbán) and TV and radio licences were abolished, and from January 2003 the approximately three million pensioners received a thirteenth monthly pension. This generosity, for which there was no money, when taken together with the modernisation plans for construction of new motorways and continuation of the lavish subsidies on the interest rates charged on loans for building houses inherited from the Orbán government, resulted in a budget deficit of 7.5 per cent of GDP in the first year of the programme. This was to put a great strain on the national budget in the coming years.

These and other measures of the Orbán and Medgyessy governments led to a 33 per cent increase in consumption by private households between 2002 and 2005, while GDP rose only by 18 per cent. In 2003 alone real earnings grew by 7.3 per cent in the private sector and 12.7 per cent in the public sector. While the Socialist-Liberal coalition partners, instead of reducing the deficit, were actually increasing it through enhanced expenditure on welfare and modernisation projects, the opposition, thirsting for revenge, was demanding the full implementation of the excessive electoral promises. Since then no government has been able to escape this vicious circle and none has ever approached fulfilling the Maastricht Criteria that Hungary had to accept before joining the EU.[2] Every single serious economist is agreed that this policy of running the gauntlet with the public budget originated in the final years of the first Orbán government; it was a fatal policy continued with a vengeance by Medgyessy.

To this day Medgyessy maintains that he acted correctly with his infamous 100-day programme: 'It is not possible to be happy in an unjust society. For this reason I kept my promises on raising salaries for teachers and lecturers, nurses and doctors etc. Later, I wanted to reduce the deficit but the MSzP lacked the necessary courage; as a party it was impatient and fearful of losing the 2006 elections'. A leading lawyer and former government commissioner for administrative reform sees his motives differently.

As an economist, Medgyessy knew that he was not doing the right thing, but behind all the wild spending of money lay his need to forge a camp of supporters. In reality he would have preferred to have organised a nationalist, Christian centre-left party. He handed out goodies because he wanted to win. He was destroyed by the party apparatus, but he also wanted to destroy it. There is no doubt he is talented, but incapable of making a decision.

One of his predecessors as Minister of Finance was even harsher:

Capable, but vain, and weak. Our worst prime minister, and the one who caused the greatest damage. He was delighted to become prime minister. He is strengthening his legitimacy by being the benefactor of the people. He has gone well beyond his election promises by introducing the first 100-day programme and then by topping this with a second 100-day programme. He will lead the country into bankruptcy.

THE MEDGYESSY PUZZLE OR THE END OF A DECEPTION

A minister who served in his government came to a similar conclusion. 'Medgyessy was the weakest prime minister, a man without charisma, who didn't work until 6 pm like the others, and could neither make a decision nor inspire as an example. He simply wanted to add to his CV the fact that he had been prime minister'.[3]

It would be easy to quote a whole series of similar assessments of Péter Medgyessy. However, the reasons for his relatively quick fall did not lie in his mistakes in financial policy, deluded as he was by his sudden and rapid popularity. Against the background of the ever more evident lack of orientation and a Socialist Party paralysed by continuous internal bickering, the Prime Minister, who had no party affiliation, did not radiate leadership and could not present ideas, let alone formulate a strategy against the revived forces of the opposition. In addition, there was the problem of his repeated gaffes in style and conduct, blown up by the media and even more by his political opponents.

One example: after his government declaration and the furore surrounding the D-209 affair, Medgyessy was holidaying with his wife at Cannes on the French Riviera when on 14 August 2002 Hungary was badly hit by particularly severe flooding of the Danube. About 20,000 people were frantically working to strengthen the defences against the floodwaters. Thousands had to be taken to safety. The Prime Minister, however, calmly remained in Cannes for another two days and only appeared on the scene on 17 August in the picturesque tourist spot of Szentendre near Budapest, which was also threatened with inundation. The 'travelling man of the world' was even more harshly criticised when at the end of 2002 he went on a winter holiday to Cuba. The arrangements were so secret that not even his government spokespersons were able to give any information as to his whereabouts to inquisitive journalists. That Medgyessy had chosen one of the last communist states for his holidays was even more grist to the mill of malicious commentators. There was a further blunder in his communications policy when he took yet another semi-secret holiday in Thailand.

On the positive side was Medgyessy's foreign policy, above all the accession to the EU and the improvements in relations with Hungary's neighbours. His presence as Prime Minister at a reception given by his Romanian colleague Adrian Năstase in a hotel in Budapest on the occasion of the Romanian national day was deemed a courageous, personal gesture, but wildly attacked by the right wing media. Medgyessy was, by the way, the first Hungarian prime minister who could speak fluent Romanian: for the first five years after the Second World War his father had headed the Hungarian trade mission in Bucharest, which enabled the young Péter to learn the language. Relations with Russia were also intensified by a number of personal contacts between Medgyessy and Vladimir Putin.

Measures taken to curtail the subsidies on the interest rates charged on loans for building houses and to reduce or postpone various items of budgetary expenditure, measures that had become unavoidable but were still relatively painless, led to a surprisingly rapid deterioration in the mood of wide sections of the population during 2003. This was reflected in the fall in the Prime Minister's popularity in opinion polls. By the beginning of 2004 the leadership in the Socialist Party was already discussing how and when it could rid itself of Péter Medgyessy. The Prime Minister had fulfilled his historical duty by winning, albeit only by a small margin, the 2002 elections for the MSzP.

The final straw was, however, a controversial personal initiative made by Medgyessy that alienated the governing parties.

THE MEDGYESSY PUZZLE OR THE END OF A DECEPTION

Upon the advice of some American media specialists he proposed the introduction of a second chamber in parliament, a reduction in the number of MPs and direct elections for the president. Additionally, he floated the idea of a common list of all parties in the forthcoming elections to the European Parliament and hinted at the possibility of a referendum on these questions. The hastily presented ideas were criticised by both the left and the right, and eventually shelved by the government.

The European elections on 13 June 2004 unsurprisingly proved to be a resounding slap in the face for Medgyessy's government and the MSzP. Fidesz won 12 seats as opposed to nine for the MSzP, two for the SzDSz and one for the MDF. Even more important, however, were the percentages: 47.41 per cent for the opposition and only 34.41 per cent for the Socialists. In the wake of the shock effect of his first personal defeat Medgyessy went on the attack on two fronts.

It was Ferenc Gyurcsány, almost 20 years his junior and the 60th wealthiest man in Hungary, who appeared in the eyes of Medgyessy to be first a potential rival and then perhaps his most dangerous rival within the ranks of the MSzP. The husband of his former chief of personal staff, Klára Dobrev and the son-in-law of Piroska Apró, who had played such a crucial role in Medgyessy's own rise to the pinnacles of government, had already repeatedly demonstrated his extraordinary talents. Behind the scenes he had played a substantial role in the election campaign, and after Medgyessy's victory he became his chief adviser in the summer of 2002.

Gyurcsány popularised such terms as 'national centre' and a 'third way' à la Anthony Giddens, the British political scientist responsible for much of the thinking behind Tony Blair's New Labour. In May Medgyessy promoted his adviser to Minister for Sport and Youth. Gyurcsány now began his carefully planned rise within the ranks of the party: first he became a member of the executive committee of the Socialist Party in March 2003 and then, the following February, party chairman for the important county of Győr-Moson-Sopron. By means of his numerous personal appearances throughout the country and the many articles he published, Gyurcsány, who had only joined the MSzP in 2000, consolidated his position.

Almost at the same time an open conflict broke out between Medgyessy and his Liberal Minister of the Economy and Transport, István Csillag. The respected economist was attacked with increasing frequency by the Prime Minister during 2003, at first internally and then publicly, for his alleged incompetence in running the huge ministry. One of its responsibilities was the building of motorways, and it was the choice between three civil engineering groups (two Austrian and one French) for the lucrative contract for the construction and management of a section of motorway that brought matters to a head. Whether the rumours about the alleged interests of the two politicians in the struggle for power hold water can no longer be ascertained. Whatever the case, in an interview given at the height of the conflict with Csillag, Medgyessy declared that his liberal coalition partner, the SzDSz, was riddled with corruption. He demanded the unconditional resignation of Csillag and announced a cabinet reshuffle, including the dismissal of Gyurcsány.

As the dramatic hours and days unfolded, it turned out that Medgyessy's ultimate challenge to his coalition partner to accept the resignation of his Minister of the Economy had failed because the Socialists took Liberal threats to break up the government seriously and, instead of Csillag, they wanted

THE MEDGYESSY PUZZLE OR THE END OF A DECEPTION

to sacrifice the Prime Minister, now little more than a 'paper tiger'. Furious with rage, Medgyessy announced his resignation at the Socialist Party congress where his successor was to be chosen, and in an emotional speech attacked unnamed rebels as the plotters behind his fall.

The era of Medgyessy's government was thus a relatively brief intermezzo before the lightning career of Ferenc Gyurcsány, a rise which nobody, including the man himself, had expected to be so rapid. Hungary was now to be ruled by the most capable, the most controversial and unpredictable, and certainly the richest politician on the left.

8

THE SENSE OF MISSION
OF AN EASILY SEDUCIBLE NATION

In 1990, in the wake of the communist implosion, the French commentator Alain Minc predicted that with the disintegration of the bloc system which had divided Europe for four decades the revenge of the nations would begin; the breakup of the post-war political order would release a renaissance of nationalist thinking, of which much could be hoped but even more feared.[1] The wars in Yugoslavia, sparked off by the pursuit of Greater Serbian hegemony and stoked by the defensive reactions of the Croats, Albanians and Bosnian-Muslims, demonstrated all too clearly to the Central and Eastern European post-communist states the catastrophic consequences of mythically charged, unbridled nationalist conflicts.

Since the enlargement of the EU in eastern European about two million members of the Hungarian minorities in Romania and Slovakia have been able to enjoy the long yearned-for freedom of movement in Europe without any visas and, with it, the freedom to travel to and from the Hungarian mother country; a privilege later extended to the 300,000 Hungarians in Serbia (even before Belgrade's possible accession to the EU). Yet, in spite of the membership of Romania, Slovakia and Hungary in the EU and NATO, we are experiencing the return of the old nationalism at the heart of Hungarian politics. Bombastic nationalist rhetoric in the Carpathian Basin, and the reciprocal racking-up of historical resentments at a pace few could have imagined, seem to demonstrate the clout which the nationalists have at their disposal to challenge the international European idea.

In his study on the 'the past neglect and present power of nationalism', published many years before the fall of the Soviet empire, Sir Isaiah Berlin wrote that nationalism was 'the elevation of the interests of the unity and self-determination of the nation to the status of supreme value before which all other considerations, must, if need be, yield at all times'. Almost prophetically, he added, 'No one has yet convincingly demonstrated that the human imagination obeys discoverable laws, or is able to predict the movement of ideas'.[2]

Hardly a country in Central Europe and the Balkans has had an open debate on its own history. The 'combination of historical memories and resentments with metaphysical and moral fanaticism' (Berlin) still remains the substitute for any critical historical consciousness. And this is the very reason why it is so very dangerous for Europe that Viktor Orbán, 'the most talented populist in Central Europe',[3] has exploited and fanned the flames of a crude nationalism wrapped up in the pieties of Christianity purely for the purpose of gaining political power and then, having achieved it, of securing his own political dominance.

THE SENSE OF MISSION

Shortly after it entered office at the end of May 2010, the new Orbán government hastily passed two controversial laws. One gave the right to a Hungarian passport to all Hungarians whether they had permanent residence in Hungary or not, whilst the other designated 4 June, the date of the signing of the Treaty of Trianon in 1920,[4] the Day of National Unity. The reverberations in the media, in the capitals of Hungary's neighbours, in the EU and internationally have been universally critical and negative. If, in the process, the overreaction in Bratislava, along with the existing anti-minority Slovak language law, was also criticised, the fact remains that most newspapers left no doubt that 'Orbán's playing with fire' and 'his messianic self-promotion'[5] were primarily responsible for the tensions between Hungary and Slovakia.

Consider first the behaviour and policies of the ruling elite in Budapest in the inter-war years (István Bibó wrote of the 'cul-de-sac character of Hungarian history'), its participation in the attacks on Yugoslavia (March 1941) and the USSR (June 1941) on the coat-tails of the Third Reich, and its assistance to the Germans in the extermination of Hungarian Jewry; then consider the tendency of the born-again Christian nationalists to collective self-glorification, paraded as it is before us in words and pictures, and the question arises: is the Hungarian nation more susceptible to the charms of the seducer than other European nations; and if so, why?[6] Is it compatible with the political culture of a democratic Europe that those such as Ferenc Gyurcsány, the Prime Minister of Hungary between 2004 and 2009, who oppose the laws on double citizenship or the Trianon Treaty remembrance day, are denounced as 'traitors of the motherland' or as 'characters' without a country?

All opinion polls and studies reach the same, indisputable conclusion: what actually encumbers Hungary is the suppression, concealing and glossing over of the truth (for a variety of reasons) about what led to Trianon, to the death warrant of the Kingdom of St. Stephen, and to the cataclysmic years between 1920 and 1989. What Nietzsche called 'cowardice in the face of reality' is certainly true in many respects for all post-communist states and by no means only for Hungary. But here we should recall the pertinent observation of the American cultural historian William M. Johnston: 'Readiness to see the world through rose-coloured glasses induced Magyars to exaggerate their grandeur, while they ignored the misery of subject peoples ... Capacity for dreaming has made Magyars superlative advocates, ever ready to defend Hungary as an exception among nations'.[7]

The communications expert Mária Vásárhelyi has revealed in a number of studies the long-term effect of the heroic sagas of Hungarian history. In polls conducted in 2005 76 per cent of those questioned held to be true the demonstrably forged saga of Simon Kézai, who was the court chaplain between 1282 and 1285, according to which the Hungarians are descendants of the Huns, while 69 per cent believed that fourteenth-century Hungary bordered on three seas (the Black Sea, the Adriatic and the North Sea). Only 9 per cent agreed that the Hungarians had always badly treated the nationalities on their territory, 17 per cent said they had done so 'partly' while 70 per cent answered with an emphatic 'no'.

As far as the *Diktat* of Trianon is concerned, Vásárhelyi discerns two principal reasons for the trauma that has dominated the Hungary psyche to this day: overshadowing everything, the aggressive, radical irredentism of the Horthy era followed by the forty years of silence under communism. Despite the Treaty of Trianon being considered an absolute taboo, 70 per cent of respondents in a 1976 research project stated that the 1920 peace agreement filled them with profound bitterness. Thus, even during the communist dictatorship, the great majority of Hungarians supported the recovery of the overwhelmingly Hungarian territories in Transylvania (Romania) and Upper Hungary (Slovakia).

Since 1989 two tendencies have stood out. The right wing has kept the Trianon trauma on the agenda as a source of nationalism, while the left has swept the problem under the carpet. As a consequence of the populist, increasingly aggressive rhetoric of the right and the passivity of the left, the right-wing interpretation of Trianon has prevailed among the adult population in the last decade. Yet, even today, more than half of the population is ignorant of the year in which the treaty was concluded. Only one adult in ten believes that the unjust treatment and the programmes of Magyarisation enforced upon the nationalities living on Hungarian territory played any important role in this Treaty which was so unfavourable to Hungary. Three times as many prefer to seek answers in the 'subversive activities of left-wing and Jewish forces', in the personal hatred the French Prime Minister Clemenceau felt for his Hungarian daughter-in-law, and in the traditional antipathy of the French towards Hungary in general.

The most explosive and spectacular change since 2002 has occurred in the current attitudes of the Hungarians regarding the consequences of Trianon. Whereas in 2002 approximately 18 per cent thought its terms should never be accepted, this proportion had risen to 45 per cent by 2010. Moreover, one person in three in this particular group maintains that no means should be discarded in the efforts aimed at reunifying the lost territories with rump Hungary. In the same period the percentage of those favouring acceptance of the Treaty fell from 34 per cent to 24 per cent, and even fewer believe that in the long term the strengthening and widening of the EU would resolve this issue.

These figures reflect a sharpening of attitudes in Hungarian society that is both alarming and at the same time absurd. As a consequence of the intensive right-wing and even extreme right-wing rhetoric, there are increasing numbers of Hungarians seeking a solution for what they perceive to be an unjust treaty not in a unifying Europe but in some sort of revenge. At the same time the replies of precisely those people who do not accept Trianon under any circumstances, and who would do anything to regain the lost territories, reveal that they have absolutely no idea about the changed demographic relations in these regions.

Only about 15 per cent have even a rough idea of the present population divisions. In Transylvania the percentage of ethnic Hungarians is just 21 per cent, yet half of those advocating its recovery for Hungary are convinced that the population is more than 50 per cent ethnic Hungarian. And it is the same in the case of the other 'lost' territories, in which the present-day percentages of ethnic Hungarians are consistently overestimated by a factor of three.[8]

The disturbing radicalisation of Hungarian attitudes illustrates just how correct the British Prime Minister Lloyd George was at the Paris Peace Conference when he twice warned of the perils of a Hungary brooding revenge for the future peace and stability of Central Europe. In 1919 he observed, 'There will never be peace in Southeast Europe if each of these newly created small nations contains a substantial Hungarian minority'. One year later he was warning once again against placing a third of the total Hungarian population under foreign control. 'There will be no peace if it turns out in retrospect that Hungary's demands are justified and that entire Hungarian ethnic groups are transferred like a herd of cattle to Czechoslovakia or Transylvania [Romania] just because the conference has declined to deal with the Hungarian question'.[9]

The monuments and gems of architecture, the birthplaces and tombs of great kings and brilliant writers in the historic towns of Transylvania and Upper Hungary can never be a matter of indifference to Hungarians. Novels and poems, paintings and family histories preserve the memories of a glorious but permanently irretrievable history.

The splendours of the past become even more opaque when it is recalled that in the century between 1910 and 2010 the proportion of Hungarians in Vojvodina (Serbia) declined from 28 per cent to 14 per cent, in Transylvania from 31.63 per cent to just below 20 per cent, in southern Slovakia from 30.30 per cent to 10 per cent. Or if, against the background of the bizarre Greater Hungary phantasmagoria of right-wing extremists, it is pointed out that in Bratislava (Pozsony)[10] today only one inhabitant in 20 is Hungarian; that in Cluj (Kolozsvár) the figure is only 22 per cent and in Košice (Kassa), the birthplace of my father (and of the famous writer Sándor Márai), only 12.6 per cent of the population are Magyars.

In the light of such statistics the position and prospects of the Hungarian minorities (290,000 in Vojvodina, 1,244,000 in Transylvania, 500,000 in Slovakia and 150,000 in Ukraine) depend very much on the attitude of the majority nation, the perceptions and behaviour of the political representatives of the minorities, and, last but not least, the neighbourhood policy of whatever government is in power in Budapest. In a previous chapter I briefly referred to the most important facts regarding the collapse of historical Greater Hungary and the consequences of the Treaty of Trianon. The development of inter-governmental relations since 1989, too, can only be understood if we carefully examine the complex array of problems regarding the minorities.

In a fatal, dialectical cycle, the relationship between majority and minority populations has been shaped by the humiliation and oppression of a once feared and envied group. Approximately 3.5 million Hungarians in Romania, Czechoslovakia and Yugoslavia were compelled to experience this role change no fewer than three times in the three decades following 1918. The abrupt metamorphosis from ruler to ruled after the Great War was followed by the two Vienna Awards imposed by the Axis Powers in 1938 and 1940, the partial recovery of the lost territories and finally, after 1945, the reversion to the position of a highly suspect and potentially irredentist minority deprived of any effective minority rights.

After the collapse of communism in Hungary, the question of the Hungarians living abroad was addressed in the very first amendment of the constitution concerning foreign policy objectives: 'The Republic of Hungary feels a responsibility for the fate of those Hungarians living outside its borders and will promote the cultivation of their contacts with Hungary'. That was a long overdue break with the four decades of making a taboo of the highly sensitive national and minority question, but the intensity of the neighbourhood policy was fated to be determined by the political priorities of governments both in Hungary and in the contiguous states.

A particular situation prevailed in the Autonomous Province of Vojvodina during Slobodan Milošević's attempt to establish a Greater Serbia. Its autonomy was abolished and the resettlement of thousands of Serb refugees from Croatia, coupled with the enormous pressure brought to bear on the Hungarian minority, further contributed to the poisoning of the atmosphere. Even after the fall of the dictatorship the strong position of the nationalists prevented a full normalisation of inter-ethnic relations.

In the 1990s the Antall and Horn governments signed neighbourhood agreements with Croatia and Ukraine, Slovakia and Romania. These included provisions on the minorities and the important principle that the protection of minorities was not exclusively a domestic concern of the states concerned, but also formed a legitimate object for the consideration of the international community. As a quid pro quo, as it were, the Hungarian government confirmed in the agreements its final acceptance of the Trianon borders. The toning down of nationalist rhetoric on the Hungarian side, pressure from the EU and the success of moderate forces even made it possible for the political representatives from the Hungarian minorities to hold positions in a number of governments in Romania and Slovakia.

Always, from the very beginning, relations between the governments in Budapest and in the neighbouring countries have primarily determined the position of the minorities and in particular their relationship with the political leadership of the majority nations. What one of the leading Hungarian intellectuals, László Szigeti, a successful publisher in Bratislava, has detected about the two main strands in the position of the Hungarians living in Slovakia since Trianon applies analogously, in spite of all the differences, to the Hungarian minorities in the other successor states of the old Habsburg Dual

Monarchy. There are two divides: one is the 'Hungro-centric' position, which in the inter-war years openly represented territorial revisionism and today is striving for the political unity of the Hungarian nation; the other is the so-called Czecho-Slovak orientation, which since 1993, when independent Slovakia came into existence, has set as its goal integration into Slovak society with simultaneous protection and strengthening of the Hungarian identity, on the basis of a compromise with the Slovaks.[11]

In the opinion of László Szarka, a respected expert on nationalities in Slovakia and the director of the Research Institute of Ethnic and National Minorities in Budapest, experience shows that a tense situation always arises when a strongly nationalist government holds power in either Hungary or Slovakia.[12] In this regard both domestic and foreign observers see the beginnings of the radicalisation on the Hungarian side in the transformation of Fidesz during the first Orbán government (1998–2002) into an 'increasingly nationalist-conservative party with a strongly populist rhetoric'.[13] The central plank of the neighbourhood policy of Fidesz was and is the 'unification of the nation beyond national borders'. Two symbolic and, from the majority nations' viewpoint, controversial steps were supposed to serve this goal.

The so-called Status Law passed on 7 July 2001 permitted those Hungarians living in the neighbouring states to apply for a Hungarian identity card allowing them to work in Hungary for three months each year and granting them a number of benefits such as reduced train fares in Hungary and free healthcare. Because of the issues it raised under international law, this public law relationship between the Hungarian state and foreign natural and legal persons (which extends to cash benefits) was sharply criticised both by the Council of Europe and by the governments of the neighbouring states, which had not been consulted on this at all. In the end something approaching 800,000 people, one third of the Hungarians in those states, had applied for this identity card by the middle of 2005, with the greatest number of applications coming from Romania, Serbia and Ukraine. For Slovak citizens, the identity card was of little practical use, especially after Slovakia, along with Hungary, joined the EU in May 2004. Moreover, it is often overlooked in Hungary itself that of the two-and-a-half million Hungarians living in the neighbouring states, 15 per cent live in mixed marriages and 20 per cent do not send their children to Hungarian schools.[14]

The other measure was the setting up of the Hungarian Permanent Conference. This body, approved by the parliament in Budapest and comprising the representatives of the minorities, the political parties and the government, was not merely consultative but also had decision-making powers; however, it did not convene between the end of 2004 and November 2010. Another organ that came into existence in this period was the Forum of Hungarian Representatives of the Carpathian Basin to which the parties in the parliament in Budapest as well as the representatives and/or parties of the Hungarian minorities in Slovakia, Ukraine, Slovenia, Romania, Croatia and Serbia belong. Viktor Orbán's remarks in May 2009, just after the European elections, about a common representation of all Hungarians from the Carpathian Basin in the European Parliament caused an uproar. The endeavour to transform, by means of the concept of a 'unified nation linked together and extending beyond nation state borders', the common historical and cultural traditions of values into the basis of an ethnically defined political nation is a heavily charged initiative in foreign policy terms, and one which in the long run could lead to the isolation of Hungary as a trouble-maker in the Danube basin.

The initiative of the World Federation of Hungarians marked an early stage in the radicalisation of Hungarian minority policies. This organisation, under the leadership of extreme right-wing nationalists, promoted a referendum on the granting of Hungarian citizenship to ethnic Hungarians living in the neighbouring states, even if they were permanently resident outside Hungary. To the surprise of many this idea, which was also supported by Fidesz, floundered badly. Only 37 per cent of the electorate went to the polls on 5 December 2004 and, instead of the 25 per cent required, only 19 per cent supported the proposition of double citizenship whilst almost as many rejected it. The failure of the referendum clearly showed that the notion of an across-the-board common destiny and community of interests embracing all Hungarians was a non-starter; furthermore, it demonstrated that such initiatives do not strengthen the will of majority nations to fulfil the justified demands of the minorities in the fields of culture and education, and that, if anything, they are ultimately counterproductive and can even bolster nationalist-chauvinist forces in Slovakia, Romania and Serbia.

Of course the Hungarians, and especially the Hungarian nationalist right, have not been solely responsible for the intergovernmental tensions in Central Europe in recent years. In June 2006 the Slovak Prime Minister Mikuláš Dzurinda was voted out of office, and with him went his economically successful government, which had been moderate on minority issues and had had the support of MPs from the Hungarian minority for seven years. It was replaced by a populist, left-wing government under Robert Fico, who found common cause with the right-wing chauvinist Slovak National Party led by the crude Ján Slota and the grouping around the discredited former Prime Minister Vladimír Mečiar. This was like throwing a match into a tinderbox. The amendment of the Slovak language law at the end of June 2009 turned the burgeoning conflict between Fico's coalition government and the Hungarian minority into an open dispute attracting international attention.

The Slovak language law has opened the floodgates to anti-minority pinpricks and harassments in daily life, in dealings with the public authorities, in education and in the workplace. It provides for fines of 100 to 5,000 euros when Slovak is not used in official statements and documents. The new law stipulates that all Slovak citizens may only speak Slovak in all public institutions such as government offices or hospitals. The exceptions are formed by communities where the minority is larger than 20 per cent. But even there notices, inscriptions on monuments, even menus have to be in both languages, with Slovak being placed before the other language.

Critics have stressed the absurd consequences of this law in healthcare. Even if they are both Hungarians a doctor must speak Slovak with his patient unless the latter does not have a good command of the language. The well-known liberal economist and commentator Tamás Bauer has observed that the various regulations mean a 'serious abasement of the Hungarians in Slovakia and are in contravention of European fundamental values'. Bauer is one of the harshest critics of Hungarian nationalists and the extreme right.

That the Hungarian card can be so easily played in Slovakia from time to time is closely bound up with the primal fears of the Slovaks that they will once again lose the lands in the south of the country bordering on Hungary.[15] It has to be emphasised that these lands belonged to Hungary for a thousand years and then, after the collapse of the Dual Monarchy in 1918, to Czechoslovakia. Apart from the short-lived fascist puppet state,[16] an independent Slovakia has only existed since its peaceful separation from the Czech lands in 1993. In addition the compact Hungarian settlement areas along the Danube have remained undisturbed. Responsibility for the historical nadir in relations between Slovakia and Hungary lies primarily with the provocations of the Fico government and in particular those of his coalition partner, the Slovak National Party. The blame cannot thus be apportioned to the Socialist-Liberal government in office in Budapest between 2002 and 2008.

Nevertheless, and without any ifs and buts, we have to recognise that the nationalist agitation of the extreme right in Hungary has always provided Slovak (as well as Romanian and Serbian) nationalists with very welcome pretexts to whip up mistrust against the large Hungarian minority. In the autumn of 2008 Slovak riot police brutally attacked fans who had come from Hungary to support the local team at a football match in the stadium at Dunajská Streda, a small town in southern Slovakia with a Hungarian majority. Admittedly, the behaviour of about 150 to 200 of these fans, who unfurled giant Greater Hungary banners calling for a revision of the Treaty of Trianon, was inflammatory. At any rate 50 people were injured, some seriously. The police arrested 31 hooligans, among them 15 Hungarians, and held them for several hours. In the wake of this rampage came a demonstration of right-wing extremists in front of the Slovak embassy in Budapest and a temporary blockade of border crossings between the two countries.

While this 'football war' has fortunately proved to be an exception, an incident involving President László Sólyom in

THE SENSE OF MISSION

August 2009 attracted international attention. Sólyom wished to attend the celebrations for the dedication of a monument to the Hungarian national saint and first king, Stephen I, in the border town of Komárno.[17] The Hungarian President wanted to take part in this official unveiling ceremony as a 'private citizen' and to hold a speech. The response of the Slovak government was to forbid entry to the president of an EU state, moreover a neighbouring one. It was a unique and outrageous episode. Sólyom demonstratively walked to the state border in the middle of the bridge over the Danube linking the two towns and before the TV cameras condemned the actions of the Slovak side as unprecedented and inexcusable. Prime Minister Fico, on the other hand, spoke of a 'monstrous provocation', of an attempt to celebrate Hungarian statehood on the soil of sovereign Slovakia.

Needless to say the claims and counterclaims on both sides are contradictory. But one fact is beyond dispute: the Hungarian organisers of this event had not invited a single representative of the Slovak state to the unveiling ceremony. Moreover, the coordination between the Ministry for Foreign Affairs in Budapest and the Office of the President left a great deal to be desired. The Hungarian foreign minister Péter Balázs confirmed this to me in an off-the-record conversation shortly afterwards on a visit to Austria. Yet a few weeks later he caused outrage in Slovakia when he casually remarked in an interview with a German newspaper: 'As the older brother we have to teach our little brother European manners'.

During his presidency (2005–10), László Sólyom made repeated 'private' visits to towns and villages in the Hungarian settlements in Slovakia, Romania and Serbia where he held speeches, laid wreaths and dedicated monuments. These trips caused great resentment in Romania and Serbia. When in March 2009 he wanted to take part in a festival celebrating the Hungarian struggle for freedom in 1848–49 in the town of Târgu Mureş (Marosvásárhely) in Transylvania, the Romanians refused to grant permission for the presidential aircraft to land, whereupon Sólyom made the journey by car.

The frequent trips of the President and the spectacular political appearances of Viktor Orbán (as an opposition leader) in the Hungarian settlement areas of the neighbouring countries were intended to underscore their ties to a unified political nation extending beyond state borders. The decision at the end of May 2010 to offer Hungarian citizenship to the Magyars in those states without any requirement of permanent residence in Hungary itself represents a turning point both for the majority nations and for the Hungarian minorities in the neighbouring countries, as well as for Hungary's position in Central Europe, with consequences that cannot yet be predicted. No politician in Hungary (with the exception of the simpletons in the far-right Jobbik Party) is demanding a revision of the Treaty of Trianon. Nevertheless, Tamás Bauer speaks 'of a new beginning of that cold war by Viktor Orbán that marked his previous period in office ... The primary losers of this cold war will be the Hungarians living in the neighbouring states'.[18]

This warning voice is, however, an exception in the Hungary of today. Instead of the Europisation we had hoped for in 1989, we are witnessing a relapse into the enemy stereotype of an unhappy past. In exile the important Hungarian Slavist Lajos Gogolák (1910–87) wrote in his profound study on the nationalities question in Hungary: 'The romantic belief mocking every sense of reality in the mission and indivisibility of the

Hungarian national state was something akin to a national lay religion'.[19] 90 years after Trianon historical myths are once again being instrumentalised in politics, in literature and in the media. The bizarre boom of 'Greater Hungary' can be seen and felt everywhere, be it as a sticker (apparently to be found on one Hungarian car in twenty), in the form of fashion jewellery or on key rings, on T-shirts or in cheap pictures.

In the four Budapest branches of the Skitia chain of bookshops it is once again possible to buy new editions of old textbooks, novels and volumes of poetry which in their day had spread the historical-political, later ethnic-racist feelings of superiority of the Magyars combined with hatred and contempt for the 'other'. It is thus no surprise that thinking in ethnic and nationalist categories is now more widespread than at any time since the Second World War. At a seminar on Central Europe held at the Academy for Civic Education in Tutzing (Bavaria), a German researcher stressed that from the Hungarian point of view the state is where the nation is. Thus, Hungary is extending its statehood well beyond its territorial borders with measures such as the law on citizenship.[20]

In contrast to Slovakia the controversial law has so far caused little commotion in Romania and Serbia, largely because of their own similar legislation regarding the Moldovans or the Serb minorities in Croatia or Kosovo. In addition, Hungarians are once again sitting (at least at the time of writing) in the Romanian cabinet, holding the positions of Vice-Premier and as Minister for Culture (!), Health and Environmental Protection, of course purely as Romanian citizens of Hungarian origin and not primarily as members of a (political) trans-border Hungarian nation.

In contrast to the former 'fraternal' socialist states, the relationship with Austria has been burdened with few or any real problems. Since the change of the system in 1989 every government in Budapest has cultivated cordial relations with the government in office in Vienna, irrespective of its political colour. In a deeper sense, for the past 25 to 30 years the Hungarians have set themselves the goal of achieving the Austrian standard of living in the 'foreseeable future' (that is, within 15 years). This aspiration is, however, fated to remain a dream rather than a reality for many years yet.

Accession to the EU has not eliminated the national problem. In view of the national sensitivities in the neighbouring countries it can come as no surprise that the vociferous incantations of the glorious past and the constant drumbeat of the political and cultural superiority of the Magyars over the present-day majority nations have engendered considerable fears. What Sir Karl Popper (1902–94), the British philosopher born in Vienna, wrote at the height of the Second World War remains true today: 'The more we try to return to the heroic age of tribalism, the more surely we arrive at the Inquisition, at the secret police and at a romanticized gangsterism.'[21]

9

THE SPLENDOUR AND DECLINE OF FERENC GYURCSÁNY

'Whoever enters public life can neither expect nor demand any clemency'.

Marie Ebner-Eschenbach

The history of Hungary after the collapse of the communist regime confirms the wisdom of the reflections of the Russian thinker and revolutionary Alexander Herzen: 'There is no libretto. If history followed a set libretto, it would lose all interest, become unnecessary, boring, ludicrous ... History is all improvisation, all will and all extempore—there are no frontiers, no itineraries'.[1]

Ferenc Gyurcsány's whole life has been a fascinating illustration of this spontaneity, and of the role of chance in Hungarian politics. When I first met him in April 2004 he was the Minister for Children, Youth and Sport in the Socialist-Liberal coalition led by Péter Medgyessy. I had read some of his articles, for example those on the necessity of discarding the paralysing post-communist ideological ballast and transforming the MSzP into a modern, open social-democratic party along the lines of the British and German models. Friends whose opinions I respected saw in him a beacon of hope. At the same time leading left-wing politicians barely concealed their opinions of the ambitious young man, calling him an 'enormously rich adventurer' and a loose cannon. Everything I had heard about him before our meeting made him look almost like a exotic bird of paradise amidst the grey suits and boring cadres of late Kádárism who were still in charge of the Socialist Party.

Our conversation in his ministerial office lasted well over an hour and was surprisingly frank. Gyurcsány was a tall, slim, athletic-looking man and made no secret of his political ambitions. In reply to my somewhat quizzical remark asking what a serious politician was doing in such a ministry, Gyurcsány said straight out that his portfolio was of no particular significance and a major department in any ministry would equally well serve the same purpose. At the same time he spoke with some pride of his election a few weeks before as the head of the Socialist Party organisation in the important county of Győr-Moson-Sopron in western Hungary.

Without openly criticising Prime Minister Péter Medgyessy, whose chief adviser he had been from the beginning of 2003 until his elevation into government, he pulled the Socialist Party to pieces, deriding it as a party incapable of deciding whom and what it represented. He himself, however, maintained close contacts with party members and visited party organisations in the various parts of the country two or three times a week. When I asked him what the point of all these activities was, Gyurcsány simply replied with a friendly smile: he just wanted to serve to the best of his ability the delayed but inevitable modernisation of the Hungarian left.

Even this first meeting convinced me that the 43-year-old Gyurcsány was probably the most gifted and most dynamic politician in the Socialist-Liberal camp. It was, however, also clear even then that his career and his wealth were not exactly the embodiment of classic socialist ideals. It is true that Gyurcsány is of unimpeachable proletarian origins, growing up in abject poverty in the small provincial town of Pápa in southwest Hungary. Yet, by the time he was 21 this talented student had already become the head of the Hungarian Communist Youth Federation (KISZ) at the teacher training college in the city of Pécs.

Several months later Gyurcsány became a full-time party functionary as secretary of the youth organisation at the local university merged with his college, earning a more than presentable salary for the time. The rise of the young party *apparatchik* in the KISZ was both rapid and smooth. By 1989 Gyurcsány had already moved to Budapest as a secretary of the National Committee of KISZ. When he (temporarily) quit politics, he was the number two in the Democratic Youth League, which though renamed was still controlled by the Young Communists; it would soon disappear.

With the demise of the old system the young man from the provinces surged forward. He was unemployed for just four months, and then his sociability eased his way into a firm of financial consultants. Like a latter-day figure out of a Balzac novel, the ambitious Gyurcsány, after his attempts to make a political career in the KISZ had ended in failure through no fault of his own, had the strength of the rebel from the provinces to conquer society and the financial world, and ultimately to win power. His friends later said he was cast in the same mould as a victor. Like many others in the post-communist world the single-minded Gyurcsány exploited the opportunities thrown up by privatisation and the transition from a command to a free market economy.[2]

Many years later he related in interviews his first steps as a budding entrepreneur: he bought himself one green and one purple suit, together with an artificial leather briefcase, in the legendary Budapest department store Corvin (which has since been pulled down). This, he thought, was how modern businessmen dressed. Driven by the will to succeed, he read specialist literature day and night and tried to learn English. For the latter, six weeks spent in Edinburgh and a month in London were of some benefit. But the most important step he took in his life as a future entrepreneur was to found with an associate the Altus Investment and Asset Management Company.

After moving to Budapest and using the money raised by the sale of the villa owned by his mother-in-law and wife in Pécs, the family was able to loan him three million forints to purchase a majority share in the Altus Company. In the early 1990s Gyurcsány, by now the father of two boys, was already being regarded as an adroit and successful businessman. An affair with Klára Dobrev, the attractive, multilingual and talented daughter of Piroska Apró, led in the autumn of 1994 to divorce and in turn to his (third) marriage. It was to be the start of a new and exciting phase in his life.[3]

That Ferenc Gyurcsány, the 35-year-old son of a single working mother, could become a forint billionaire within just four years was little short of sensational. The media paid the requisite homage to his achievements. However, the fact that Gyurcsány's image in modern Hungarian history is more controversial than that of almost every other politician is primarily due to his family connection with Piroska Apró, an influential businesswoman and a top civil servant. How else could even such a talented young man have turned three million forints into three billion in just a few years? When a journalist asked him in the autumn of 1996 whether he had always wanted to be a businessman, Gyurcsány replied, 'No ... I thought that I'd make a very good politician, I thought one day I'd be prime minister. My poor country—as if it doesn't have enough problems without me! ... Today, I'd laugh at myself, but then I quite seriously believed in all of this'.[4]

Eight years later the apparently modest entrepreneur had indeed become Prime Minister of Hungary. József Debreczeni correctly observes that Gyurcsány's career was unprecedented in Hungarian history; it was in fact a phenomenon. In the post-1989 era Gyurcsány was the first billionaire to become a top politician. Not only that, nobody had ever risen so quickly to the very summit of power: in 2002, Gyurcsány was not even in parliament; by 2004 he was Prime Minister.

How did this almost unimaginable stroke of luck even become possible? We have already described (in Chapter 7) the fall of his predecessor as prime minister. Péter Medgyessy, who bore much of the blame for his own demise, had brought the young billionaire back into politics, first as his chief adviser and then as a cabinet minister. Today Medgyessy concedes that Gyurcsány was not the actual mastermind behind his fall; moreover, he was not the victim of a putsch led by his opponents, as he had originally claimed, but rather of his own miscalculations and amateurish behaviour. And as power drained away from Medgyessy, that most charming but politically weak of men, a 'cartel of fear' was spawned in the party leadership. Initially unsettled and then outraged by the suicidal, dilettante antics of the Prime Minister, it acted with lightning speed to topple Medgyessy, no longer an election winner but a liability to the Socialist Party, and to designate as his successor the uncharismatic but dependable Péter Kiss, who after two stints as Labour Minister was directing the prime minister's office.

The vote in the party Presidium in favour of Kiss went off smoothly without any opposition. The party grandees, however, had not reckoned with their own grassroots. Within 24 hours the representatives of the party's various factions, its youth wing, supporters in the provinces and, above all, its disgruntled activists had forced the calling of an extraordinary party congress to choose Medgyessy's successor. Kiss, who was only two years older than Gyurcsány and had also begun his career in the Communist youth organisation, was an experienced functionary who had made his way to the top through the party and was therefore respected by his comrades. However, the communication experts gave him no chance whatsoever against the charismatic Viktor Orbán.

In this situation Gyurcsány's friends and soon Gyurcsány himself suddenly sensed an opportunity for his own candidature. Under normal circumstances this would have been an enormous risk for the Sports Minister, who had only joined the MSzP four years previously and had in the meantime quit the government. However, in just a week's intensive campaigning on the telephone, Gyurcsány and his closest advisers were able to turn everything around and win over the support above all of the representatives from the provinces. In the preliminary vote in the parliamentary party, Kiss was still ahead and Gyurcsány came third behind the future Finance Minister János Veres. But in the vote in the party executive Kiss received only a few more votes than Gyurcsány and both had to be nominated by a reluctant party leadership as candidates for the party congress to be held the next day, 25 August 2004.

Although the hapless Kiss was supported by several members of the party Presidium and also by the ex-Prime Minister Gyula Horn, he suffered a crushing defeat. Of the 623 delegates, 453 (73 per cent) voted for the outsider, Ferenc Gyurcsány, who had become the symbol of a rank and file revolt unheard of in the history of the Hungarian Socialist Party. In *Die Welt* of 28 August 2004 I wrote, 'Now the political future of the Socialist-Liberal coalition depends on whether Ferenc Gyurcsány, this fascinating and polarising figure, will turn out in the end to be the gravedigger or the reformer of the Hungarian left'. On 29 September 2004 Ferenc Gyurcsány was elected Prime Minister by the Socialist-Liberal majority in parliament.

In subsequent conversations with his biographer József Debreczeni, Gyurcsány spoke unusually forthrightly about the events which had led up to his capturing of the premiership. But in his characterisations of his political associates and of ministers dismissed from his first government, he was also much too candid and acerbic both in his contempt for others and in his description of his feelings at moments of personal success. Although in interviews and off-the-record remarks he often pointed out that men at the top are nearly always toppled by their own side, he himself forgot much too often Churchill's warning: 'In politics, especially at the top, there is no friendship'.

That the Socialist-Liberal coalition was able to win the April 2006 parliamentary elections and increase its majority from ten to 36 seats was primarily due to Gyurcsány. He was, despite a speech impediment (now overcome), a brilliant speaker, though at times he was barely able to conceal his arrogance in debates with his political opponents. In a decisive television debate broadcast on 5 April 2006 he succeeded in trouncing his opponent Viktor Orbán. According to the polls conducted afterwards, 54 per cent of viewers put Gyurcsány as the winner of the debate as against just 23 per cent for Orbán.

The man who at the time of his rise to the political top ranked 60th on the list of the 100 richest entrepreneurs in Hungary possessed a fortune of 3.5 billion forints (approximately 14 million euros at the 2004 exchange rate) in a country where about 20 per cent of the population was living below the poverty line. That he, as already mentioned, had married into the Apró family and moved into an elegant three-floor villa in the fashionable hills of Buda has contributed to the invidious and recurring mythmaking surrounding him. It was this factor that made Gyurcsány from the very beginning the target of media attacks, often well below the belt.[5]

Debreczeni concluded his biography of Gyurcsány, published in 2006, with an appreciation of Gyurcsány's almost unbelievable political achievement in leading the government from the almost hopeless situation in the summer of 2004 to victory in the spring of 2006. At the end of the book the victorious Prime Minister reflects on his feelings in the moments of jubilation and passionate applause: in contrast to Orbán he would not like to have—and this is true of his wife too—any contact with the enthusiasms of the masses and rejects any cult of personality. In retrospect, after his political debacle, such concerns ring hollow today. To the rhetorical question I posed in the summer of 2004 ('gravedigger or reformer of the Hungarian left?'), which was also widely reported in Hungary, a former close colleague of Gyula Horn observed at some point, perhaps in 2008, in a short SMS to me: 'No doubt—he is the gravedigger'.

Without the least idea of his approaching disaster, Gyurcsány ended his 14-page-long postscript (entitled 'After the victory') to Debreczeni's biography with the words: 'I know that the fate of democratic politicians is ultimately the loss of power. I know: in the end I will fail in the personal sense. The question is whether as a politician you have four or eight years ... In the end you lose. The arcane and immutable sympathy of the people decides the fate of politicians'. Then in the next sentence, and in full consciousness of his victory, he bragged:

I'm not really interested in the things that are said to me like, for example, that 'you will certainly go down in the history books as the first politician able after 16 years [of democracy] to extend his term of office as prime minister into a second one'. That something like this has never happened before does not interest me at all ... Nor, to be honest, does it concern me what they will write about me in history books. What interests me is the task facing me. Hungary interests me.

The flame of this perhaps greatest political talent in the postcommunist history of the Hungarian left flared but briefly. Ferenc Gyurcsány turned out to be (in the sense of Jacob Burckhardt's reflections on history) a 'man of momentary greatness', in which a short phase of history is intensified. He was above all the champion who for the first time since the changes of 1989 led the left to victory in two consecutive elections. Victory—but to what purpose? Personally, Gyurcsány wanted to put 'social-democratic signals' into the market economy, as Bruno Kreisky had tried to do in Austria in the 1970s, and Tony Blair and Gerhard Schröder also tried three decades later. However, the seeds of the future defeat were already sown in the unprecedented victory.

The political honeymoon came to an abrupt end within a matter of months. Gyurcsány's popularity fell from 55 per cent in April to 34 per cent in August 2006.[6] No other government had had to swallow such a rapid, massive decline in popularity. In the election campaign of 2006 both parties had promised, as in 2002, that things would only get better. Gyurcsány concealed the gravity of the economic situation and remained silent about the planned belt-tightening measures while his opponent Orbán even promised a 14th monthly old-age pension payment and radical tax cuts, as well as cheaper gas and electricity prices.

The disappointment of the public was great, probably for the simple reason that Gyurcsány had already been in office for two years and, after his many election promises, now unexpectedly set about consolidating an economy that had tumbled into a crisis. It only added insult to injury when, having introduced a package of cuts that included increases in gas prices and taxes, he casually let slip the remark that 'they wouldn't really hurt'. At the same time Gyurcsány failed to convince his own party of the need to take courageous and unavoidable but unpopular steps and initiate the necessary radical reforms to deal with the structural weaknesses of the ailing economy. The contemporary historian Zoltán Ripp has pertinently noted that the Socialist Party was not an organisation of people sharing the same opinions but rather one of people concealing different views.

Meanwhile, the defeated (but, contrary to the predictions of some Western observers, far from finished) Viktor Orbán had easily survived his third defeat (1994, 2002 and 2006). Even during the summer break immediately after his latest electoral setback he began, with unbroken lust for power and unprecedented ruthlessness, to set the stage for a turnaround in Hungarian politics. He gave the signal for an open declaration of war in an extraordinarily biting speech delivered before a mass meeting in Transylvania and then expounded on it in detail in a series of articles in the Fidesz mouthpiece *Magyar Nemzet* (29 July, 5 August and 11 September 2006).

Orbán painted a gloomy and alarming picture:

> For the first time since the change of the system an open, organised political lie has been committed ... Hungary's real problems are, in spite of the repeated and widespread political platitudes, not of an economic nature. The true problem is the lying by the government, the conscious distortion of the facts, the policy without a binding mandate and the fact that Hungarian democracy has not been able to defend itself against any of this. The Gyurcsány package [of budgetary cuts] is not a democratically mandated government programme but an arbitrary *Diktat*—not legitimate. The government has no right to implement the Gyurcsány package. Until the beginning of the winter there will be no dialogue between left and right, but an embittered and outraged country will be confronting its illegitimate government.

Orbán may well already have had in his possession the evidence for the campaign against 'Gyurcsány's government of liars'. At least this is what most serious commentators thought before the local elections on 1 October, where the opposition won a great victory.

Soon after the publication of the three newspaper articles, a 'political atomic bomb' (József Debreczeni) exploded in Hungary on 17 September 2006. On radio and television, on websites and for days afterwards in the newspapers, extracts were made public from a speech held by Gyurcsány almost four months previously at a closed meeting of some 200 Socialist members of parliament in the holiday resort of Balatonőszöd on Lake Balaton. In this passionate and rousing improvised speech, peppered with coarse, even at times vulgar language, Gyurcsány sought to convince his comrades, who were both cynically indifferent to and fearful of the anger of the people, of the inevitability of painful reforms. In substance, Gyurcsány openly conceded that he, his government and party had been lying 'morning, noon and night' to the Hungarians before the elections. This speech, which lasted for some 25 minutes, made history in Hungary and has irreversibly changed the country.

To this day it has remained a secret how the extract made its way from the government holiday home into the public arena. Who leaked the explosive recording of an internal meeting of the Socialists to the media and, possibly even prior to that, to the opposition? Both before and since his resignation I have spoken about the Őszöd affair on a number of occasions not only with Gyurcsány himself but also with four other members of the party Presidium, as well as with an array of political observers. Nearly everybody, and that includes József Debreczeni, the biographer of both Gyurcsány and Orbán, is convinced that Viktor Orbán and/or his people knew about the tapes in the summer before Fidesz began its campaign against the 'government of liars'.

The respected German political scientist Karl-Dietrich Bracher once observed: 'Words do not only make history. Words can also make history happen, can distort reality'. Bracher warned that even 'the implicit association between historical keywords and their political substance can counter their degradation to naked means of manipulation'.[7] This is exactly what happened with this speech, which in its context was nothing less than an impassioned appeal for honesty in politics. For this reason, the most prominent Hungarian writers ranging from Péter Nádas to Péter Esterházy have—in spite of or perhaps just because of its profane language—lauded the style and moral substance of Gyurcsány's speech.

In my opinion the Őszöd speech, to quote the saying attributed to Talleyrand, was not a crime but an irreparable political error. The media and Gyurcsány's political enemies have always cited only the grievous and cynical sounding confessions of a deliberate lie, ignoring the context, the text as a whole. This would have of course confirmed that Gyurcsány was in reality trying to make a break with the politics of lies. It is in this fatal distortion of the true purpose of the speech that Gyurcsány's personal tragedy lies, a tragedy that he has presumably still not yet completely comprehended.

It should suffice to quote just a few verbatim extracts from Gyurcsány's speech:

We had almost no other choice [than the package of cuts] because we have fucked it up. Not just a little bit but totally... No other country in Europe has committed such stupidities as we have. It can be explained. Obviously we have been lying our heads off for the last one-and-a-half, two years. It was quite clear that what we were saying wasn't true ... And in the meantime, we have, by the way, been doing nothing for the past four years. Nothing. You can't name me one single important government measure we can be proud of, apart from pulling the government in the end [i.e. after the fall of Medgyessy] out of the shit again. Nothing. If we were forced to give an account of what we've been doing in the past four years, what could we say?

... Reform or failure. There is nothing else. And when I say failure, then I'm speaking about Hungary, about the left and, to be quite honest, about myself.

I've almost killed myself the last one-and-a-half years having to pretend that we were governing. Instead we've been lying morning, noon and night. And I don't want to do that any more. Either we do something about it, and you have the man for this, or you carry on with somebody else … To sit around in endless committees where in the end we can never agree on any laws, where we always end up with the same old compromises just so that we don't have to change anything because doing something different would damage somebody's interests: for this another Madame is needed …

Before we turn to the frenzied consequences of the revelations, we have to raise the question of who leaked the damaging extracts of this speech to the media or to Gyurcsány's political opponents (or to both), and why. There have been investigations, insinuations and inconsistencies but to this day the hard facts have remained a carefully guarded secret.

The best informed sources in the Socialist Party assume that there are two possible versions. The first, widespread in the upper echelons of the party, is that the Prime Minister's spin doctors and media advisers, impressed by the passion and courage of the speech, passed it on to the media, though without Gyurcsány's knowledge, and the text was then handed on to Fidesz. I have heard this variant over and over again from high-ranking party members, including two former party leaders. On the other hand, Gyurcsány himself, his family and journalists still loyal to him are firmly convinced that he was betrayed by rivals and conspirators from within the party who actively wished to rid it of the hated parvenu in this perfidious manner. Several names, above all that of a long-serving treasurer and that of a deputy chief of the party, are often mentioned in Gyurcsány's immediate circle and by those still sympathetic to his cause.

Whatever the truth of the matter, the infamous 'lie speech', stripped of its context, quoted *ad nauseam* over the length and breadth of Hungary as needed by his opponents, and fre-

THE SPLENDOUR AND DECLINE OF FERENC GYURCSÁNY

quently reported on abroad, irrevocably destroyed the Prime Minister's credibility. Orbán called him a pathological liar and his government's measures a 'dilettante package'. Some believe that Gyurcsány could have prevented the worst if he had quickly and publicly, this time without the crude language, given a forthright speech. In any case, Orbán now gave the green light for a campaign that was to generate an echo worldwide, and in Hungary itself would also lead to the rise of the extreme right.

10

THE POWER OF THE DISCREET PRESS BARONS

'The press has only one impeccably honest section: the classified ads'.

Kurt Tucholsky

The media landscape in Hungary today reminds us of the famous statement made by Paul Sethe, the founding editor-in-chief of the conservative *Frankfurter Allgemeine Zeitung*. In a letter to *Der Spiegel* magazine of 5 May 1965 Sethe, who later became a leader writer for other German quality papers, wrote: 'The freedom of the press is the freedom of 200 rich people to disseminate their opinions'.

Now, in tiny Hungary there are only relatively few (forint) billionaires to whom Sethe's remark could be applied. More pertinent is his observation about the dissemination of opinion. Hungary's discreet oligarchs, who today can be considered press barons, do not generally spread their own views in the newspapers, magazines, TV and radio stations, and internet portals they directly or indirectly control. Without exception, all the media they own, whether it is 100 per cent or only in part, have for years only followed one line, namely that of Viktor Orbán's Fidesz (Alliance of Young Democrats); it was not least thanks to the backing and adroit deployment of the right-wing media empire that Fidesz was able to win the parliamentary elections in the spring of 2010 so convincingly. It should also be noted that the openly extreme right-wing Jobbik party, together with its notorious and (until recently) uniformed Hungarian Guard, have also considerably benefited from the benign reporting of these very same media.

On the initiative of the late Peter Galliner, director of the International Press Institute (IPI), and together with some other Western journalists, I organised both before and immediately after 1989 a number of workshops and seminars for journalists in Hungary (as well as other former Eastern Bloc countries).[1] At the time we did not think, even in our wildest dreams, that Western press and media concerns so admired by the young Hungarians working in the media would start firing independent editors-in-chief instead of defending the young democratic press; equally remote was the idea that they were capable of making rotten compromises with the post-communist or right-wing populist parties and their press and propaganda bosses.

All the post-communist states have witnessed considerable changes in their media—sadly, not all of them beneficial. At first glance, the situation in the Hungarian print media does not seem to differ greatly from the trends prevailing in Western

THE POWER OF THE DISCREET PRESS BARONS

Europe: tabloids and free newspapers have gained ground while sales of quality papers have collapsed; online newspapers have flourished and the growing influence of advertisers, as a consequence of the financial crisis, can be observed in Hungary just as elsewhere.

Nevertheless, it is only in Hungary that there has arisen such a sharp and to date unbridgeable gap between the populist newspapers supporting the right and the centre-left press. In the period immediately after the change of the system this divide, of course, reflected the real political differences in the country. At the same time the struggle first for the control of public radio and television, and subsequently for the print media, has led to further polarisation. I have experienced at first hand this process, which has proven so bewildering to many foreign observers.

In my roles as a foreign correspondent for the *Financial Times* and as editor-in-chief of the East European department of the Austrian public broadcaster ORF, I had over the years maintained close working contacts with many television and print journalists during the long Kádár era; moreover, after its collapse I gave numerous interviews to the new free media in Hungary. Through my work with IPI I was also for a short period a member of the foreign advisory board for the Hungarian state broadcaster Magyar Televízió (MTV). When, for example, in March 1994 the managing director appointed by the Antall and Boross governments fired 129 radio reporters and editors overnight, I was invited, together with other Western journalists, by a newly founded media club in Budapest to speak about the situation and provide some background information on the rights of employees of the Austrian ORF. Soon after the 1994 election victory of the Socialist-Liberal coalition many of those sacked were rehired, while some leading journalists on the right were forced to retire.

In order to be able to understand the present topsy-turvy world of the Hungarian media, we have to glance at the past. It was widely assumed at the time that during the four decades of communist rule many journalists both at home and abroad were active as 'informal collaborators'[2] and agents, some even as 'top secret' officers for the state security services. These suspicions have since been fully confirmed. I have written on a number of occasions about my own perplexing experiences with this bizarre world.[3] When at the end of 2005 the historical archive of the state security services finally made available to me 395 pages of the operational material and files they held on me (though it has to be said that overwhelmingly they dated from the 1958–1966 period only), I described the sometimes outrageous, sometimes ludicrous events in a lengthy article in the literary weekly *Élet és Irodalom*. With the aid of the files of informants' real and cover names, I was able to identify some of these informers.

Anyone who had for many years struggled against the 'the institutionalised system of the lie in public life', such as the historians János Kenedi and Krisztián Ungváry,[4] welcomed my article, but otherwise it was greeted with a stony silence. Many Hungarians still regard the deeds of the 'IMs' and other informers as a peccadillo. This attitude was and is the consequence of the experience of the overwhelming majority of Hungarians who were compelled to come to terms and make the necessary arrangements with the Kádár regime in the 1970s and 1980s.[5]

Those who embrace the imperatives of forgetting and even more of denial have openly or cryptically cast suspicion on the authors of research reports and studies, who are attacked as denigrators of Hungary or as tools of their political opponents (no matter of which side). The young and courageous Ungváry estimates that between 1950 and 1990 some 200,000 people were active for longer or shorter periods of time as agents or informers of the political police. According to Kenedi, at the time of the change of the system there were still 11,000 agents on the books. In an interview he gave me at the end of 2004 he guessed that 50–60,000 members of the political and administrative elite of the old regime had been involved in working as agents or informers.[6] During the Socialist-Liberal coalition nothing at all ever came of the 'file revolution' promised at the time of the secret service affair concerning Prime Minister Medgyessy. Obviously, too many prominent people in the Socialist Party and the state bureaucracy had also been involved in intelligence activities both at home and abroad.

Nothing could illustrate the absurdity of the situation better than the witch-hunt against Krisztián Ungváry conducted by unmasked 'informal collaborators' and their overseers. After this independent and free spirit exposed a whole row of church dignitaries (including the last three chairmen of the Catholic Bishops' Conference and Cardinals László Lékai and László Paskai) as informers, he was sued by one of the bishops named. Although Ungváry even produced documentation, the bishop's former secret service handler came to his aid in court, denying that the churchman had ever supplied him with any secret reports. The same bishop who before the collapse of the Kádár regime had, as Ungváry has maintained, done dirty work for the communists, subsequently popped up in the elections of April 2010 as a vociferous patron of Fidesz...

Although bold documentary films have been made about the entanglement of many Hungarian bishops in Budapest and

Rome, the episcopacy, in spite of the plucky initiatives of Asztrik Várszegi, the arch-abbot of Pannonhalma, has to date nipped in the bud each and every investigation into the past. In another case, a current Constitutional Court judge, who is alleged by Ungváry to have closely cooperated with the Ministry of the Interior at the University of Pécs during the communist regime, successfully sued *Élet és Irodalom* and the researcher, who were fined over 10,000 euros by the Supreme Court for having failed to prove the correctness of the accusations.

Élet és Irodalom has indeed a special place in the Hungarian media landscape. In addition to articles and novellas written by Hungary's most prominent writers and critics, this literary weekly has for years published reports and investigative pieces on corruption, black market dealings and other dubious transactions in all parties (including some about the family of Viktor Orbán). In addition it has regularly exposed other well-known personalities. In January 2006, for example, I revealed that the sporting legend György Szepesi, using the cover name 'Galambos', had since 1950 submitted to the secret police reports on hundreds of people, not only my friends and myself, but also many sportsmen and civil servants.[7]

I was personally shaken by the well-researched report of a film critic that between 1957 and 1961 an old acquaintance, the Oscar winner and internationally famous director István Szabó, had written 48 reports on his colleague for the Ministry of the Interior. Many familiar names from the world of the liberal arts and the media elite issued a statement in solidarity with the great artist, without of course actually addressing the accusations. The author of the original article, and not Szabó himself, then became the target of a venomous whispering campaign about his possible motives.

A similar campaigning role is fulfilled by *Magyar Narancs* (Hungarian Orange). This left-liberal weekly has in recent years reported *inter alia* on the unbelievable bribery scandals in the upper echelons of the city bureaucracy in Budapest, which is dominated by the Socialists. It has also published numerous critical essays not only on Fidesz or Jobbik politicians but also on political figures of the Socialist and Liberal parties. However, to this day a remarkable truce has by and large been maintained between Fidesz and the Socialist Party regarding the role of the secret services and their networks. This is not unrelated to the fact that both political camps are well anchored in the no fewer than five (!) secret service agencies in Hungary. Innumerable turncoats can be found in the highest ranks of the civil service and the courts. The words of the Polish satirist Stanisław Jerzy Lec (which needless to say date from the communist period) are particularly applicable to many of these people: 'It is difficult to recognise who is voluntarily swimming with the tide'.

In the first years after the political change in 1989 the sympathisers of the Liberals and the erstwhile reform-communists stamped their mark on the world of the media. But the struggle for the control of Hungarian radio and television began even under the Antall government. In 1990, quite literally overnight, one of the most talented reform journalists, Endre Aczél, together with his team, was fired on the flimsiest of pretexts from his job as editor-in-chief of TV news and magazine programmes on MTV. The change served as a preparation for the ultimately failed plan to form a government of the Democratic Forum with the Pozsgay wing of the post-communists (which was shortly to sink without a trace).

This particular earthquake was followed by larger and smaller aftershocks in the public media. Thus, at the end of

2009 the managing director of the public broadcaster MTV, in full expectation of what seemed to be a certain Fidesz election victory in 2010, terminated with immediate effect the contract of the longtime producer of the 'Sunrise' breakfast show; the best editors (including Endre Aczél) had already been replaced under pressure from Fidesz by opportunistic (and more pliable) presenters. The very next day Viktor Orbán pointedly gave an interview to MTV; until then the Fidesz people had boycotted the channel on account of its alleged left-wing bias.

Much more significant were the adjustments made by journalists, newspapers, the private TV broadcasters and owners of internet portals. Since his surprising electoral defeat in 2002, Orbán has single-mindedly pursued the building up of a media empire controlled by his rich supporters, a process already begun in his first period in office. Using funds from undeclared and unknown sources, at the end of the 1990s the Orbán group financed the transformation of *Magyar Nemzet*, the traditional newspaper of the intelligentsia,[8] into a vocal, bellicose organ supporting Fidesz. Today, two once respectable daily newspapers, several weeklies, free newspapers distributed on the Budapest underground and in the residential areas, two TV and two radio stations are the principal transmitters of Fidesz's political message. They serve at the same time as offensive platforms for the numerous Fidesz campaigns against its political opponents and their leaderships.

The fate of the former communist government newspaper *Magyar Hírlap* was somewhat different. A centre-left-leaning newspaper in the period immediately after 1989, it experienced some tumultuous years: briefly owned by the controversial British media mogul Robert Maxwell, it was sold to the Swiss publisher Jürg Marquard, then to the Swiss Ringier Group, and finally to its employees. In September 2005, the loss-making newspaper was acquired by the (forint) billionaire Gábor Széles (currently the fifth wealthiest man in Hungary with a fortune of 300 million euros). This politically ambitious entrepreneur, who initially was close to the MDF, turned demonstratively to Orbán's party, and *Magyar Hírlap* acquired a hard right-wing, nationalist editorial line. Independently minded journalists were quickly weeded out: the veteran editor-in-chief was fired in the autumn of 2006 and every second member of the editorial staff has since either been dismissed or quit the paper of their own volition.

Széles once compared himself with Artur Görgey, the commander-in-chief of the Hungarian forces in the 1848–49 War of Independence; and in the same interview he compared Viktor Orbán, a man he greatly admires, with Lajos Kossuth, the legendary political leader of the revolution of 1848. Born in 1945 and an electrical engineer by training, Gabor Széles is said to have laid the foundations of his fortune during the communist era when he headed large state-owned microelectronic and computer enterprises. There were many other similar careers among the captains of industry and top bankers, who, in the last years of the Kádár regime, created with state permission islands of capitalism in Hungary and then, after the collapse of communism, turned these into empires worth billions with the support of politicians on both the left and the right.

The tragic fate of the entrepreneur János Fenyő, however, illustrates just how an all too aggressive approach can under certain circumstances provoke dangerous reactions. Having lived for many years in the USA, he returned to Hungary, allegedly as a photo reporter, and built up a media concern, Vico, which owned 13 newspapers with a circulation of 14 million copies. However, Fenyő's ostentatious lifestyle aroused considerable envy. On 11 February 1998 the 44-year-old media baron was shot almost 30 times on the streets of Budapest at the height of the rush-hour when his car stopped for a red traffic light. Neither his assassin, who jumped out of a car and disappeared on foot, nor the driver of Fenyő's car was ever found. In later years, there was from time to time some speculation about an Albanian gangster and his employer, supposedly a rival businessman in the media world.

Tamás Gyárfás, the owner of the company which produced the 'Sunrise' breakfast show for MTV until its contract was abruptly terminated for purely political reasons, has not exactly gone hungry either: he is still one of the hundred richest Hungarians. However, it may also be noted that there are among the forint billionaires several entrepreneurs who, like my first Hungarian publisher, have remained true to the left.

Apart from Gábor Széles, who in 2007 founded Echo TV, an extreme right-wing channel, there is a whole bevy of forint billionaires from the circle around Viktor Orbán who since 2002 have systematically collaborated in the creation of a right-wing media hegemony. In the last decade a new TV station (Hír TV, modelled on CNN), new radio stations (Inforádió, Lánchíd Rádío), as well as weekly magazines, have all been launched. A certain Tamás Vitézy (64th on the list of billionaires) on his own admission initially lost billions when he founded *Helyi Thema*, the free newspaper for the Budapest underground. Today he prints 1.2 million copies weekly, each one of which, to quote him, 'should serve the spirit of Viktor Orbán'.

Not all of Orbán's friends, assistants and poodles speak so blithely. In the foreground, those playing a role are figures like his former spokesman Gábor Borókai, once the general director of Hír TV and now the publisher of the weekly newspaper *Heti Válasz*. His company, Infocenter RT, displays spectacular growth and is absolutely loyal to Orbán. Following the purchase of the weekly *Heti Válasz* and Lánchíd Radio in the autumn of 2009 (incidentally with the approval of the Socialists), it also succeeded in taking over, without any tender, one of the two important radio bands which had previously been operated by foreign companies but had now become free.

By coincidence the majority owner of Infocenter was one Dr Tamás Fellegi, who in the 1980s had been one of Orbán's university tutors and who after his return from the USA, where he had worked as a guest lecturer, was promoted into the innermost circle of advisers around the Fidesz boss. He was seen as the best educated among the super-rich and at the same time by far the richest among the leading courtiers fawning around Orbán. Before the second round of voting in the parliamentary elections in 2010 Fellegi gave up his holdings to party friends so that after the anticipated Fidesz victory he could take charge of the key Ministry for National Development.

In addition to the more 'traditional' newspapers, television and radio stations, Fidesz is also careful not to ignore the new electronic media. Two further forint billionaires, Zoltán Speder (with 28 billion no. 18 on the list) and Kristóf Nobilis (17 billion and no. 28), own the business newspaper *Napi Gazdaság* and the online business journal portfolio.hu. Hungary's most visited internet portal, index.hu, also belongs to their empire, as do a tabloid magazine, a car magazine and other companies. Recently, the corporate group of the two billionaires has completely bought out Hungary's only radio news station, Inforádió, and its website inforadio.hu. Finally, the billionaire István Töröcskei (no. 42 among the super-rich with a fortune of 12 billion forints) is, together with other investors, the owner of Hír TV and the newspaper *Magyar Nemzet*.

Ten to fifteen years ago Fidesz and right-wing political scientists asserted that the left controlled 80 per cent of the media. The claim was of course much exaggerated, even if there can be no denying that left-liberal journalists set the tone. Today, two-thirds of young journalists freely concede that their sympathies lie with the right: hardly surprising given its overwhelming media preponderance. Networking with one another, they are also beginning to shape, even dominate, the programming of the private broadcasters. According to the leading liberal, independent researcher in communications studies, Mária Vásárhelyi, there is no transparency whatsoever regarding the sources of the financing of the seemingly inexorable rise of the rightwing media, and the business criteria on which it is based.

The central figure not only in the media but also in the entire financial world of the Fidesz camp is Lajos Simicska. This gifted man, the conductor who orchestrates the acquisition of economic power and influence, has long held the purse-strings of Fidesz. Perhaps Orbán's oldest friend (together with László Kövér, the president of the parliament), in 1998 Simicska was forced to resign as the president of the Hungarian Tax and Revenue Office after facing widespread criticism. For years he has been the boss of MAHIR, the largest advertising agency in Hungary. He is also the coordinator for all larger financial and media transactions in the country, as well as for the private fortune of the Orbán family.[9]

The tight-knit network of connections, barely perceptible to the broad mass of Hungarians let alone foreign observers,[10] and the subtle division of labour regarding the allocation of capital and personal relationships within the media empire loyal to

Fidesz have been laid bare both by Mária Vásárhelyi and, more recently, in some headline stories in the independent business weekly *Figyelö*. Vásárhelyi sees three main strands in the media controlled by or close to Fidesz: a moderate conservative one, a nationalist-populist one and an extreme right-wing, racist one. Accordingly, Inforádió and the weekly *Heti Válasz* are aimed at the moderate audience; Hír TV, Lánchíd Rádió and the daily *Magyar Nemzet* at the nationalist-populists; and the daily *Magyar Hírlap*, the weekly magazine *Magyar Demokrata* and Echo TV at the radical, extremist and racist elements in society. In addition to these, there are free newspapers, websites and ever more intensive connections with the entertainment channels and tabloid newspapers.

The power of the politically corrupt press is always and everywhere the same: it is the power of concealment. The observation made by the Polish satirist Stanisław Jerzy Lec during the communist era in his own country is equally valid today for much of the Hungarian media: 'The view to the world can be blocked with a newspaper'. Consequently, as before 1989, the newspapers and broadcasters mentioned above are silent on Western criticisms about anti-Roma, anti-Semitic and racist gaffes in Hungary, just as they are about critiques levelled at the political style of Orbán and his entourage.

The critical reports and commentaries about Hungary published in the *New York Times* or the *Washington Post*, in the *Neue Zürcher Zeitung* and the *Tagesanzeiger* (Switzerland), in *Die Zeit*, *Die Welt*, the *Süddeutsche Zeitung* (Germany) and *Der Standard*, *Die Presse* and *profil* (Austria) are hardly ever quoted in detail and never reprinted in the pro-government media in the country itself. Only in occasional surveys, and then written in a ridiculing or aggressive style, can we find some sentences ripped out of all context and then frequently misquoted. Thus, apart from diplomats and the few linguistically proficient specialists, the right-wing, conservative and nationalist elite learns almost nothing of how it and Hungary are perceived in the Western media.

In the perverse world of the Hungarian media a broadcaster such as the erstwhile US-run Radio Free Europe (RFE), which used to broadcast news and commentaries in Hungarian from Munich to communist Hungary day and night (just as it did to all other states of the Soviet Bloc in their own languages), would be of immense importance. Unfortunately, for financial reasons and because of the advance of the internet, all the Western broadcasters such as the BBC, Deutsche Welle or Voice of America have ceased broadcasting to Hungary. In the communist era, one Hungarian in four was a regular listener of RFE. Additionally the state news agency provided high-ranking bureaucrats in the party and state apparatus, as well as 'reliable' intellectuals, with collections of articles marked 'secret' or 'top secret' originally published in the 'hostile' Western press.

Consequently, it is hardly surprising when today even members of the Catholic, moderate-nationalist middle classes loyal to Orbán react with shock, surprise, irritation or even anger on hearing from foreign friends or visitors about the disquieting picture of Hungary portrayed in the world's media. A well-known German journalist, who several years ago published in an internationally respected newspaper a very critical but completely honest article about the political and ideological background to the anti-Roma and anti-Jewish excesses in Hungary, was practically excommunicated by the family of his Hungarian wife, who had been living and working in the West for many years.

Instead, what can be heard time and time again is that it is the agents and controllers of foreign, above all Jewish, finance and capital (who want to buy everything up) and even more the traitors of Hungarian origin (who at home and abroad mislead foreign journalists) who are to blame for the distorted picture of Hungary. It remains incredible to me how the top civil servants or those close to the centre of power, even during the Antall government and then even more openly in the first Orbán government, behaved just as the communist agitprop functionaries had done in another age. They continued to compile black lists of awkward foreign correspondents. During the eight years in opposition the right-wing press never once shied away from either personal vilification or the use of what was by European standards an unbelievably acerbic tone.

Paradoxically, those journals which describe themselves today as 'middle-class daily newspapers' remind us both in style and content not only of the communist propaganda sheets, but also of the propaganda of the extreme right in the 1930s. Here are just a few examples taken from a paper I gave at a conference of journalists held in Budapest in February 2008, that is, during Gyurcsány's government. First, László Tőkéczki in *Magyar Nemzet* (23 February 2008): 'What distinguishes minister Péter Kiss together with comrade Gyurcsány is the shameless political lie. And this sells like hot cakes in the West, especially in that colourful, left-wing and materialistic environment which has almost nothing sensible to tell the outside world'.

The leading Fidesz politician László Kövér called Gyurcsány a 'paranoid Nero', who 'in his despair fills the key positions of power with political adventurers' (*Magyar Demokrata* 27 February 2008). In the same issue, a 'philosophy graduate and investment adviser' wrote the following: 'At present it appears that the fate of the EU (and with it that of the USA) depends on Hungary. The leading political circles in the USA have not yet recognised the crisis as they are fully preoccupied with their own problems in Iraq and Iran, with the presidential elections and the credit crisis ...' He also wrote that Gyurcsány, 'supported in equal measure by the Slovak, Serbian, Romanian and Russian secret services, is following a script to hand over the Carpathian Basin, Ukraine and the Eastern Balkans to the Russians ...' (Attila Szabo Olgyay).

One year later, an article in the weekly *Magyar Demokrata* calling for a 'cultural police' caused a particular uproar. Special three- or four-man squads, it proposed, should assume the honourable duty of combing through libraries and other cultural institutions, and cleanse them of 'anti-Hungarian filth', by which is meant the books of such outstanding writers as Péter Esterházy, György Spiró, Péter Nádas and others. Years ago, Orbán personally visited the editorial offices of *Magyar Hírlap* and *Magyar Demokrata* and called them, together with *Magyar Nemzet*, his 'favourite newspapers'.

As for the veracity of the personal and political attacks made by these newspapers, Mária Vásárhelyi has pointed out that since 2002 *Magyar Nemzet* has been compelled by the courts to print more than 200 corrections of approximately 450 untrue or illegal statements. Even this figure, Vásárhelyi believes, is just a fraction of all the virulent fallacious attacks made by the Fidesz newspapers. Of the countless examples, the case of the former MDF MP and the biographer of Orbán, József Debreczeni, stands out as a particularly shocking one.

In the spring of 2006 this spirited journalist was accused of 'having gone into politics as founder of the MDF on the instructions of the secret service'. The charge, originally made in an anonymous letter, was quickly spread by the obscure right-leaning Havaria Press news agency and immediately blown up into a scandal by *Magyar Nemzet* and Hír TV. Even after the absurdity of this risible accusation had been proven by the secret service officer named in the letter, it took two years for the courts to rule that the three Fidesz mouthpieces should pay Debreczeni compensation. Not a single report on the outcome of this case was carried by Havaria Press, *Magyar Nemzet* or Hír TV; nor is it to be found in the archives of *Magyar Nemzet*. According to Vásárhelyi, the often invented slanders and untruths spread against Socialist and Liberal politicians, well-known journalists and public figures have undoubtedly contributed to the demoralisation of the centre-left in Hungarian politics.

Those foreign correspondents who criticised not only the Socialist-Liberal government of Gyurcsány but also Fidesz and Viktor Orbán whilst in opposition have themselves become targets. Here we might name Ulrich Schmid, the Eastern Europe correspondent of the *Neue Zürcher Zeitung* between 2002 and 2008, the *Tagesanzeiger* reporter Bernhard Odehnal or Gregor Mayer of the DPA and *Der Standard*, the Austrian quality daily newspaper. They were attacked by emigrant groups in Switzerland, which are dominated by the far right. In letters and petitions the emigrants and their accomplices demanded the removal of journalists who twisted 'historical facts'. In the meantime the Orbán propagandists, now restored to power, can press forward with their witch-hunt against correspondents and commentators on a much broader scale, even through diplomatic channels.[11]

In this regard, the conclusion reached by the writer Péter Nádas about seven years ago has proved all too true: there is a 'bond of matrimony between Horthyism and Kádárism' in Hungarian society and politics. The nostalgic memories of personal security and (in comparison with other Eastern Bloc countries) modest prosperity in the Kádár era go hand-in-hand with the undifferentiated condemnation of the achievements of democracy since the collapse of the communist regime, resulting in the bizarre delusion of a 'socialism without communism and a capitalism without private property and competition' (Mária Vásárhelyi).

Approximately 60 per cent of Hungarians see their country as the loser of 1989. No fewer than three-quarters of young people believe in the possibility of a new system change with the renationalisation of key companies and a reckoning with the guilty politicians who have so damaged the country. Two-thirds of Hungarian adults believe that 'the country still serves the interests of foreign powers' and that 'Hungarian interests are not regarded as an absolute priority by the government in office'.

These absurd opinions in a country which has now been independent and free for more than 20 years and has determined its own fate in free elections are naturally just as unreal and politically dangerous as the misinterpretations of Hungarian history outlined above. But they explain how the bitter and almost infinite disappointment of many in the country, especially the young, was so successfully exploited by the unbridled power politician Viktor Orbán between 2007 and 2010. The Socialists and the Liberals (who have now sunk into oblivion) had undoubtedly caused considerable harm to Hungary and had themselves fallen into a morass of corruption and scandal.

It was in these years that the die was cast in favour of the right-wing populist and nationalist course under Orbán. This

THE POWER OF THE DISCREET PRESS BARONS

was also due to Orbán's discreet, wealthy and unquestioningly loyal media barons who, from the beginning to the end of the 'political civil war', proved themselves to be confident and unscrupulous vassals. The core of this strategy was the campaign for the political annihilation of Ferenc Gyurcsány, by far the most capable politician on the left.

11

COLD WAR AT THE TOP—ORBÁN VERSUS GYURCSÁNY

The years between 2006 and 2010 produced one of the strangest and most exciting duels in modern European history: the (for Hungary) decisive battle between two extraordinary but totally different politicians, Ferenc Gyurcsány and Viktor Orbán.

Both were representatives of the same generation. Orbán had lost three elections against Socialist candidates: in 1994 against the post-communist veteran Gyula Horn, in 2002 against the smooth and congenial upper-middle class gentleman Péter Medgyessy, and in 2006 against the self-made man from the lower classes Ferenc Gyurcsány. Of his three defeats Orbán, a professional politician to the core, found the last particularly intolerable and unjust.

The following four years witnessed almost a life and death struggle as Viktor Orbán not only destroyed Ferenc Gyurcsány, the surprise winner of the poll in April 2006 and a man just two years his senior, by means of an unprecedented personal and political demolition campaign, but also crushed all his left-wing, liberal or moderate conservative rivals. His irrepressible will to triumph, his skills in correcting in a second any political or tactical mistakes, his talent for the timely sidelining of potential or putative competitors and his cynical determination to win over 'Homo Kádáricus' and sections of the extreme right by means of a mélange of nationalistic, clerical and left-wing populist language formed the background to his epochal election victory in the spring of 2010.

Even then, the breakthrough would not have been possible, or at least not on this scale, if the following factors had not prepared the ground for Orbán and his Fidesz Party:

(1) Ferenc Gyurcsány's catastrophic secret speech about lying to the public in May 2006; the inability of an otherwise inspired politician and communicator to govern purposely and convincingly with a team, and his failure to distinguish the significant from the trivial; Gyurcsány's chronic lack of strength to curb his impulsive temperament and his tendency to rhetorical sleights of hand in interviews instead of courageously facing unpopularity. There is not a single other head of government in a modern state who, like Gyurcsány, would for years write a generally accessible blog, with many details from his personal daily life, or divulge details about explosive internal party matters to his biographer. A humane, extremely sympathetic amateur in the revolting snake pit of the old communists and left-wing careerists pretending to be social democrats.

(2) The Socialists (MSzP), who were in office for 12 of the first 20 years after 1989, were not only unable but also

unwilling to convincingly face up to the inheritance of the Kádár regime and transform themselves into a Western style social democratic party. Only Ferenc Gyurcsány tried to accomplish this, but he failed abysmally. Many of his closest colleagues devoted incomparably more time and energy to undermining him as party and government leader than to mounting a defence against the challenge coming from the right. The Socialist Party elite not only failed in this political battle but was also mired in a swamp of corruption, above all in the electorally decisive capital, Budapest.

(3) The failure of the Liberal Party (SzDSz), which in 1989–90 had launched the most vehement attacks on the ruling communists. By joining the Horn government between 1994 and 1998 the Liberals actually lost a part of the critical middle-class electorate. Owing to the internal party battles between the intellectuals and the young politicians, the civil rights activists forfeited their credibility. In the 2002 and 2006 elections they served merely as a stepping stone to power (albeit a rather uncomfortable one) for the Socialists, who otherwise would not have had a viable parliamentary majority. That it was the liberal Gyurcsány of all people who, through his rash acts and gaffes, forced his pivotal and hopelessly divided left-of-centre allies from mid-2008 first into opposition and finally into political oblivion may be considered a macabre footnote in the never-ending story of the atrophy of the incessantly squabbling liberal elite.

(4) The incompetence, cowardice and rivalry of the ministers responsible for economic policy and their top-ranking civil servants in the governments of Medgyessy and Gyurc-

sány; the political failure of the capable Minister of Economics Lajos Bokros, engineered by his jealous rivals, and the belated and fragmentary reaction of Gyurcsány to the global financial crisis of 2008. Thanks to the crisis management skills of Gordon Bajnai (born in 1968), who filled the office of prime minister between March 2009 and May 2010 with great courage and competence, Hungary was able to avoid the threatening financial collapse. The crisis package came, however, far too late to be of any aid to the discredited Socialist minority government politically.

(5) Thanks to the systematic inflammatory campaigns of the right-wing and extreme right-wing media the phenomenon of the apparently inexorable rise of the radical right, so reminiscent of the 1930s, has repeated itself in Hungary. Many disappointed and angry voters from the poorest sections of the populace or from among the losers of the economic crisis of that fatal decade supported the Arrow Cross Party in 1939, instead of the Social Democrats, in working-class and mining districts. That in Hungary in 2010 almost as many people voted for the radical right-wing, anti-Semitic and extremely nationalistic Jobbik Party (the name is a pun on 'on the right' and 'better') with its paramilitary arm, the Hungarian Guard, as for the Socialists was a resounding slap in the face for the MSzP.[1] At the same time the breakthrough of Jobbik, an organisation that openly exploits the symbols of the Arrow Cross Party, among young voters was also a warning to Orbán that he could lose their support by pursuing policies that were too conservative and too cautious.

It is against this background that we should now closely examine the dramatic events in Budapest in the autumn of

COLD WAR AT THE TOP—ORBÁN VERSUS GYURCSÁNY

2006 and their political fallout over the following years. Some of these events I witnessed, like most people, as a viewer of television news reports, but others were recounted to me by various politicians who were sometimes secret but often open political rivals.

Though Viktor Orbán launched his invidious witch-hunt after his defeat in 2002, the actual beginning of the particularly 'hot autumn' of 2006 was marked by the publication and immediate nationwide dissemination of the juiciest extracts from Gyurcsány's secret 'lie speech'. The attacks of Orbán and his henchmen against the left (which they claimed to be anti-nationalist for 'genetical reasons') and against the 'illegitimate' government of Gyurcsány, illegitimate because he won power on the basis of a lie, served consciously and unconsciously as the beginning of the unrest which has destroyed Hungary's image in the world as a stable and peaceful democracy based on consensus for many years to come.[2]

The same evening as extracts from Gyurcsány's speech were broadcast, members of the hard right, football hooligans and supporters of Jobbik gathered in front of the parliament building and started chanting for the Prime Minister's resignation. The demands of the demonstrators, who were immediately recognisable by their dress and by their curved red and white striped Árpád flags,[3] did not change for the days and weeks they remained on the streets. On 18 September the incensed mob moved from the parliament to the nearby television centre, which was soon stormed and partly set on fire. The police were taken by surprise and clearly overwhelmed.

In the following two days there were serious clashes between these far-right demonstrators and the police. Ahead of the nationwide local elections, Orbán played political roulette as

171

he bet everything on a successful mobilisation of the masses, turning the elections into a 'referendum' on the government. On the same night as the Socialists and their Liberal coalition partners suffered significant losses, the opposition leader demanded the resignation of the 'pathological liar' at the head of the government.

Shortly after the closing of the polling stations, in a speech broadcast on television President László Sólyom effectively recommended the replacement of the controversial Prime Minister. Orbán then presented the two government parties with a 72-hour ultimatum to remove Gyurcsány. The unprecedented intervention of the conservative Head of State contributed to the emergence of a highly dangerous situation. Far from acting as an intermediary, Sólyom's trenchant comments fanned the flames in a country where there was already little or no willingness for dialogue.[4] After his convincing victory in the local elections, Orbán held a mass meeting in front of parliament in order to maintain the momentum of the demands for Gyurcsány's resignation. In response to Orbán's ultimatum, Gyurcsány called for a vote of confidence in parliament; this he won by 207 votes to 167.

Nevertheless, the protests and clashes continued and reached their climax on 23 October 2006, a day of profound symbolism as it marked the 50th anniversary of the Hungarian uprising. Extreme right-wing organisers succeeded in mingling their violent thugs with the tens of thousands of peaceful Fidesz supporters who had just left a mass meeting addressed by Orbán. Reacting to their failure some weeks earlier, the poorly led police displayed towards the crowd a disproportionate harshness, not to say brutality, even against the peaceable participants from the Fidesz rally. There was, as always, a lighter moment: in a bizarre scene, one shown repeatedly by the international media, a far-right pensioner seized control of an old tank that had been wheeled out as an exhibit for the 50th anniversary celebrations and drove it around in the middle of Budapest.

That all this took place in the presence of dozens of foreign heads of state and government only contributed to the negative reaction to these events worldwide. The unrest, which lasted for several weeks, shocked the country: 326 civilians were injured (16 badly) as were 399 police officers (47 seriously). In a newspaper article the human rights activist Ferenc Donáth described the siege and temporary occupation of the MTV building as a violent attempt at a putsch.[5] He sharply criticised the playing down of the 42-day-long public agitation in front of parliament by the opposition. During this six-week period hard-right extremists read out the names of alleged Jewish politicians and journalists, as well as the addresses of judges and public prosecutors who had handed out sentences to the violent disturbers of the peace.

While the memory of the violence on the margins of the failed attempt to topple the Gyurcsány government quickly faded, the random but undoubtedly brutal acts of the police have been kept very much alive in the reports and commentaries of the right-wing press.[6] During the disturbances the Jobbik Party stood out as 'the now best organised political force on the right' (Gregor Mayer). This grouping, founded in 2003, profited the most from the 'hot autumn', the same fateful autumn that Gábor Vona, a 28-year-old teacher, was elected chairman of the party. Admitted some years previously by Orbán to his so-called 'citizens' league' loosely associated with Fidesz, Vona energetically set about building up a network among the young.

In recent years Krisztina Morvai, a university lecturer in the field of penal law and a successful top far-right candidate in the European elections, has appeared next to Vona as the figurehead of the Movement for a Better Hungary (Jobbik). A well-known feminist and (until recently) the wife of a prominent liberal TV journalist of Jewish origins, she made a complete political about-turn following the refusal of the Socialist-Liberal coalition to prolong her tenure on a UN human rights committee. After the disturbances in October 2006, the embittered but pugnacious Morvai founded a commission to investigate the police attacks and, in doing so, began to show solidarity with convicted Jobbik supporters. She achieved notoriety in a reader's letter to the literary weekly *Élet és Irodalom* (14 November 2008) in which, with an unmistakeable anti-Semitic undertone, she divided the Hungarians into 'our equals' (*magunkfajták*) and 'those of that ilk' (*magukfajták*).

In her speeches Morvai has repeatedly warned against Hungary becoming a second Palestine and has railed against 'Zionist criminals'. When a Hungarian manager living in New York, describing himself as a 'proud Jewish Hungarian', harshly criticised her on a Hungarian website, the mother of three daughters flew into such a rage in her reply that the following outburst was quoted in several newspapers: 'I'd be happier if those who award themselves the title of proud Hungarian Jews played with their tiny little circumcised dicks rather than defame me ...'[7]

The radicalisation of Hungarian politics has also been mirrored in the erosion of trust in democratic institutions. As opposition leader, Viktor Orbán dictated the pace after the failure of his 72-hour ultimatum in the realisation of his gloomy scenario. It was the prelude to the 'power of fear' in

Hungarian politics. Thus he declared a total boycott of the 'illegitimate' Prime Minister by withdrawing the entire Fidesz parliamentary party from the debating chamber whenever Gyurcsány announced he would speak in parliament.

The music accompanying the war of annihilation against Gyurcsány was provided by a media campaign which was unprecedented in its style, vocabulary and frequency of attacks, a campaign reminiscent of a bizarre mixture of the Third Reich's *Völkischer Beobachter* and a Stalin-era issue of *Pravda*. Two decades after the collapse of communism, the writer György Dalos observed that even in the first years of freedom 'the ghosts of the past filled the rhetoric of the political discourse with apparently forgotten anti-Semitic, chauvinistic, anti-European content. Instead of a political culture, Hungary has found itself saddled with one of hatred'.[8]

The impression of calm after the storm soon proved deceptive. In a startling series of articles in various Socialist and Liberal publications, József Debreczeni, who as his biographer probably knows Orbán better than anybody, warned of the fatal consequences of the policy of total confrontation championed by the Fidesz leader. He expressed 'the most serious concerns' about the nationalistic, hate-filled, aggressive, populist, xenophobic and barely concealed anti-Semitic path of the party, which had definitively lurched to the right. At the same time he noted the helplessness, confusion and fears prevailing on the centre-left.

At the beginning of 2007 a statement by Orbán in the right-wing, conservative pro-Fidesz weekly *Heti Válasz*, published with the sensational headline 'There is nothing to negotiate!', shocked even those who had been critical of Gyurcsány since his 'scandalous speech'. Orbán openly threatened the Socialist

Prime Minister, indeed the whole ruling elite, with criminal proceedings and rejected any dialogue with Gyurcsány, the 'pathological liar who threatens democracy'. Moreover, he made no secret of his hopes that only 'the political and social dissatisfaction' of the people could force a change either through a government of experts or early parliamentary elections. An editorial in *Magyar Nemzet*, a newspaper close to Fidesz, stated the case even more precisely: Orbán's vision of public outrage meant that the drastic budget cuts advocated by Gyurcsány's government would result in an explosive situation.

In this sense the founding of the Hungarian Guard, which attracted worldwide attention, was a development that in every respect confirmed the dire premonitions of critical observers and caused immense damage to Hungary's international standing. On 25 August 2007 the whole eerie oath-taking ceremony of the first 56 members of the Guard was enacted at Budapest castle; to make matters worse, it took place practically beneath the balcony of Sándor Palace, the Office of the President of Hungary. The Guards wore black waistcoats over white shirts, black caps, black trousers and leather boots. In both their cut and colours, and above all the reappearance of the red and white striped Árpád coat of arms on the brims of their caps and as arm badges, their uniforms revived memories of the nightmare times of the winter of horror of 1944–45 when members of the Arrow Cross committed acts of indescribable cruelty in Budapest at the behest of the Third Reich.

The television pictures of the military-like parading and shouting of orders, the ceremony surrounding the oath taking, the blessing of flags by Catholic and Protestant priests and the outfits so reminiscent of those worn by the Arrow Cross, as well as the bombastic pronouncements of the national mission to rescue Magyardom (which was fatally threatened 'physically, psychologically and spiritually'), all taken together stunned commentators from the international media and enraged many others, not least Jewish organisations. Lajos Für, the Minister of Defence in the Antall government, appeared next to Gábor Vona at the ceremony. After the swearing of the oath and cheered on by a crowd several thousand strong, he presented the Guards with certificates bearing their names. Für's presence at the macabre event was supposed to symbolically lend Jobbik's paramilitary unit an air of respectability.

During the bizarre parade, and especially later, both Hungarian and foreign observers judged the silence of the State President curious, not least because the oath-taking ceremony had taken place beneath the windows of his official residence. Only two weeks later did László Sólyom make any comment on the episode in a long-winded speech given on the occasion of the opening of the autumn parliamentary session. As in subsequent newspaper interviews, so in this first, belated response, Sólyom condemned not only the organisation of this event by the far right, but also the manipulation of fears that it had aroused.[9] The most frequent criticism laid at Sólyom's door was that he always remained silent when he should have spoken out, and always said something when it would have been better to keep quiet.

In an extremely critical commentary on Sólyom's presidency the Hungarian film director and translator László Kornitzer drew attention to an aspect of the controversy which had hitherto gone unmentioned within Hungary itself.

You have to imagine a situation in which 2,000 neo-Nazis want to swear an oath on the lawns of Schloss Bellevue in Berlin, the official residence of the German president. Far and wide, there are no police to be seen, also no president, not even a hint of his shadow as a ghost behind the curtains of one of the palace's windows. The ceremony lasts two hours and is even broadcast on television; then the neo-Nazis march off, unchallenged, with their heads held high and their destination unknown. Unimaginable. Yet that is exactly what happened in Budapest in the summer of 2007 without the president feeling the need to say a word on this incident.[10]

In one paragraph of his speech to parliament Sólyom warned, out of respect for the survivors of the Holocaust, against using the Árpád flag. What was at issue here? The Árpád flag with its red and white stripes is one of the 12 historic flags of Hungary and was in use until the thirteenth century. The Arrow Cross Party chose this flag as its own in the 1930s. In 1944 the Árpád stripes became a symbol of the mass murders committed by the members of the Arrow Cross paramilitary wearing them as armbands.[11] I still have vivid memories of witnessing as an adolescent the murderous operations of the fascist thugs with their red and white armbands in the besieged Hungarian capital between October 1944 and February 1945. But Sólyom was incorrect when he referred only to Jewish victims. As a consequence of Hitler's scorched earth tactics in the dying months of the war, tens of thousands of civilians, as well as Hungarian, German and Soviet soldiers, also died.

Instead of clearly condemning the right-wing extremists, Fidesz politicians blatantly exploited the founding of the Guard for their anti-Gyurcsány campaign. For this reason the then vice-chairman of Fidesz explicitly declared that the forming of the Guard was to be understood as a reaction to the personality and behaviour of Ferenc Gyurcsány. The tragic events in the following two years and the international uproar they spawned fulfilled the gloomy prognosis. The genii Viktor Orbán had conjured up in his thirst for power had spun out of control.

12

THE ROMA AND JEWS—TARGETS OF THE EXTREME RIGHT

Jobbik and its paramilitary wing, the Hungarian Guard, can attribute their rapid rise to their systematic and rampant hate campaign against the Roma. Moreover, venomous and barely veiled articles against foreign (above all Israeli) businessmen and investors, as well as Hungarian liberals and in particular Jewish intellectuals, are regularly published on their websites and in their publications.

The opinions expressed by Péter Nádas, one of the most important Hungarian novelists, in an interview printed in the Austrian newspaper *Der Standard* on 5 September 2009 are shared by most of my friends and acquaintances in Hungary:

There is no functioning state in Hungary. The state has been corroded by corruption ... Every government to date bears a responsibility for this, but naturally none of them wishes to admit this. The state has for all intents and purposes collapsed. The left has completely failed. The liberals have also failed. They are all corrupt ... The extremists on the right dominate the media and public discourse. I can't leave my flat any more without being forced to look at their heinous slogans.

The Roma, who are almost universally, even in specialist literature, called Gypsies in Hungary, first arrived in the Magyar kingdom in the 16th century. According to a survey conducted by the EU in seven Central and East European countries, all the Roma living in Hungary claim that Hungarian is their mother tongue. The representatives of this largest ethnic minority in Hungary (estimated at 600–700,000 people or 6–7 per cent of the total population) believe they are discriminated against at every level: social, cultural, intellectual and political. Approximately 90 per cent are of the opinion that the discrimination against them is widespread and is also much stronger in Hungary than in any other European country; 62 per cent claim to have personally experienced discrimination in the past 12 months.[1]

There is no question that the Roma have been the biggest losers of the change of system in 1989 and the collapse of the old heavy industries. Today four-fifths of Roma are unemployed, and because of high birth rates long-term unemployment is even more pronounced amongst women. Two-thirds of Roma are estimated to be affected by segregation and oppressive poverty, often living in squalid shacks in northern and eastern Hungary. In spite of some measures to alleviate this, Roma children, owing to their low educational level, do not share the opportunities available to their non-Roma Hungarian counterparts.

A successful experiment, and one that is unique throughout Europe, is to be found in Pécs: the first Roma grammar school, the Gandhi Gymnasium, which was founded in 1994 on the initiative of the sociologist János Bogdán.[2] But overall, more than half of Roma children never complete elementary school; the Roma account for only 5 per cent of those taking high-school leaving exams and a mere 1 per cent of those in higher education. Life expectancy among the Roma is about eight to ten years less than the average in Hungary.

In view of the unemployment, the socially neglected minority ghettos and the lack of hope for of any social advancement, it is hardly surprising that petty crime in the shape of stealing chickens or robbing grocery stores is part and parcel of life in the poorest regions of Hungary. But the tragedy that took place in Olaszliszka, a village in northeastern Hungary, on 15 October 2006 was of a completely different order. While driving through the Roma quarter Lajos Szögi, a school teacher, had an accident with a small Roma girl, slightly injuring her. When he got out of his car, he was attacked by incensed Roma who believed the girl was dead: Szögi was killed on the spot. The police immediately arrested several suspects. Although the crime was clearly both spontaneous and unpremeditated, following a complex trial lasting 3½ years and exploited to the full by Jobbik and the right-wing press, six men were given prison sentences of 15 to 30 years (practically life); two minors received ten years each.

The brutal murder in Olaszliszka with all its gruesome details (the school teacher was killed before the eyes of his two daughters sitting in the car) provoked a nationwide outburst of verbal and physical attacks on Roma. Polls suggest that approximately 80 per cent of Hungarians, not least because of the systematic witch-hunt conducted by Jobbik and the right-wing media against 'Gypsy criminals', are ill-disposed towards the Roma.[3]

According to a poll prepared by the International School Psychology Association, one grammar school pupil in two in Hungary would not sit next to a Roma in the classroom.[4]

Late at night on 8 February 2009 three popular handball players of a local team in the town of Veszprém in western Hungary were involved in a nightclub fight. The Romanian Marian Cozma was stabbed; the other two players suffered critical injuries. The fact that the attackers were Roma fuelled the debate on 'Gypsy criminality' sparked off a few days earlier by a statement made at a press conference by Captain Albert Pásztor, the police chief in the important industrial town of Miskolc. Pásztor had said quite openly that Gypsies were responsible for most robberies; he went on: 'the many sweet little Gypsy children all too often become tough and ruthless criminals ... Any cooperation with our fellow countrymen from the minority simply doesn't work ...'[5]

Within 24 hours Pásztor had been fired. Yet, equally quickly and with just a warning, he was reinstated 24 hours later. The explanation for this bizarre turn of events was quite simple. Almost immediately, a coalition backing the police chief had formed in the town, one which had not existed before and which stretched from the Socialists to the local Jobbik organisation. This loss of face, which owing to internal party pressure was embarrassing even for the Prime Minister, confirmed the bitter words of the bold reporter Szilvia Varró of the weekly magazine *Magyar Narancs* during a long conversation with me about the situation of the Roma:

Olaszliszka was only a pretext. The right-wing extremists, such as the Hungarian Guard, have been growing in strength since the autumn of 2006. Their website, Kuruc.info, is on line again; the national security authorities have not been sufficiently energetic in shutting down the server ... There are cases where the police have even protected the meetings of Jobbik against the Gypsies. The attacks demonstrate that the far right is becoming more and more self-confident. There are just as many racist Gypsy-haters in the Socialist Party as everywhere else in Hungary. In its eight years, the Socialist government has done nothing to get rid of the ghettos, nothing to create jobs etc. This has prepared the ground for the radical right. The Hungarians have no real contact with the Roma, not at home, not in the workplace, not at school. The cancerous evil is ghettoisation. The Hungarian Guard and the Roma murders interact as a catalyst in the Gypsies' finding of themselves—strengthening of identity, radicalisation, fear.[6]

Not only Szilvia Varró but also many other observers have pointed out that a Jobbik trade union grouping has been formed within the ranks of the police with about 5,500 members (or approximately 10 per cent of the police force). Citing two pro-Fidesz newspapers, *Magyar Nemzet* ('Again Gypsies commit murder') and *Magyar Hírlap* ("These murdering animals were Gypsies, once again Gypsies'), János Kis observes that the right-wing press had a field day after the murder of the handball player in Veszprém.

Kis, a liberal professor of political science and of philosophy at the Central European University in Budapest, found it even more damaging and disturbing that, within 48 hours of the murder in Veszprém, the Fidesz party Presidium hastened to declare the 'dramatic increase in the serious crimes committed by people of Gypsy origin'. With this choice of words the Presidium made an entire ethnic group accountable for the criminal acts of a few individuals. 'Thus, Fidesz has crossed a line, one which a responsible political force should not overstep'.[7]

While the campaign with the war cry 'Gypsy crime' was running at full steam in the right-wing and extreme right-wing media, the Hungarian Guard appeared in a number of high profile (and highly theatrical) events, such as the ceremonial induction of 600 new Guards at the historic Heroes' Square in Budapest on 15 March 2009, the National Day. Much more dangerous, however, was the martial parading up and down of the Hungarian Guard at weekends in towns and villages with a relatively large proportion of Roma. Though they carried no (visible) weapons, the Guards in their black uniforms, marching in step to military commands, wearing bovver boots, camouflage or combat kit, spread a climate of fear among the Roma. Their spokespersons behaved as if they were the protectors of law-abiding Hungarian citizens against the evil machinations of the criminal Roma.

Here and there the police tried to keep a cordon between the Guards and the intimidated villagers, who were embittered by the provocations coming from outside their communities. Instead of trying to calm things down, the Guards and their Jobbik backers enflamed the situation everywhere they went. Whenever the paramilitaries, always dressed in black, appear in villages, their intention is to march through Roma ghettos with the sole aim of cowing the locals. Fear and terror are often also spread by the bands of motorcyclists rigged out in black leather roaring up and down the narrow streets of Roma communities. As a particular provocation, they call their convoys 'goy columns' after the Hebrew word for non-Jews.

It is no wonder that leading international newspapers and broadcasters have reported worldwide on the absurd but menacing parades of the black jackets in an EU state.[8] In retrospect the choice of the village of Tatárszentgyörgy for the first big march of almost 300 men and even a few dozen women in the autumn of 2007 may have been a particularly macabre coincidence.[9] A quarter of the 1,800 inhabitants of this small village, some 50km southeast of Budapest, are Roma. A Jobbik leader demanded the segregation instead of integration of the Roma, as well as the reintroduction of the death penalty; he also assured the 'populace which was threatened by Gypsy terror' that 'You are not alone!' Thanks to a large police presence, the march went off without incidence.

However, 14 months later Tatárszentgyörgy was once again in the headlines. In the night of 22–23 February 2009 unknown perpetrators threw an incendiary device onto the house of the 27-year-old Róbert Csorba. The family fled from the burning house at the end of the so-called *ciganysor* (Gypsy Row). The arsonists then shot down in cold blood Csorba and his five-year-old son, whom he was carrying in his arms. The twin murder was the beginning of a terrifying wave of attacks which left six dead and very many injured. The Roma in Tatárszentgyörgy tried to organise their own self-defence by means of voluntary patrols, but soon were forced to abandon these for lack of money. Four alleged suspects were arrested in the summer of 2009; to date, however, the public prosecutor still has not pressed charges. The four arrested were not members of the Hungarian Guard but of a far-right group which is also said to have been responsible for shootings and bomb attacks on the homes of Socialist politicians.

The close connection between the Guards and Jobbik, and their joint instrumentalisation of alleged 'Gypsy crime', have played a decisive role in the mobilisation of potential voters. The young political scientists whose work we have already mentioned above[10] point to the complex impact of the media: the series of horrifying murders of Roma and above all the detailed reporting on these have contributed to the unease and atmosphere of resentment against the Roma ('There's always something going on with the Gypsies ...'). Jobbik received almost half a million votes (round 15 per cent) in the European elections, yet it would be wrong to conclude that it is recruiting mainly from among the poorer, uneducated sectors of society. Its voters were as often as not university graduates and members of the middle class, by no means people who could be seen as losers of the change of system or the global economic crisis. They were younger than average, male rather than female, and tended to live in small communities.

Although both the Fidesz leadership, in the person of Viktor Orbán, and the right-leaning media, not to speak of the churches, have all remained silent on the Hungarian Guard (or at best have reacted very cautiously), in July 2009 the appeal court in Budapest finally disbanded the Guard and its sponsoring organisation led by the Jobbik boss, Gábor Vona. The response was to immediately refound the militia as the New Hungarian Guard. According to the weekly *Figyelö* (25 February 2010), in early 2010 this had 3,000 active members and more than 10,000 supporters. At the beginning of July 2010 a Hungarian National Guard was brought into being again under the overall control of Gábor Vona, in clear defiance of the court ruling. Around 1,000 people took the oath of loyalty to the Guard. Several Jobbik MPs spoke at the ceremony.

If the blatant and crudely expressed hatred of the Roma has been the 'open secret' of the political success of Jobbik, then anti-Semitism has also had a 'significant' influence on the growth in support for radical political groups.[11] The findings of the opinion polls referred to in Chapter 4 are of course not only due to failure to come to terms with the past, especially the silence on or trivialisation of the Hungarian share in the mass extermination of Hungarian Jews. Even before the last two major elections in Hungary (the European elections in June 2009 and those for parliament in April 2010), Ulrich Schmid, the former East European correspondent of the *Neue Zürcher Zeitung*, wrote a painstakingly researched article on the growing anti-Semitism. This caused a storm of outrage among emigrant associations, which are often led by right-wing extremists, as well as among the newspapers and political parties concerned.

In Hungary since the regime change the pat answer, as common as it is mendacious, has always been that there is no anti-Semitism in the country and the allegations of anti-Jewish tendencies, from whatever quarter they come, can be traced back 'for 20 years to the same overwhelmingly liberal sources'. Even the editors of the allegedly moderate pro-Fidesz weekly *Heti Válasz* repeat this and see 'behind this evident tendency foreign secret services interested in the destabilisation of Hungary'. Yet it would seem as difficult to accuse Ulrich Schmid of any such intention as it would the correspondents of other internationally well-known newspapers. The reasons for the right-wing indignation can be found in Nietzsche: 'The truth finds the fewest advocates, not when it is dangerous to speak it, but when it is boring'.

Schmid's findings are sobering: 'There is a massive and alarming anti-Semitism in Hungary'; the situation is not yet dramatic, but it is serious enough:

Parties which nurture feelings of resentment are gaining support. And whilst it is true that paramilitary formations ... primarily rail against 'Roma criminals', they equally mean the Jews. An incomprehensibly malicious hatred of Jews manifests itself in football stadiums. Anyone who has witnessed such outbursts would never again have any inclination to play it down. In the pages of many newspapers disrespectful innuendo about this or that Jew, or Jews in general, has almost become de rigueur.

The occasion for this stocktaking was a notorious, openly anti-Semitic article in *Magyar Hírlap*, a daily newspaper once known for its liberal views, on 18 March 2008. The author who, in the words of the novelist Péter Esterházy, had composed what was 'by a long way the vilest article of recent years' was a certain Zsolt Bayer, a well-known journalist, a founding member of Fidesz and part of Orbán's inner circle. His 'miserable article, barely worth mentioning' (Esterházy) first denounced by name several Jewish journalists and concluded with an unprecedented, openly anti-Semitic outburst: 'In 1967 Jewish journalists in Budapest still reviled Israel. Today, these very same Jewish journalists revile the Arabs. And Fidesz. And us. Because they hate us more than we hate them. They are the Jews who vindicate us. And let's say it: their sheer existence justifies anti-Semitism'.

In an open letter more than a hundred prominent Hungarian intellectuals protested to the owner of the newspaper, the industrialist Gábor Széles, that such anti-Semitic attacks had hitherto been known only in the extreme right-wing press of the 1930s and 1940s. By printing this article the newspaper had 'crossed an important line in the Hungarian media. Hitherto, those in the Hungarian press and in public life who were called anti-Semites by their critics had always immediately rejected the accusation. The author [of this article], however, consciously admits his anti-Semitism'.

The brave stand of Ibolya Dávid, president of the small conservative opposition party MDF, attracted particular attention. The former Minister of Justice in the first Orbán government wrote in an open letter that it was scandalous, outrageous, baffling and abhorrent that such an article was ever allowed to see the light of day. The author's action was especially infamous because one of the main targets of the right-wing, nationalist attack was the Catholic publicist Rudolf Ungváry, a prominent civil rights campaigner, one of the few active civil rights fighters before the collapse of the communist regime. In contrast his attacker was an opportunist journalist who since 1989 had swung effortlessly from left to right and who had for some years worked for the newspaper *Népszabadság*, the former mouthpiece of the Hungarian Communists.

We can say in general that a prominent characteristic of the mendacious atmosphere of Hungarian politics and media is that both are populated by people who demonstrably won their spurs in the old communist apparatus and who now, as convinced, well-drilled anti-communists, gratuitously slander left-wing or liberal politicians and journalists, men and women who in many cases were once their colleagues. Thus, for example, the co-founder of the Hungarian Guard, and the editor-in-chief of the far-right weekly *Magyar Demokrata*, had worked for years as a loyal editor for the official communist newspaper on the desk covering so-called party affairs. For many years *Magyar Demokrata* has published articles such as the one lauding the notorious Holocaust denier David Irving as a 'champion of free thought' (9 March 2006) or celebrating Waffen SS officers as heroes of the failed attempted breakout in the battle for Budapest (8 February 2007). Such newspapers and broadcasters in the right-wing media empire[12] have exercised considerable clout in winning over for Fidesz the large and electorally strong right wing. Shortly after the publication of the disgraceful anti-Semitic article referred to above, which was cited with much glee, its author, broadly smiling and very ostentatiously, celebrated together with Viktor Orbán the anniversary of the founding of Fidesz, a scene that was repeated one year later. We can hardly be surprised to learn that in the autumn of 2008, in an extraordinarily aggressive tone, the same Zsolt Bayer was making 'avaricious, insatiable Jewish financiers [responsible for] the American and ultimately worldwide economic crisis' of that year. Whatever happens in Hungary, be it financial aid for the needy Jewish Community or the first visit of the Nobel Peace Prize winner Elie Wiesel, the lap-dog journalist courtiers orbiting around Orbán never fail to use the opportunity to awaken anti-Semitic resentments.

All this has created an atmosphere of fear and a feeling of exclusion in the Jewish community in Hungary. Not a single person on the moderate right has ever publicly called to order the anti-Roma and anti-Jewish rabble rousers or the thugs responsible for the brutal attacks on gay rights rainbow parades. We could fill pages with quotations from the virulent speeches of Jobbik and, on occasion during the 2010 election campaign, of Fidesz politicians. It is not only the Jews but also liberal and conservative circles who have been outraged by the inflammatory erosion of taboos.

It is like living in a world turned upside down. The German news magazine *Der Spiegel* has reported how on the National Day at the monument for Sándor Petőfi, the poet of national liberation, situated on the banks of the Danube, Jobbik party members and passersby sympathetic to their cause started chanting 'Jewish swine! Jewish swine!' or 'Into the river with you!' The target of their abuse was the (former) liberal mayor of Budapest, Gábor Demszky, who was once one of the few bold opponents of the Kádár regime. Not far from that scene on the Danube, where in the winter of 1944 thousands of Jews were shot and their bodies thrown into the river, there is today a small monument comprising sixty bronze shoes; recently somebody stuffed hacked-off pig trotters into these shoes. Also not so long ago, in a community in eastern Hungary, in spite of protests and exposés in the liberal press, a teacher was made head of the local school after he had had himself photographed in an SS uniform 'just for fun' and had, moreover, ridiculed the Holocaust on the internet; he is a history teacher. His colleagues told reporters that it was none of their business what he did in his spare time.

Not only the universities but also high schools have become the stage in the struggle with right-wing extremists. In a school in Budapest, for example, the head teacher, who had held the post for thirteen years, was anonymously attacked on the far-right website Kuruc.info because he urged a pupil not to wear a polo shirt adorned with images of Greater Hungary and the Turul bird.[13] The rabble-rousing website responded by publishing his name, photo, telephone number and e-mail address with the comment that the man was a Jew. After these details were posted, under the title 'Jewish head teacher terrorises patriotic pupils', the man received a flood of vile, anti-Semitic hate messages.

Magyar Hírlap headlined a similar case on its front page. At his school in Székesfehérvár in western Hungary, the liberal head teacher, a member of the SzDSz, banned the wearing of a school cap with the red and white Árpád stripes and a badge of Greater Hungary; the chair of the local Jobbik Party brought up the case in the steering committee of the town council. And from what I hear all these cases are just the tip of the iceberg. Friends and acquaintances in Budapest tell me how their children or grandchildren have been confronted by racist teachers or fellow pupils, or else they have witnessed similar incidents involving Roma or Jewish classmates.

And the adults? A well-known radio journalist, a friend of my wife, relates how she was abused in a Budapest bus by uniformed right-wing radicals, without any reaction from the other passengers. A similar story was told us by another elderly journalist. Or then there is the example of Orthodox Jews who, on account of the insults hurled at them, no longer openly wear their yarmulkes but keep them hidden under baseball caps. Or the case of a celebration of the Sabbath in which a window in the flat where it was being held was broken by a stone thrown from the street. Individual incidents, undoubtedly, and certainly not comparable to the mass marches and acts of violence perpetrated in Roma communities; but, nonetheless, an intolerable affront for people of Jewish origin, who themselves, or their parents and grandparents, could say with the exiled German writer Hans Sahl:

> *We are the last.*
> *Ask us.*
> *We are competent.*

The crude anti-Jewish propaganda peaked on the eve of the 2010 parliamentary elections. At the beginning of the year, the Jobbik weekly magazine *Barikád* published on its title page a photomontage showing the Benedictine monk and patron saint of Budapest, Gellért, standing on the Buda side of the Danube and waving a menorah instead of a cross over the city. The point being made was that Israeli investors—which for everybody meant simply the Jews—wanted to buy up the country. According to a report in the business newspaper *Figyelö*, Jobbik held 4,000 election meetings before the first round of voting; in the same period, the Jobbik website had on average half a million hits a day.

In this connection the ceremonial presentation of a documentary film about István Csurka at the Uránia National Film Theatre in Budapest should also be mentioned. The 78-minute-long film portrayed this once talented dramatist, who until Jobbik arrived on the scene had been the front man for far-right anti-Semites. The weekend supplement of *Magyar Hírlap* opened with a full-page, and fulsome, report on the Csurka film. Yet Csurka was the internationally notorious leader of the Hungarian Justice and Life Party, which when it was formed in 1993 was the first extreme right-wing party after the collapse of communism; he sat in parliament with his group between 1998 and 2002; in addition, he was the founder of *Magyar Fórum*, the first openly anti-Semitic newspaper in the country.

The fact that Mátyás Szűrös was seated immediately on the right of Csurka in the VIP box at this film premiere was of great symbolic significance. Szűrös was the most prominent, and in the eyes of the left and liberals, the most despised turncoat from the old days. After 1989 he served briefly as the provisional State President, but before that, in the Kádár era, he had been a long-serving Ambassador in Moscow (a position of trust of the first rank), and finally secretary of the Central Committee as well as a member of the Politburo. Szűrös and Imre Pozsgay are always welcome guests at the biggest Fidesz events.

Because of the seemingly inexorable advance of the extreme right, above all in the ranks of the youth—thanks to the internet, and in view of the lack of massive counter-demonstrations of the left, the liberals, the democrats worried about Hungary's image—pessimistic observers were already seeing the return of the ghosts of the 1930s. Some journalists and writers had begun making comparisons with the Weimar Republic. But things have not yet gone so far, as was shown by the mass protests against the Orbán government which have erupted since the spring of 2011.

The behaviour of young people in the 2010 parliamentary elections is no doubt a consequence of the swing to the right in the media, of the erosion of the left, the liberals and moderate conservatives. No fewer than 23 per cent (almost every fourth person in the 18–29 age group) voted for Jobbik, only 10 per cent for the Socialists; among the 30–39-year-olds, Jobbik received 18 per cent of votes, twice as many as the Socialists.

All this shows that the challenge from the right, just as in the inter-war years, will dominate the political landscape in the coming years. But even after Jobbik took up 47 seats in the new Hungarian parliament, I still believe that the real danger comes not from the neo-fascists or those who seek solutions in violence, but rather from the 'fine' silence of the political right around Orbán and (with a very few exceptions) the Catholic and Protestant churches.

We must of course always keep before our eyes the warning of the French thinker and politician, Alexis de Tocqueville (1805–59): never take the end of an act for the end of the play.[14]

13

THE POLITICAL SUICIDE OF THE LEFT

'A white lie is always forgivable. But anybody who tells the truth without having to deserves no leniency'.

Karl Kraus

The landslide victory of the right in the elections of April 2010 came as no surprise to either side. A sinuous path led from the mega-scandal of Gyurcsány's May 2006 secret speech, exploited by his political enemies as a constant indictment against the government, via the setbacks at the referendum of 9 March 2008 and at the European elections in May 2009, to the catastrophic defeat of the Socialist minority government. The period of seeming Socialist domination between 2002 and 2010 was in reality the political suicide of the entire left and the liberals, a suicide committed in instalments.

Because of his double role as both Prime Minister (2004–09) and party chairman (2007–09) Ferenc Gyurcsány's personality lay at the very heart of the public and private debates inside and outside the Socialist Party. One of the issues considered by the exiled German sociologist Norbert Elias (1897–1990) was how, as a rule, social processes lead to the unplanned; that in the struggle for the aspirations harboured by social groups, and especially by the powerful, what they originally set out to achieve is seldom how things ultimately turn out. We have already seen in Chapter 9 how this self-made (forint) billionaire, after the failure of his predecessor Péter Medgyessy, convincingly defeated Viktor Orbán in the 2006 elections (even though the polls all showed Fidesz well in the lead) and rescued power for the Socialist-Liberal coalition. Gyurcsány alone could justifiably call the victory his own. In a party in which the cowardice of the leadership obstructed its view of reality, and the top party officials had for decades made themselves very comfortable within a client system nourished on corruption, Gyurcsány emerged as somebody who could act as a liberating force.

However, from the beginning to the end unsettled questions about credibility and responsibility pursued Gyurcsány and, with him, the whole leadership. Even in the months before the publication of his cathartic, but politically disastrous speech to the Socialist MPs at Őszöd, Gyurcsány's government had already, between June and August, been paying the price for its broken promises and for its silence on the true financial situation in the country. It was predictable that until the final, bitter moment the Fidesz opposition would exploit the 'lie speech', which had been served up to it (by whomever) on a silver platter, as ammunition in its campaign to utterly destroy the 'illegitimate' Prime Minister. Peering into the abyss, Socialist politicians had to outwardly back the reform programme of their leader, who was widely perceived as by far the ablest talent on the left. Yet, behind the masks they wore, the leading party and government officials were embroiled in incessant internal intrigues and often interested solely in their survival at the top.

In those years I met Gyurcsány several times for informal interviews. I was certainly not alone in being impressed by his creativity, his energy and his frankness. But over time the truth of what his close colleague Viktor Szigetvári said of Gyurcsány to his biographer, József Debreczeni, became more and more evident: 'A political strategist of genius, but less so as a manager'. Although Gyurcsány won the party chairmanship with the support of 89 per cent of the congress delegates at the beginning of 2007, this fact did not alter the conclusion of the liberal philosopher János Kis: 'Gyurcsány is the prisoner of those political forces which heaved him up into the position of head of government. But he began the remodelling of the left at the very moment when his image collapsed and then delivered himself up to the very people who he should have neutralised in the interest of the modernisation of the party'.

The aura of power lent to Gyurcsány by his holding the twin positions of Prime Minister and party leader was deceptive. His room for manoeuvre was appreciably limited by the dynamics of a threefold crisis: financial, social and political. While the Socialists were preoccupied with their own identity crisis and the undermining of Gyurcsány's position, the trench warfare and intrigues of their SzDSz coalition partner also continued. The Liberals had been the driving force behind privatisation and reform of the healthcare system. The opposition had, however, cleverly organised a campaign collecting signatures for a referendum against the already approved introduction of fees payable when visiting a GP or hospital (at a maximum of 24 euros per person per year these were not particularly burdensome) as well as planned tuition fees for university students. Despite the reservations of some constitutional lawyers, the Constitutional Court approved the holding of the controversial referendum.

The result of the referendum in March 2008 was a shattering defeat for the government. Over half of the electorate took part with more than 82 per cent rejecting the introduction of the new fees: 3.4 million Hungarians opposed and only 640,000 supported what was in truth a moderate, but poorly presented reform proposal. The government immediately complied with the vote and scrapped the healthcare and tuition fees. The outcome of the referendum was a huge vote of no-confidence in the Socialist-Liberal government. The Socialists, in a state of shock at the dimension of the defeat, shelved their plans for the restructuring of state social insurance and Gyurcsány began to speak of 'velvet reforms'. Some observers thought that Gyurcsány should have resigned at this point. Following the defeat in the referendum the conflict within the coalition between the Socialists and the Liberals on the question of reform of the healthcare system now came to a head and the SzDSz ministers quit the government. From May 2008 onwards Gyurcsány led a minority government, though he was able to rely on the support of the majority of Liberal MPs in important votes.

Although the government succeeded in reducing the budget deficit from almost 10 per cent to 3.8 per cent of GDP in two years, the onslaught of the global financial crisis immediately put enormous foreign pressure on Hungary: the country faced insolvency. Only through a massive and, at the time, unique standby credit of 20 billion euros provided by the IMF, the World Bank and the EU was the country able to survive the first phase of the global crisis. The significance of this international bailout can be measured by the fact that the credit was three times as great as the total net foreign exchange proceeds of all the privatisations between 1989 and 2007. Furthermore, had it not been for the austerity programme implemented by the Gyurcsány government, the international community would not have been prepared to grant Hungary such a large emergency credit.

Nevertheless, the Gyurcsány government soon ran into a hopeless situation. The strict financial restraints imposed by the international financial institutions, as well as the ideas put forward by the Reform Association founded by independent and respected Hungarian economists, forced the government to consider further public expenditure cuts in the social services. GDP fell sharply in the first quarter of 2009; the contraction for the whole year was almost 7 per cent. Further radical cuts were necessary to cope with the crisis. At the same time, within the Socialist Party itself, the resistance of its various left-wing factions to further drastic measures was growing. This collective denial of reality, dressed up in left-wing rhetoric, was the main reason Gyurcsány was not able to push through the reforms that he himself saw all too clearly to be necessary.

It should also be remembered that throughout this period Fidesz, supported by the head of state, was calling for early elections rather than reforms; on top of this, the opposition was demanding further increases in state expenditure. The highly emotional, almost hysterical character of Hungarian politics contributed naturally enough to the growing mistrust of the country among observers from the European Union and international finance. Moreover, in the spring of 2009, at an EU summit on the global economic crisis Gyurcsány, quite precipitately and without any proper preparation proposed a credit package amounting to 160 to 190 billion euros for the new member states, an idea that was publicly rebuffed in Warsaw, Prague and Bratislava. This politically self-inflicted wound, the subsequent rejection by the president of the European Central Bank of the Hungarian wish for closer cooperation with the Eurozone, and Gyurcsány's continuing catastrophic opinion poll ratings were crucial factors behind his decision to announce his resignation as Prime Minister at the party congress held on 21 March 2009.

In a long and passionate speech, Gyurcsány signalled his intention to remain leader of the Socialist Party. The delegates, as ever, hung on his every word and the departing head of government retained the party leadership with an impressive 85 per cent vote. Even his closest colleagues assumed that Gyurcsány already had a successor tucked up his sleeve. However, a weeklong public, and increasingly embarrassing, search for a candidate acceptable to the party Presidium and the parliamentary party, as well as to the SzDSz, ended with a bombshell: Gyurcsány also resigned as party leader. It would be idle to speculate how many names, whether 12 or 18, were put forward in the tragicomic search for a crisis manager. The undignified procedure, together with the repeated indiscretions (by cell phone) of the various participants at the meetings of the party leadership, presented a picture of political squalor, cronyism and corruption, which left even seasoned observers speechless.[1]

In his 1856 book *The Old Regime and the Revolution* Alexis de Tocqueville observed that 'experience teaches us that the

THE POLITICAL SUICIDE OF THE LEFT

most dangerous moment for a bad government is when it begins to reform itself' and that politicians often fall when they, for whatever reasons, are judged unworthy of the leadership role entrusted to them. His words perfectly describe the situation in Hungary 150 years later. The claim made in a leading article in the Fidesz newspaper *Magyar Nemzet* at the beginning of 2010 that the economic and social position in the country was worse than after a world war[2] was of course nonsense, but fully in accord with the reckless cheap propaganda of an opposition assured of victory. The campaign of annihilation against the Socialist-Liberal coalition in general and against Gyurcsány as the principal scapegoat in particular must, however, been seen as the consequence, and not the cause, of the failures of the Medgyessy and Gyurcsány governments.[3]

I had the opportunity to interview Gyurcsány shortly after his twin resignations. In the garden of his house on Szemlöhegyi út on Buda hill he was still very embittered when he spoke of the disgusting intrigues he had witnessed in the days after he quit the post of prime minister and his party sought his successor. It was then that he had understood that he had no hope of remaining party leader either. Gyurcsány told me in confidence that he had from the very beginning wanted as his successor the Economics Minister Gordon Bajnai, the man who was finally acceptable to the Socialists and Liberals. Bajnai's name had been the last on the list of candidates. The fact that in the meeting of the party Presidium he had first put forward other names was due to his conviction that Bajnai would otherwise have been regarded merely as a Gyurcsány clone and that this would have immediately torpedoed his candidature. Be that as it may, the election of the 41-year-old economics expert proved ultimately to be a stroke of good fortune for

Hungary—even if it had come far too late for the now totally discredited Socialist Party.

The reforms pursued by the independent Prime Minister, who insisted on the symbolic salary of one forint a month, brought Hungary back from the brink. The economic correspondent of the conservative *Frankfurter Allgemeine Zeitung*, like her colleagues in other leading foreign newspapers, was favourably impressed. Commenting on his year in office, she wrote, 'Bajnai's crisis management is highly admirable. It should be continued ... At any rate it would be desirable for the Hungarians that the sober work of the outgoing government, one which has not been solely concerned with handing out electoral bribes, is continued. For this has restored trust in the stability of the country and has benefited the people'.[4]

What had happened? What had Gordon Bajnai been able to achieve in little more than a year?

In the spring of 2009 Hungary was teetering on the precipice. For about ten years the country had been living on tick. There were 1.7 million consumer loans denominated in foreign exchange. Approximately a third of those employed were operating in the shadow economy. The Hungarian employment rate, at 57 per cent, was well below the EU average and that of all other new member states: Slovenia 68 per cent, the Czech Republic 66 per cent, Slovakia 61 per cent and Romania 59 per cent. More and more Hungarians were receiving benefit payments from the state. In 2007, for example, a new male pensioner received a pension that was worth more than his last net wage. State indebtedness rose between 2001 and 2008 from 66 per cent of GDP to almost 80 per cent. The highest ancillary wage costs in the EU formed the other side of an inflated welfare state, which had been 'born too early' (János Kornai).

Against the background of the enormous foreign exchange debts, due to high domestic interest rates, and the fact that at times the international capital markets could not be tapped—even though half of Hungarian government stocks were in Western pension funds—the forint kept slipping into the danger zone against the euro.

In this situation Gordon Bajnai decided to shoulder the risk himself and have the Socialist and Liberal MPs sign a mandate giving him practically unrestricted powers to undertake radical reforms. Because of the justified fears of early elections and certainly not because of any sudden, newfound enthusiasm for reform, the Socialist-Liberal parliamentary majority gave Prime Minister Bajnai and his talented (and non-party) Finance Minister Péter Oszkó (36) practically carte blanche for the implementation of the most radical budgetary cuts of the previous 15 years. Predictably, the Fidesz opposition voted against the rigorous austerity package. Moreover, the fact that in such a situation the opposition leader, Viktor Orbán, for the entire duration of the interim government (20 April 2009 to 29 May 2010) turned down every invitation made by the Prime Minister to hold talks (only at the burial of the Polish President Lech Kaczyński in Kraków in April 2010 did Orbán deign to exchange a few words with Bajnai) spoke volumes about the political climate in the country.

In his inaugural speech and in numerous interviews with both domestic and foreign media the former top manager made no secret of the depths of what was very much a home-grown crisis. Caught in a trap of self-delusion Hungary had practically forfeited the ten-year head start it had enjoyed after 1989. Bajnai once cited Edmund Burke (1729–97): 'Every political decision is a choice between the unpleasant and the intolerable'. The most important and most painful cuts comprised the ending of the 13th monthly payment to pensioners and the 13th payment for employees; the freezing of salaries in the public sector; the raising of the retirement age from 62 to 65; the 8 per cent reduction in the ancillary wage costs paid by companies; cuts in social spending; the lowering of maternity (and paternity) leave from three to two years, and the raising of VAT from 20 to 25 per cent. In total the austerity measures amounted to 5 per cent of GDP in 2009–10.

Bajnai said, 'It's my job to rescue the country', and he kept his word. In March 2009 the exchange rate was 1 euro to 315 forints; since June 2009 it has stabilised between 270 and 280 forints. The premiums for loan default insurance for Hungarian bonds lay at the beginning of the Bajnai government at 630 base points; they had fallen to under 200 by May 2010.

The modest and likeable Bajnai once told me that he had fully anticipated the noisy protests of one hundred thousand angry people on Kossuth Square after he entered office and announced his drastic austerity programme. Yet one year later, in an interview in the *Frankfurter Allgemeine Zeitung* (28 May 2010), he was praising 'the Hungarians' particular maturity and ability to act rationally ... The budget cuts have been implemented without a single strike, without a single mass demonstration'. Unexpected approval came from Vienna where on 6 March 2010, at the height of the Greek financial crisis, the *Neue Kronen Zeitung*, a tabloid not known for its finesse or mincing of words, wrote that 'Greece could learn from Hungary'.

The success of the crisis management of the Bajnai government was highly regarded internationally, praised by people ranging from US President Barack Obama to leading officials of the IMF and the EU. Although the cooperation between

THE POLITICAL SUICIDE OF THE LEFT

veteran Socialist ministers and independent experts in the cabinet served the country well, their efforts were of little benefit to the Socialist Party, which was still formally in government. The politicians and propagandists of Fidesz, with Orbán in the vanguard, continued to blast away with all guns blazing; the attacks were now increasingly aimed at Bajnai personally. So close to its long-yearned-for election victory Fidesz was not prepared to alter its tactics of blocking the work of the government.

The Socialists had fallen into a maelstrom of economic crisis and bribery scandals, much hyped by the media. The gap left by the fall of the charismatic and reform-minded Ferenc Gyurcsány is so great that in the foreseeable future no current politician on the left can fill it. The experiment of morphing the former post-communist party into a social-democrat one has failed for many reasons, some of which have been discussed here. József Debreczeni's final word on Gyurcsány's government is that he was a 'kamikaze prime minister'.

This great political talent had neither the time nor the room for manoeuvre to govern the country and fundamentally reform his party. Politically inexperienced and attacked on all sides, Gyurcsány failed after four and a half years in both tasks. Benjamin Disraeli (1804–81), the great successful outsider in British politics, said in Westminster (28 February 1859) that 'Finality is not the language of politics'. This is very much true of both Ferenc Gyurcsány and his successor Gordon Bajnai. And for this very reason, both remain the targets of a vicious campaign headed by their victorious opponent Viktor Orbán, a man who in the long term is striving for total control of political life in Hungary.

14

ORBÁN *ÜBER ALLES*—HUNGARY AT A DEAD END

'All this amounts to the reestablishment of authoritarian rule under a paper-thin veneer of democracy in the heart of Europe'.

Paul Krugman

Viktor Orbán and his Fidesz party won a landslide victory in the parliamentary elections in April 2010. There can be no doubt that Orbán's successful 'revolution in the polling booth' has put an end to the liberal democracy existing in Hungary since 1990 and has smoothed the path to a populist autocracy.

Today, almost two years after Fidesz's triumph, it is evident that the institutional checks and balances on the executive have practically disappeared. Already in his closing speech delivered at the end of the first session of the new parliament,

Orbán could justifiably boast that the 'national centre' had achieved more in 56 days than the Socialist-Liberal coalition had in eight years. Looking back on the 20-year history of democracy in Hungary, it is indeed without precedent that the constitution was amended no fewer than ten times in the government's first year in office, an achievement crowned, thanks to its huge majority, by the enactment of an entirely new constitution that entered into force on 1 January 2012. In all, by the end of the 2011 parliament, 'little more than a rubber stamp',[1] 350 laws—including 25 so-called 'fundamental' laws which may be amended only by a two-thirds majority in any subsequent parliament—had been passed in a frenzy of legislation. Even if a new government wins a simple majority, basic policies instituted and key officials appointed (for a term of six to nine years!) by the Fidesz government cannot be changed. Nobody can any longer doubt that Viktor Orbán, the most experienced and most ruthless Hungarian politician, will strive to achieve the vision he articulated in his notorious speech at Kötcse on 5 September 2009: establishing a permanent hold on power for a period of 15 to 20 years. It is not only the hapless, weak left-liberal opposition but also independent and respected European and American observers, including the Nobel Prize winner Paul Krugman and the great Polish freedom fighter Adam Michnik, who have concluded that Viktor Orbán and his party have captured the state on behalf of Fidesz. They have bluntly stated that 'Hungary is not a constitutional democracy' but a state sliding into authoritarianism. 'All this amounts to the reestablishment of authoritarian rule under a paper-thin veneer of democracy in the heart of Europe and it is a sample of what may follow much more widely if this depression continues'.[2] Charles Gati, the Hungarian-born US academic, summed up his impressions after a year-end visit to his native country: 'Hungary is no longer a Western-style democracy. It is an illiberal or managed democracy in the sense that all important decisions are made by Orbán; it is similar to Slovakia under Vladimir Mečiar and Poland under the rule of the Kaczyńskis'.[3]

Before analysing the dramatic consequences of this 'constitutional revolution by legal means',[4] we have to raise the question how it was possible for Orbán's party to achieve such an astounding electoral victory. Although only one third of all eligible voters actually voted for Fidesz, because of the disproportionate and distorting electoral system the party was able to win 68 per cent of the seats in parliament. In the two rounds of voting on 11 and 25 April 2010 Fidesz, together with its insignificant political ally the Christian Democratic People's Party (KDNP), won almost 53 per cent of the vote, but managed to capture over two-thirds of the seats in parliament. Turnout was a mere 64 per cent. We must remember the fact that József Debreczeni was the first to point out: the approximately 2.7 million votes for the Fidesz party ticket, just over half of all votes cast, amounted only to a third of the electorate in Hungary and a quarter of the entire population. Debreczeni bluntly describes Orbán's claims that Fidesz represents the 'undivided will of the Hungarian nation' and the 'system of national cooperation' as a 'falsification of history'[5] built on a tissue of lies. In a recent article Charles Gati correctly stressed that

the misleading 'fact' of a two-thirds mandate ('voting booth revolution') has been used day in and day out by the Fidesz propaganda (and believed by most foreign governments) to justify all the radical laws and regulations Orbán and his parliamentary majority have introduced since mid-2010—even though during the campaign

Fidesz uttered not one word about a new constitution, media law, electoral law or religion law.[6]

The sanctimonious and hypocritical style of the new system was quickly reflected in a government decree instructing the authorities to hang the Declaration of National Cooperation (in a 50 x 70cm glass frame) on the walls of public buildings. The Declaration not only repudiates the 'negative inheritance of the past 20 years' but also includes the statement that 'Hungary has recovered its ability and right to self-determination'. As if this was not bad enough, the Declaration goes on to state that it 'recognises and respects' the revolution fought out within the framework of constitutional law. With this Declaration Fidesz openly rejects all the positive achievements of the change of the system in 1989–90. The economist and MEP Lajos Bokros emphasised early the fact that 'none of the Fidesz initiatives implemented so far ever appeared in the party's election manifesto and therefore, logically, they have no mandate from the electorate'.[7]

Nevertheless, the 'historic act of the nation' has subsequently produced dramatic changes to which we will later return. First of all, the implications of the shift to the right permeating Hungarian society must not be ignored. Thanks to the massive publicity about the provocative acts of the Hungarian Guard, the new radical right-wing grouping, Jobbik, was able to win 17 per cent of the vote and 47 parliamentary seats. This extremist party represents an even greater potential threat because it is highly popular amongst the young with almost 25 per cent of voters aged between 18 and 29 supporting it. Through their often extremely nationalistic and xenophobic, anti-Roma and anti-Semitic rhetoric, the right-wing media, including the pro-Fidesz newspapers, have become accomplices of this far-right party. The popularity of Jobbik among young voters has also been promoted by the extreme right-wing internet portals kuruc.info and barikad.hu. It should also be underlined that neither before the European elections of June 2009 nor in the campaigning for the parliamentary and local elections of 2010 did Viktor Orbán and his party unequivocally and publicly dissociate themselves from the radical right. When asked at a student meeting held behind closed doors in 2009 (that is, before the parliamentary elections) how he thought he would deal with Jobbik, Orbán light-heartedly replied that he would give them a clip around the ears and send them packing...

Both Hungarian and foreign observers drew attention to an episode of symbolic significance that occurred during the very first session of the new parliament. Before the Jobbik leader Gábor Vona took the oath with the other parliamentarians, he took off his jacket. Underneath he had on a waistcoat strongly reminiscent of the one worn by the banned Hungarian Guard. Orbán and the Fidesz MPs ignored the provocation, acting as if nothing had happened. At the end of the sitting they all sang the Székler hymn together.[8]

As far as government policy is concerned, Orbán quickly acted to take the wind out of Jobbik's sails. He had the national issues upon which the hard right was noisily insisting rushed through parliament. Hence a law was quickly passed which gave ethnic Hungarians living abroad the opportunity to fast-track Hungarian citizenship, even if they lacked permanent residence in Hungary. After initial vague denials, parliament later adopted a law which allows ethnic Hungarians—which included members of Hungarian minorities in the neighbouring countries—to vote in Hungarian elections. As a prelude to this nationalist offensive, on 4 June 2010 the 90th anniversary of the signing of the Treaty of Trianon, the 'Day of National Unity' was elevated to a public holiday. As the *Neue Zürcher Zeitung* observed, Fidesz had outflanked Jobbik on the right in questions of national identity.[9]

The ideological and political proximity between Fidesz (262 MPs) and Jobbik (47 MPs) gives the governing party the opportunity to pursue a two-track policy: on the one hand, Fidesz is seeking to weaken the group of unreconstructed extremists and, on the other, it is striving to gradually absorb those careerists in Jobbik ready to make the necessary compromises. Thus it hopes to strengthen the basis for an all-embracing right-wing party.

It must be remembered that the nationalist offensive and the right-wing, conservative clerical course of Orbán's government initially met with little resistance in society at large. Polls revealed that a great majority wanted a strong government which could implement its policies without internal party conflicts. About 50 per cent of those polled in a survey conducted at the same time as the parliamentary elections supported a state of affairs in which only one dominant party ruled.[10]

On account of their incompetence in government mixed with corruption scandals and constant infighting, the Socialists have had to absorb significant losses amongst all sectors of voters. Particularly alarming from their point of view was the fact that among voters aged between 18 and 39 they had been overtaken not only by Fidesz but also by Jobbik. In this age group the far right-wing party won more than twice as many votes as the Socialists. It is also symptomatic that between 2006 and 2010 the MSzP's popularity fell to just one third among pensioners. In contrast, Fidesz was able to garner 60 per cent of their votes. In addition, the left-wing, populist rhetoric of the

Fidesz government against the international financial institutions active in Hungary has not been without its effect. Opinion polls taken between 2010 and 2012 seem to support those analysts who doubt whether the hopelessly divided Socialists will be able to win back from Fidesz the bulk of their traditional supporters in the foreseeable future. Contrary to the optimism expressed relatively early by some on the centre-left,[11] in my view there is nothing to suggest that the Orbán regime could be seriously threatened by the left in the foreseeable future. A genuine threat to Orbán could only come from the right in the event of an economic crisis. In view of the weakness of the political opposition, the crisis of the Socialist Party (MSzP), exacerbated by the departure of Ferenc Gyurcsány and his followers, and the gerrymandered districts created by a new election law render any change of government at the next parliamentary elections extremely unlikely.[12]

The two former major parties, the liberal SzDSz and the moderate centre right MDF, failed to leap the 5 per cent hurdle in the 2010 elections and both have completely vanished from the scene. The surprising success of the new 'eco-green' party LMP (Lehet Más a Politika, in English 'Politics can be different') is above all a consequence of the disappearance of these liberal and moderate groups. Nationwide, the LMP won 7.5 per cent of votes and in Budapest 10 per cent, which gave it a total of 16 seats in parliament. Its mainly youthful MPs speak out forcefully against both the Fidesz and the radical right, but they also dissociate themselves sharply from the Socialists. In the local elections in the autumn of 2010 and a couple of by-elections in 2011, the LMP failed to increase its share of the vote. In January 2012 internal stresses and conflicts over future strategy, pitting the advocates of a 'going-it-alone' line against those willing to forge electoral coalitions with the Socialists, led to the resignation of the leader of the parliamentary group.

Back in power after two major defeats at the polls in 2002 and 2006, Fidesz found itself after its electoral triumph in a very comfortable position since it was almost inconceivable that the left-wing and eco-green opposition parties would work together with the radical extremist Jobbik right. The Declaration of National Cooperation mentioned above identifies 'work, home, family, health and order' as the pillars binding together 'the new political and economic system achieved through the democratic will of the people' and the 'members of the multifaceted Hungarian nation'. The preamble of the Declaration, which proclaims the 'day of national unity', also says that 'God is the master of history'. The new constitution, in addition to this reference to God, also pays tribute to the Christian roots of the Hungarians, the Holy Crown of Saint Stephen and the inseparable common bonds linking all Hungarians, whether living in Hungary or abroad, in a united Hungarian nation. Furthermore, it requires all citizens to behave in accordance with vaguely defined moral standards and Christian values, outlawing abortion and same-sex marriages. The constitution, called 'the basic law' and rushed through parliament without a nationwide debate or a referendum, 'recognises the role of Christianity in preserving nationhood' and holds that 'the family and the nation constitute the principal framework of our coexistence'. Yet, despite the lip-service repeatedly paid to religious beliefs, a new law on the status of religion has reduced the number of state-recognised churches to only fourteen, excluding the adherents of the Methodist and Mormon religions as well as scores of other churches.

ORBÁN *ÜBER ALLES*—HUNGARY AT A DEAD END

Listening to the speeches of Orbán and the declarations of his acolytes from Fidesz, with all their nationalist and populist pathos, the author is reminded of the opinion expressed by the former German Chancellor Helmut Schmidt: 'Educating the people towards an ideal or a canon of values is not really the business of politics and certainly not the business of governments. Of course there are always going to be politicians proud of following pedagogical or educational principles ... I am profoundly suspicious of political leaders who wish at the same time to be cultural leaders'.[13]

When in his comprehensive biography of Viktor Orbán entitled *Arcmás* ('Image'), as well as in a whole series of articles, József Debreczeni warned of the consequences of Orbán's unbridled opportunism and insatiable lust for power, even some centre-left critics of Fidesz thought his analyses were excessively pessimistic. In the epilogue to his book published in 2009 Debreczeni wrote: 'We can take it for granted that Viktor Orbán will regain the mandate to form a government which he lost eight years ago. Once he is in possession of a constituent majority, he will turn this into an impregnable fortress of power ... Nobody should have any doubts that Orbán will recklessly and utterly make use of this power.'[14]

It is unnecessary to emphasise that the sequence of events under the Orbán government has completely confirmed Debreczeni's gloomy predictions and has made ludicrous the words of a liberal commentator who before the elections welcomed not only a Fidesz victory, but even one with a two-thirds majority. It is of course undeniable that the image of the centre-left camp between 2002 and 2010 was both pitiful and unsavoury, one marked by nepotism, obscure networks and a general political immorality. The internal party conflicts, especially the almost incessant debates about the role and future of Ferenc Gyurcsány, have prevented the Socialists from becoming a powerful opposition force in the foreseeable future. The spectacular defection of Katalin Szili, the former Speaker of parliament, from the Socialist Party after the electoral defeat confirms in retrospect the doubts surrounding her dilettante bid for the office of state president. Gyurcsány's instincts in opposing her candidature for the highest office in the land in June 2005 have thus been proved correct. But at the time, as so often afterwards, he was not determined and resolute enough to act. Even before his notorious speech admitting lying to the public, Gyurcsány had already let slip through his fingers the opportunity to knock his party into shape, a Socialist Party that was certainly no longer communist but still far from being social democratic. In the following years a wry remark made the rounds of the deeply disappointed left: 'Whilst Gyurcsány has good intentions and is ineffective, Orbán has bad intentions and is highly effective'. In this context the role of the SzDSz as the grave diggers of the centre-left must also be mentioned. In government the Liberals proved themselves simply incapable of finding a common standpoint on even the most elementary of questions. At the same time, just like many Socialist politicians, they set themselves up comfortably and enjoyed the tangible fruits of power.

Orbán has apparently laid the foundations for his dream of a 'central political force' on the basis of a well-thought-out script. In a major analysis of the first 18 months of the Orbán government, the former Prime Minister Gordon Bajnai concluded that this government had not *used* the historic opportunity to 'restart' country, but *abused* it: 'By now, it is apparent, that Fidesz, or at least its leadership, had previously concocted its plan to liquidate the third republic'.[15] Hence the incredible pace of the changes.

The first significant step towards the unprecedented concentration of power was the election by parliament of a new head of state. Calculating that two-thirds of MPs would automatically nod through his wishes, Orbán decided to nominate Pál Schmitt, a member of the fencing team which won two Olympic gold medals and former Deputy Minister of Sport under the communist regime. Even some of his close associates were said to have been surprised and upset by this unusual choice. In an unusually sharp tone the respected economist János Kornai noted that 'The state president is neither independent nor does he embody the unity of the nation. He is a compliant party hack'. In the same article he went on:

Wide-ranging debates and consultations are non-existent. The parliament has deteriorated into a voting machine, laws are churned out at an incredible speed ... The key position of the chief public prosecutor has been filled with a reliable supporter of the ruling party ... The legal authority of the constitutional court as the highest guardian of the constitution has been brutally curtailed. When it had the audacity to criticise the plans of the government, the independent budgetary board was dissolved without further ado.[16]

It should be noted that this devastating indictment was published at the beginning of 2011. Since then virtually all independent institutions, as well as the legal and media landscape, have been transformed by the government's relentless centralisation, filling all key positions with Fidesz stalwarts and allies. The media law package was the first move that caused an international outcry, alarming respected international NGOs and the representatives of the Organisation for Security and Cooperation in Europe (OSCE), the Council of Europe and the

United Nations. The fact that as of 1 January 2011 Hungary took over the rotating chair of the Council of the European Union for six months almost inevitably gave a powerful fillip to the debate in the European and even the US media. The European Commission also intervened and by mid-February 2011 an agreement had been reached between the Commission and Hungary. This, however, was mainly technical in character and according to the former and current OSCE media representatives, as well as experts of the UN and the Council of Europe, has not gone nearly far enough.[17]

Events since the setting up of the National Media and Telecommunication Agency with unprecedented powers have fully confirmed the worst fears about the threats to press freedom. The new five-member Media Council was packed with Fidesz acolytes and had a chair who was appointed by the Prime Minister for a nine-year term. This board can review the compliance of all public and private media with a vague standard of political 'balance' and 'proper' news coverage. At the end of 2011 the 'old' Constitutional Court declared as null and void some of the most controversial paragraphs of the media law, those concerning protection of sources and 'balanced coverage'. However, the basic structure of the 'single media governance pyramid' with powers for content control extending over all media, including the print and on-line press, for punishing or even bankrupting any news organisation with large fines, and the total merger of the public service media, as well as the state news agency, have been left untouched.

As Miklós Haraszti, the Hungarian-born former OSCE media representative, has put it:

The National Info-communication Authority and the Media Council, both headed by the same person, appointed by Viktor Orbán, has authority over all audiovisual, print and Internet-based media ... The media regulatory boards, all named or dominated by candidates of the ruling party, have been made into a rubber-stamp, protected by strict secrecy rules; the various boards in effect are 'departments' of the Authority that is practically a Media Ministry ... However the single greatest danger for the freedom of the press lies in the arbitrary licensing provisions, the parallels of which can only be found in some post-Soviet countries.[18]

The correctness of the warnings voiced by both domestic and international critics has been fully borne out by subsequent developments. National broadcasters are now totally in Fidesz hands. All independent surveys published about the new media regime have unanimously concluded that the newscasts and features programmes on politics on both radio and television are dominated by pro-government statements and reports (often accounting for 75 per cent of their content). This unique national media conglomerate, financed from tax revenues but divested of any public control, with all key editors or producers appointed from the top without the positions being advertised, simultaneously produces and controls all programmes with a total budget exceeding the combined financial resources of the private broadcasters. The private and independent broadcasters and newspapers have become, with few exceptions, increasingly self-censoring. This is partly due to the main weapon of the Fidesz government: cutting off directly or indirectly the financing of critical media through advertisements placed by companies and institutions, directly or indirectly controlled by the state or by Fidesz allies.

The clumsy editing and selection of the news remind listeners and viewers of the Soviet manipulation of photographs and history. 'In this regime only good things happen', remarked a sacked editor of the evening news programme of the public TV network. The restructuring of the national broadcasters and the state news agency (MTI) was used to kick out without any explanation or chance of appeal almost 1,000 employees, including many able and seasoned journalists, editors and experts. Nobody disputes that the public media have been notoriously overstaffed and top executives overpaid. The point is, however, that political reliability has been the reason for the summary dismissal of many employees. As a result levels of professionalism have become dismal. Worse still, an extreme right-wing editor (previously spokesman of the Jobbik party) was put in charge of all news programmes after flagrantly forging a report insinuating ludicrous allegations against Daniel Cohn-Bendit, the Green politician in the European Parliament and a sharp critic of Viktor Orbán. Somewhat later the former Hungarian Chief Justice was airbrushed out of footage shown on state television.[19]

The potentially most devastating blow against the rest of the independent-liberal media was the decision taken by one of the Fidesz-controlled media regulatory boards to award the broadcasting frequency used by Klubradio, the liberal radio station with over half-a-million regular listeners, to an obscure new outfit promising more Hungarian music. The silencing of this immensely popular broadcaster was decided on despite a protest movement launched by private news portals and on Facebook ('One Million against the Media Law') mobilising tens of thousands of peaceful protesters in Budapest on 23 October 2011 (the 55th anniversary of the 1956 uprising). This was followed by an even larger demonstration outside the Opera House on 2 January 2012 against the constitution which had come into force a day earlier. The way in which state television and the right-wing print media have reported on these events, and on the international condemnation of the erosion of democratic norms, reminds me of how communist regimes once managed the news in Hungary and elsewhere in the Eastern Bloc.[20] Incidentally, it has been widely noted in western Europe that it was not the leaders of the European Union but Hillary Clinton, the American Secretary of State, who took the lead in loudly and clearly censuring Orbán's authoritarian slide, expressing concern about the excessive concentration of power in the 'politically-appointed' Media Council and the non-renewal of Klubradio's licence.[21]

Despite the numerous protests of international journalist organisations such as Reporters Without Borders or Freedom House, as well as by the Hungarian opposition as shown in the Budapest demonstrations, the centralised day-to-day control of the bulk of the electronic and print media by the top Fidesz political and financial echelons appears to be irreversible in the foreseeable future. The road to a veiled censorship and to self-censorship, just like the one brought to perfection under the Kádár regime, now stands open. However, it has to be remembered that it is not only the media landscape that has been transformed. As the former premier Gordon Bajnai has succinctly put it: 'The spine of Hungarian democracy has systematically been broken, one vertebra after another ... In 2012, Hungary is lumbered with a government that is performing badly, but is very difficult to vote it out of office. This is the worst possible combination for the young Hungarian democracy'.[22]

It is no longer only the left and liberal opposition in the country itself but also major European and American newspapers that maintain that the Hungarian government is undermining democracy, centralising power and destroying pluralism. The new constitution and a series of fundamental laws also give the ruling Fidesz party sweeping powers over the constitutional order, above all the judiciary. The jurisdiction under the constitutional court has been restricted, which means that it can no longer fulfil its function as the ultimate institution to safeguard legality and review any law pertaining to taxes and austerity measures. The rules of access to the court have also been changed, making it impossible for individuals to challenge the constitutionality of laws without first going through a lengthy process in the ordinary courts. Last but not least, the government has increased the number of judges and appointed several former Fidesz ministers and MPs to the bench. All these changes made against the background of a compliant head of state confirm the conclusion drawn by the Princeton academic Kim Lane Scheppele that the old Constitutional Court as a major check on governmental power is now 'functionally dead'.[23]

Mandatory early retirement of judges at the age of 62 instead of 70 means that 270 judges will be forced to retire. The new law was also formulated in such a way as to remove the president of the Supreme Court, András Baka, on 1 January 2012 although his mandate only expired in June 2015. The new legislation provides that the president of the Court must have at least five years of Hungarian judicial experience; thus Baka was 'disqualified' because his 17 years of experience as a judge on the European Court of Human Rights do not count. This flimsy pretext was invented to remove a conservative, but independent and internationally respected judge because he had publicly opposed the retroactive changes in the criminal law and the setting up of a new National Judicial Office. Its president will in future have 'inordinate and uncontrollable power over judicial administration which is unprecedented in Europe',

Baka said. He added that his removal was unlawful and unprecedented.[24]

The independence of the judiciary is becoming a fiction, with the new president moving judges around at will and having unlimited power to replace and appoint judges, as well as to decide which court deals with which case. The head of the new judicial office and the chief public prosecutor are permitted to choose which judge will hear which case. The chief of the newly constituted supreme judicial authority elected by parliament for nine years is Tuende Hando, president of the Budapest Labour Court. She happens to be the wife of the chair of the Fidesz group in the European Parliament, who is said to have written the preamble of the new constitution on his iPad on the train between Brussels and Strasbourg. Mrs Hando is moreover a former college roommate and lifelong friend of Mrs Orbán. If we add that the Chief Prosecutor is himself a highly controversial Fidesz loyalist, the sharp criticism of the new legal landscape by the purged Chief Justice is more than understandable.

Other controversial changes much criticised by liberal and left-wing intellectuals involve the change of the name of the country in the new constitution, removing the word Republic and leaving it officially just Hungary. There has been a drift towards an authoritarian government in other areas too. The erosion of independent institutions includes a threat to the independence of the national data-protection authority and a change in the rules for the composition of the five-member Election Commission, which is in charge of the legal supervision of elections. After the victory of Fidesz the commissioners were replaced, without being allowed to finish their terms, by five members of the ruling party.

The wave of politically motivated purges affecting the public media has also hit the scientific community, above all the various institutions under the umbrella of the Academy of Science, as well as the theatres and publishing. Here again it was a question not only of an overdue reduction in the number of superfluous administrative staff but also of weeding out politically 'unreliable' officials. The dismissal of civil servants and academics with only two months' notice and without any reason needing to be given was a disquieting and unprecedented measure. The president of the Academy and former Fidesz Minister of Culture József Pálinkás backed the dismissal of seven outstanding philosophers from the Institute of Philosophy, which sparked off an international scandal. The respected philosopher and essayist Sándor Radnóti circulated worldwide a petition against the purge signed by several thousand scholars in Hungary and abroad. Nevertheless, the sacking of philosophers not only continued but was combined with a kind of revenge operation. Hand in hand with a vicious public campaign in the Fidesz media against Radnóti and two other internationally known philosophers, Ágnes Heller and Mihály Vajda, a criminal investigation has been launched against them and other academics as to whether they have misused government funds for international research projects. They have rejected the totally unfounded charges and sued the newspapers in question.

At the same time events in the world of arts and culture have confirmed the timeless relevance of the observation made by the British historian Lewis Namier: 'The first and most elementary requirement in government is a routine of decent administration'.[25] The lack of independent and incorrupt officials is a deeply rooted evil in most East European countries, and not only in Hungary. Thus the primary loyalty of state and regional bureaucrats is in general not to a given institution but to the person who appoints them.[26] This is how the regional and urban administrations controlled by Fidesz dominated assemblies replaced some two dozen theatre directors, including outstanding producers. An international scandal was sparked off by the sacking of the long-serving director of a major Budapest theatre and the appointment of a right-wing actor who used to perform at events organised by the Jobbik party. But what provoked angry public protests in the capital and outrage in the international media was the fact that the mayor of Budapest not only overruled the recommendations of the programme council but appointed along with the controversial actor the notorious, wildly anti-Semitic writer and editor István Csurka as a kind of co-director of the theatre. Following a wave of protests and renewed anti-Jewish insults by Csurka in his weekly *Magyar Forum*, the mayor withdrew his appointment but comforted the new right-wing director that he could nevertheless stage Csurka's successful plays in the theatre...[27]

While comparisons with Belarus or Ukraine seem exaggerated, there are disquieting signs in the almost totally revamped judiciary landscape which may yet become the harbingers of politically motivated prosecution. For example, when the state television cameras could record for viewers a former high official being taken away to a police station with his hands shackled at six in the morning this was widely regarded as an attempt at intimidation. Attempts have also been long under way to charge former Socialist prime ministers with criminal economic mismanagement on the pretext of their being directly responsible for the rise of state indebtedness during their terms of office. Through the officials the Fidesz government has been putting into place, and owing to a constitutional amendment, retroactive political and criminal charges have become possible. Thus the statute of limitations for prosecuting crimes committed during the communist period has been lifted, the former Communist Party branded as a criminal organisation and the Socialist Party defined as its legal successor.

In addition to the centralised control of the political, financial and technical instruments of the state, a new election law, passed as usual in a flurry without a wide public debate, should make the Fidesz 'revolution' irreversible and perpetuate Orbán's power. Apart from reducing the number of MPs from 386 to 200, it provides for a single round voting system on the basis of new electoral districts with their boundaries drawn in such a way that no other party besides Fidesz is likely to win elections.[28] As Gordon Bajnai puts it, the new rules ensure a good 30-yard advantage for Fidesz in a 100-yard sprint. A Hungarian think tank has estimated that with the revised constituency boundaries Fidesz would have also won the two previous elections they actually lost. The boundaries of the electoral districts, as well as tax and fiscal policy decisions, cannot be changed in the future by a simple majority vote but only by a two-thirds majority.

A change of government will be nearly impossible under the new constitutional rules. Even if despite the electoral law an opposition party alliance won at the polls, the Fidesz office holders in charge of key institutions appointed for six- to nine-year terms can stay in office for another term unless (and this is most unlikely) a two-thirds majority can be achieved to decide otherwise. The example of the national budget council was singled out justly by Professor Scheppele in her study. It can veto any future budget that increases the national debt. Its members, chosen for terms of six to twelve years, can only be replaced when their terms are over if two-thirds of parliament agree on their successors. Constitutionally, parliament must pass a new budget by 31 March of each year. If parliament fails to agree, the head of state can dissolve the legislature and call new elections. And in theory this can be repeated until an acceptable government is voted back into power. The *Financial Times* aptly summed up the situation after the enactment of the new constitution, the passing of new basic laws and the gerrymandering of the electoral system: 'Together they bestow inordinate power on the ruling Fidesz party. The prime minister can claim to have won the 2010 election fairly. Now he is deploying a two-thirds majority in parliament to deny opponents the same possibility'.[29]

When considering the recent spate of lengthy and sharply worded reports and comments of the international media on the Orbán government, we can say without exaggeration that apart from the first phase of the Kádár regime after the crushing of the 1956 revolution and its persecution of the freedom fighters, no single Hungarian government has ever had such a poor reputation. It has to be recognised, however, that it was not the slide into authoritarianism alone, but rather the mixture of economic blunders combined with the arrogant and erratic public behaviour of the government on the international stage, and the discriminatory measures taken against foreign banks and investors coupled with an unprecedented smear campaign against the head of the Hungarian central bank, which so seriously harmed Hungary's image in the world.

As described in earlier chapters, no one can doubt that the past Socialist-Liberal governments were primarily responsible for the relative economic decline of Hungary in comparison with Poland, Slovakia or the Czech Republic. Incompetence, corruption and infighting in both coalition parties (Socialists and Liberals) time and time again frustrated and blocked economic reforms. However, governments, the markets and financial commentators have all acknowledged that after asking for and accepting a €20 billion aid package from the EU and the IMF, the Bajnai cabinet in 2009–10 then implemented substantial cuts in expenditure and reduced the budget deficit, and after a recession of 6.3 per cent, the country was put back on the path to growth.[30]

How then was it possible that by the end of 2011 Hungary found itself in the midst of an economic and financial crisis much more serious than that of 2008? Public debt has reached a historical peak of 82.4 per cent, the forint's exchange rate has slid to a historic low, dropping against the euro by almost 20 per cent; three rating agencies have downgraded Hungary's public debt to junk status, its 10-year bonds have topped 10 per cent, far above sustainable levels. The outlook for the coming years is bleak, with all major international institutions predicting the highest debt and lowest growth among the East European member states of the European Union. On the eve of renewed pleas for urgent aid from the IMF and the European Central Bank to once again save Hungary from state insolvency, independent and even conservative economists in Hungary, as well as foreign experts, have almost unanimously blamed the erratic, bizarre and contradictory economic policy dictated by Prime Minister himself and obediently executed by his Minister of the Economy György Matolcsy.

Fidesz won the elections by promising radical tax cuts to its traditional supporters in the middle and upper-middle classes and also promising an end to austerity and, at the same time, an

ORBÁN *ÜBER ALLES*—HUNGARY AT A DEAD END

increase in welfare benefits to low income groups and pensioners (most of them traditional Socialist voters). Orbán's request for a practical doubling of the (originally projected) budget deficit in 2010 to 6–7 per cent was flatly refused by the IMF and EU experts monitoring the country's financial situation following the 20-billion-euro loan. The Prime Minister's reply was to storm out of the talks with the IMF in July and launch his 'war of independence' against foreign capital, which was celebrated and trumpeted by the government's propaganda apparatus and the right-wing media. He introduced a 16 per cent flat tax, costing 2 per cent of GDP, and other costly measures.

The government abruptly nationalised the private pension funds (to the tune of nine billion euros) and levied retroactive windfall taxes on the foreign banks and multinational companies in the retail, energy and communications sectors (about three billion euros), as well as forcing the banks to renegotiate at an arbitrary low rate the hundreds of thousands of mortgages taken out in Swiss francs and euros. However, such wilful and heavy-handed measures only served to make the country's economic problems in fact far worse by scaring off foreign investors and undermining confidence. Faced with the imminent threat of insolvency and confronted with a spirited defence of the independence of the National Bank by its Governor András Simor and the European Central Bank, the beleaguered Orbán government appears, at the time of this writing, to have changed its tactics in favour of a tactical withdrawal from some extreme and untenable positions. In a devastating analysis of the self-defeating economic policy conducted by the government since its seizure of power, Tamás Mellár, the former president of the Central Office of Statistics and a respected conservative economist, has publicly warned against continuing the nationalistic campaign against 'the conspiracy of international finance'. He has also predicted an inevitable state bankruptcy if the Orbán government merely makes some minimal adjustments for the sake of new IMF and ECB credits. Since the next general elections are due only in 2014 and Viktor Orbán rules supreme over his Fidesz party, his policy options will shape the future of Hungary. As the astute Columbia University professor of History István Deák noted in the spring of 2011, 'For all intents and purposes Hungary has become a one party state'.[31] A disillusioned writer and former civil rights activist against communism, György Konrad, already sees Hungary as 'a junk country, with a junk administration and a junk prime minister'.

Those who know him and his career do not regard Viktor Orbán as a conservative politician. Moving from left to right since 1993–94, he is a master tactician, a gifted populist, a radical and consummate opportunist, a ruthless power politician who believes not in ideas but in maximising his power without any compunction, giving vent to Hungarian nationalism or tapping into fear and prejudice at a moment of crisis. For him order is guaranteed not by freedom, but by a strong leader; for him, still only 49, leadership embodies the traditional, patriarchal way of thinking and the ingrained attitudes of crowds, hundreds of thousands strong, drawn from the Hungarian countryside.[32]

Regarding other countries of Central Europe, the question arises whether the Orbán government will continue with the same aggressive nationalism that Fidesz pursued whilst in opposition, to silence domestic criticism. And how will the political elites of Slovakia, Romania and Serbia, infected with the same deeply rooted virus of nationalist prejudices, react?

ORBÁN *ÜBER ALLES*—HUNGARY AT A DEAD END

The great political theorist István Bibó (1911–79) in his essay 'Distorted Hungarian State of Mind, Hungarian History at a Dead End' (1948) noted a particularly interesting and peculiarly Hungarian phenomenon:

In decisive moments, especially between 1914 and 1920, and between 1938 and 1944, the country has, in a fateful way, proved to be incapable of acting in accordance with its true situation and its actual assets ... The Hungarian nation in these decisive moments—in the political, social and intellectual sphere—could not find or put into power those leaders who could have well expressed and found its needs, interests and path.

It seems that after the 20-year democratic intermezzo the current ruling elite of the country, temporarily still supported by a relative (though by no means a two-thirds) majority in society, sees the salvation of the nation in once again pursuing the path of clerical neo-conservativism and ethnic nationalism which followed in the wake of Trianon. What France and Germany, Italy and Austria have finally achieved after decades of tenacious struggle is the victory of a Europe bound by a common destiny and based on mutual interests over an introverted protectionism and a suicidal nationalism. It is true that at Trianon Hungary lost 45,000km² of territory with a purely Hungarian population and 20,000km² with an ethnically mixed population. But we should also remember that, as the briefest glance at a history book will reveal, in the last century alone Austria, France, Germany and Italy have also had to confront similar tragedies, losses and injuries to national pride. The lasting peace between Paris and Bonn, as well as, for example, the durable compromises between Rome, Vienna, Bolzano and Innsbruck regarding South Tyrol, could serve as examples for Hungary and its neighbours as ways of overcoming the barriers between them and, at some stage, jointly facing up to the unfortunate inheritance of Trianon. The demons of the past and the chimera of various political systems have to be forgotten in the national interest. Hungary too has to come to terms with the bitter lessons of history.

NOTES

1. A FUNERAL AS THE END AND THE BEGINNING

1. 2,652 people died and almost 20,000 were wounded as a consequence of the fighting between 23 October and 31 December 1956. On the Soviet side there were 669 dead and 1,541 wounded. Estimates of the total number of refugees range between 180,000 and 200,000.

2. A HALF-HEARTED CHANGE

1. For an analysis of the events and consequences of the 1956 revolution see the author's *The Hungarians, 1000 Years of Victory in Defeat*, London 2003 and *One Day That Shook the Communist World: The 1956 Hungarian Uprising and Its Legacy*, Princeton 2008.
2. Years later, in an interview with me about 1956, the role of Imre Nagy and János Kádár held with Kryuchkov (1924–2007) in Moscow on 26 September 2005, the former KGB boss still praised Kádár as a 'high-minded communist, who was always loyal'.
3. Initially, Grósz impressed many, including me, as a populist but competent 'doer', a man fully at ease with the media. My overestimation of him proved to be, perhaps, my worst misjudgement in all my years as a reporter on Hungary. Cf. the author's *Das*

eigenwillige Ungarn ('Stubborn Hungary'), 2nd edition Zürich/Osnabrück 1988.

4. The reference is to the murders and other outrages committed by units composed of extreme nationalistic and violently anti-Semitic officers in 1919–20, the early phase of the rule of Admiral Miklos Horthy. See also Chapter 4.

5. The peace treaty signed in the Trianon summer palace in the park of Versailles on 4 June 1920, and perceived as the 'Trianon Diktat', marked the end of historical Greater Hungary. The victors of the Great War divided two-thirds of its territory and 40 per cent of its population among the three neighbouring states of Romania, Czechoslovakia and Yugoslavia. Hungarians accounted for 3.2 million of the ten million people living in the newly separated lands and half of these lived in enclaves directly on the borders of the three successor states. Between 1938 and 1941 Hungary won back 40 per cent of the territories lost at Trianon in accordance with the Vienna Arbitration Awards imposed by the two Axis powers. Hungary paid a high price (900,000 dead and 40 per cent of its national wealth) for its disastrous wartime alliance with Hitler's Germany. With the defeat of the Third Reich, Hungary lost all the territories it had regained in 1938–41, plus three additional villages in Czechoslovakia.

6. Zoltán Ripp, *Rendszerváltás Magyarországon 1987–1990* ('The change of the system in Hungary 1987–1990'), Budapest 2006, and Rudolf L. Tőkes, *Hungary's Negotiated Revolution*, Cambridge 2006.

7. The enormous importance of the international shortwave radio stations in the undermining of all communist regimes should be stressed.

3. JÓZSEF ANTALL—A POLITICAL PHENOMENON

1. For the informants' reports on Antall, see János M. Rainer, *Jelentések Hálójában—Antall József és az Állambiztonság Emberei 1957–1989* ('In the network of reports—Antall József and the state secu-

rity agents'), Budapest 2008. Biographical details are taken from József Debreczeni, *A miniszterelnök* ('The prime minister'), Budapest 1998, and Sándor Révész, *Antall József távolról* ('Antall József from a distance'), Budapest 1995. See also Anna Richter (ed.) *Ellenzéki Kerekasztal Portrévázlatok* ('Sketches of portraits from the opposition round table'), Budapest 1990, esp. pp. 153–69.
2. For Birós' remarks, see the interview with him in *Puha diktaturától kemény demokráciáig* ('From soft dictatorship to hard democracy'), Budapest 1994. In the meantime this erstwhile high-ranking official in the Ministry of Education under the communist regime has become a vociferous nationalistic and barely veiled anti-Semitic columnist in the pro-Fidesz daily *Magyar Hirlap*.
3. See Debreczeni, pp. 115 ff.
4. Debreczeni, p. 190.
5. See Eszter Rádai, *Penzügyminiszterek reggelire* ('Finance ministers for breakfast'), Budapest 2001, especially the interviews with Ferenc Rabár, Mihály Kupa and Iván Szabó.
6. See the appendix of documents in Imre Kertész, *Briefe an Eva Haldimann* ('Letters to Eva Haldeman'), Hamburg 2009.
7. Cf. Zoltán Ripp, *Eltékozolt esélyek?* ('Wasted opportunities?'), Budapest 2009.

4. THE ROOTS OF HUNGARIAN ANTI-SEMITISM

1. Horst Krüger, *Ost-West-Passagen. Reisebilder aus zwei Welten* ('East-West passages. Travel pictures from two worlds'), Hamburg 1975.
2. Cf. Julien Benda, *La trahison des clercs*, Paris 1927; trans. *The Treason of the Intellectuals*, Piscataway 2006.
3. Imre Kertész, *K. dosszié* ('K. file'), Budapest 2006.
4. *Die Welt*, 7 November 2010; see also the author's commentary 'Der Heilige Krieg der Ultras' ('The crusade of the ultras') in *Die Welt*, 17 November 2010.
5. For a detailed description, see the author's *The Hungarians: A Thousand Years of Victory in Defeat*, London 2003.

6. Under the terms of the 1867 Austro-Hungarian Ausgleich or Compromise, Austria conceded the return of sovereignty to the Kingdom of Hungary. With a few exceptions, the territories of Austria and Hungary, known henceforth as the Dual Monarchy, were now governed by separate parliaments and ministries but had a single head of state, the reigning member of the Habsburg family.
7. István Bibó, *Zur Judenfrage* ('On the Jewish question'), Frankfurt am Main 1990. This essay, first published in 1948, still remains today probably the best contribution on this subject, not least because it was written by somebody who was neither a Jew nor a communist or socialist, but a progressive middle-class thinker.
8. Gyula Juhász, *Uralkodó eszmék Magyarországon 1934–1944* ('Domineering ideas in Hungary'), Budapest 1983.
9. Christian Gerlach and Götz Aly, *Das letzte Kapital. Der Mord an den ungarischen Juden* ('The final chapter. The murder of the Hungarian Jews'), Stuttgart 2002.
10. For the figures, see Ignác Romsics, *Magyarország története a XX. Században* ('Hungary's history in the 20th century'), Budapest 1999; see also László Varga, 'Ungarn' ('Hungary') in Wolfgang Benz (ed.), *Dimensionen des Völkermordes* ('Dimensions of the genocide'), Munich 1991. On the persecution of the Jews, see Randolph Braham, *The Politics of Genocide*, 2 vols, New York 1994.
11. Cf. Mária Vásárhelyi, *Csalóka emlékezet* ('Deceptive memory'), Bratislava 2007, and her articles in the weekly *Élet és Irodalom*, 10 February and 1 October 2010.

5. GYULA HORN AND THE RETURN OF THE POST-COMMUNISTS

1. Citing Horn's participation in the wave of reprisals against the revolutionaries in 1956–57, President László Sólyom refused to honour the former Prime Minister with Hungary's highest award on the occasion of his 75th birthday in 2007.

NOTES pp. [75–88]

2. See my background interview with Békesi on 9 April 2010; also the interviews with Eszter Rádai in January 1998 and Katalin Bossányi in October 1999. All published in Hungarian publications.
3. In the Tocsik affair both coalition parties stood accused of exacting and receiving 112 million forints each as a kickback for placing contracts with the lawyer Márta Tocsik. Cf. Ferenc Kőszeg, 'Sakk! Matt?' ('Check! Mate?') in *Élet és Irodalom*, 15 August 2008.
4. Medgyessy was the young star of the Kádár era: while still in his forties he was Minister of Finance (1982–87) and then Vice-Premier (1987–90). His premiership (2002–04) is considered in Chapter 7.
5. No government since 1989 has so far been able to resolve the issue of the tens of thousands of files on past agents, informers and their 'minders' in the secret service during the four decades of communist rule.
6. See the author's *Best of Paul Lendvai. Begegnungen, Erinnerungen, Einsichten* ('Best of Paul Lendvai: Encounters, memories, reflections'), Salzburg 2008, pp. 81–100.

6. THE YOUNG COMET—VIKTOR ORBÁN

1. In 1955 the 32-year-old András Hegedüs was nominated prime minister by the Politburo of the Communist Party and shortly afterwards elected to this post by the toothless parliament. His position, however, cannot be compared in any way to that of a freely elected head of government in a democracy.
2. Hans Kohn, *Wege und Irrwege. Vom Geist des deutschen Bürgertums* ('Paths and false paths. On the spirit of the German bourgeoisie'), Düsseldorf 1962.
3. For a discussion of the meaning of the national myth see Chapter 8.
4. Additionally, Debreczeni has written the first major biographies of two other recent Hungarian prime ministers, József

237

Antall (1998) and Ferenc Gyurcsány (2006). Both of these books and the two on Orbán have to date been published only in Hungarian.
5. Unless otherwise mentioned, all the quotations and details are taken from Debreczeni's two books.
6. See Ludwig Helms, 'Leadership-Forschung als Demokratiewissenschaft' ('Leadership research as the science of democracy'), and Claudia Ritzi and Gary S. Schaal, 'Politische Führung in der "Postdemokratie"' ('Political leadership in the "post-democracy"') in *Aus Politik und Zeitgeschichte, Beilage der Bonner Wochenzeitung Das Parlament* 2–3/2010.
7. Quoted from an interview with Katalin Bossányi in *Mozgó Világ* 1999/10.
8. For details on the quarry, real estate, vineyard and winegrowing transactions of the Orbán family, see pages 245–74 of Debreczeni's second biography *Arcmás* ('Faces'), Budapest 2009.
9. See Zita Mária Petschnig, 'A magyar gazdaság az uj évezred kezdetén' ('The Hungarian economy at the outset of the 21st century') in *Pénzügypolitikai stratégiák a 21. század kezdetén*, 26 January 2006.
10. For details, see *Anti-Semitic Discourse in Hungary in 2000*, Budapest 2001 and *Anti-Semitic Discourse in Hungary in 2001*, Budapest 2002.

7. THE MEDGYESSY PUZZLE OR THE END OF A DECEPTION

1. The author's interview with Péter Medgyessy took place on 6 May 2010. See also István Perger, Pál Köves, Gergely Varga, Vera Németh, Zsolt Gréczy, *Medgyessy*, Budapest 2004; Péter Medgyessy, *Polgár a pályán* ('A bourgeois on the field'), Budapest 2006; Ervin Csizmadia, *A Medgyessy-talány* ('The Medgyessy riddle'), Budapest 2004.
2. Under the terms of the 1992 Treaty of Maastricht, government deficits may not exceed more than 3 per cent of GDP and gov-

ernment debt 60 per cent of GDP; moreover, inflation may not be higher than 1.5 percentage points over that of the three EU member states with the lowest rate of inflation; long-term interest rates may not be higher than two percentage points of those in the three member states with the lowest inflation.
3. These four anonymous quotations were all recorded by the author on tape during interviews conducted in Budapest at the end of 2009 and the beginning of 2010.

8. THE SENSE OF MISSION OF AN EASILY SEDUCIBLE NATION

1. Cited in Michael Jeismann and Henning Ritter (eds), *Über neuen und alten Nationalismus* ('On new and old nationalism'), Leipzig 1993.
2. See Isaiah Berlin, *Against the Current*, London 1980, p. 339 and p. 353.
3. The Swedish journalist Richard Swartz, writing about Hungary in the *Süddeutsche Zeitung*, 30 April 2010.
4. See Chapter 4.
5. See the leading article in the *Neue Zürcher Zeitung*, 29–30 May 2010. At the end of May and beginning of June 2010 numerous major European newspapers such as the *Süddeutsche Zeitung, Die Welt, Die Zeit* (Germany), *Der Standard, Die Presse* (Austria) and *Le Monde* (France), as well as an array of newspapers in Slovakia, the Czech Republic, Romania and Serbia, wrote in similar vein.
6. This very question, but with reference to the German nation, was posed and discussed by the former German Chancellor Helmut Schmidt with the German-born American historian Fritz Stern; see C.H. Beck, *Unser Jahrhundert* ('Our century'), Munich 2010, p. 51.
7. See William M. Johnston, *The Austrian Mind*, Berkeley 1983.
8. The author is indebted to Mária Vásárhelyi for these figures taken from a lecture she gave at a conference on the Treaty of Trianon held in Budapest June 2010.

9. Cited by Ignác Romsics, *A trianoni békeszerződés* ('The Trianon Peace Treaty'), Budapest 2007, pp. 178–82.
10. The present-day Slovak capital is of special significance to the Hungarians. Owing to Ottoman incursions into the country it became the capital of Hungary in 1536 and its kings and queens were crowned in St. Martin's Cathedral between then and 1830. Pest only replaced Bratislava as the capital of Hungary in 1848. In 1910 41 per cent of the population was Hungarian.
11. See the interview with László Szigeti in the Budapest weekly *Magyar Narancs*, 5 September 2009.
12. See the interview with László Szarka entitled 'Politikai értelemben nem létezik Kárpátmedence' ('In a political sense, there is no Carpathian Basin') in *Élet és Irodalom*, 12 December 2008.
13. Cf. Herbert Küpper, 'Ungarn und die magyarischen Minderheiten in den Nachbarstaaten' ('Hungary and the Hungarian minorities in the neighbouring states') in *Ost-West Europäische Perspektiven—Schwerpunkt Ungarn*, Freising 2/2007. For a critical consideration of the unilateral Hungarian measures, but also of Slovakia's blunder with its language law, see the essays of Tamás Bauer published in the literary weekly *Élet és Irodalom* between 2008 and 2010; see also the article by Csaba Tabajdi, a Socialist MEP, entitled 'A nemzet mindannyiunké' ('The nation belongs to all of us') in *Népszabadság*, 21 May 2010.
14. See the interview with László Szarka, fn.12.
15. The First Vienna Award arbitrated by the foreign ministers of the Axis Powers, Ribbentrop and Ciano, on 2 November 1938 granted Hungary some of the territories lost at Trianon. Budapest regained control over 11,927km^2 of Czechoslovak territory and 1,060,000 inhabitants, of whom 84 per cent were Magyars according to the Hungarian census of 1941 but only 57 per cent were according to the Czechoslovak census of 1930. After the Second World War the Hungarians also suffered the consequences of the notorious Beneš decrees: 36,000 were expelled, 45,000 deported to Bohemia and Moravia, and 70,000 were relocated in Hungary following a population exchange (Slovaks from

Hungary, Hungarians from Slovakia) and approximately 350,000 were forcibly (though intermittently) 're-Slovakised'.
16. To counter the political turmoil in Slovakia following the German occupation of Czechoslovakia, in March 1939 Hitler threatened to annex some of Slovakia and partition the remaining territories unless the country declared independence and placed itself under German protection. A former Catholic priest, Jozef Tiso, headed a strongly right-wing and anti-Semitic regime between March 1939 and April 1945, an 'independent nation' that existed solely at Hitler's grace and favour.
17. This town, which straddles the Danube, was divided into two after 1918. Today, the Slovak part is known as Komárno and the Hungarian part as Komárom.
18. *Népszabadság*, 21 May 2010.
19. Lajos Gogolák, 'Ungarns Nationalitätengesetze' ('Hungary's nationality laws') in *Die Habsburgmonarchie*, Vienna 1980, p. 1263.
20. Karl-Peter Schwarz, 'Staatsbürgerschaft jenseits der Grenzen' ('Citizenship across borders') in *Frankfurter Allgemeine Zeitung*, 26 May 2010.
21. Karl Popper, *The Open Society and its Enemies Volume One*, 4th edition, London 1962, p. 200.

9. THE SPLENDOUR AND DECLINE OF FERENC GYURCSÁNY

1. Cited in Isaiah Berlin, *Russian Thinkers*, pbk. edn. London 1978, p. 92.
2. For the sometimes controversial deals Gyurcsány made at the time and which have been much exaggerated by his political foes, see József Debreczeni's biography, pp. 81–166.
3. For details, see Chapter 7.
4. *Népszabadság*, 21 September 1996.
5. Antal Apró (1913–94), a construction worker and pre-war communist, held high office throughout the four decades of commu-

nist rule in Hungary: a member of the Politburo, head of the trade unions, president of the parliament. His wife and son also filled important positions. His daughter Piroska Apró, an economist, had many jobs, including Deputy Minister for Foreign Trade, head of Prime Minister Gyula Horn's personal staff, chair of the board of the Magyar Hitelbank etc. Her husband Petar Dobrev worked in the Bulgarian foreign trade organisation. Their daughter, Klára Dobrev, was *inter alia* deputy secretary of state in the National Development Agency. The marriage between Klára Dobrev and Ferenc Gyurcsány (his third) has produced two children. Gyurcsány's two sons from his second marriage also live partly in the villa in Buda which Antal Apró's widow and daughter purchased after his death and later reconstructed.
6. The author would like to thank Endre Hann, the head of the Media opinion research centre in Budapest, for making the polling data on Gyurcsány and his successor available.
7. Cf. Karl-Dietrich Bracher, *Schlüsselwörter in der Geschichte* ('Key words in history'), Düsseldorf 1978, p. 11 and p. 53.

10. THE POWER OF THE DISCREET PRESS BARONS

1. See Chapter 3, p. 00.
2. Inoffizieller or Informeller Mitarbeiter (often abbreviated to IM) were informants in East Germany who secretly passed information to the state security service without formally being employed by this organisation.
3. See especially my memoirs *Blacklisted: A Journalist's Life in Central Europe,* London 1998 and the chapter 'Michael Coles Glück und Ende oder Die Geschichte einer gescheiterten Anwerbung' ('Michael Cole's luck and end or the story of a failed recruitment') in *Best of Paul Lendvai. Begegnungen, Erinnerungen, Einsichten* ('Best of Paul Lendvai. Encounters, reminiscences, reflections'), Salzburg 2004, pp. 81–100.
4. See János Kenedi, *Kis állambiztonsági olvasókönyv I–II* ('Short reader on state security'), Budapest 1996, and Krisztián Ungváry

and Gábor Tabajdi, *Elhallgatott mult* ('Concealed past'), Budapest 2009.
5. See Chapter 2 for details.
6. *Der Standard*, 30 December 2004.
7. Szepesi, one of Hungary's most popular sports commentators since 1945 and a former member of the IOC and FIFA, has never denied my revelations. Nevertheless, he has continued to be an honoured citizen of Budapest. On 15 March 2008, the Hungarian National Holiday, he distributed, in his role as chair of the Committee of the Golden Pen, prizes to journalists of outstanding merit ...
8. *Magyar Nemzet*, founded in 1938 by progressive, middle-class journalists, was brought into line first by the extreme right during the war years and then, after 1945, by the Communist Party.
9. For the connections, which go back to their student days, and the activities of this multifaceted fixer, see especially József Debreczeni's second biography of Orbán, Budapest 2009.
10. See Balázs Sipos, *Média és demokrácia Magyarországon—20 év után* ('Media and democracy in Hungary—20 years on'), Budapest 2010; Mária Vásárhelyi, *Foglalkozása: ujságiro* ('Profession: journalist'), Budapest 2006, and her essays in *Élet és Irodalom*, 19 June 2009, 23 April 2010 and 25 June 2010. For the superrich, cf. the annual volumes Top 150 (*Népszabadság*) 2008 and Top 100 (*Napi Magyarország*) 2010. In the figures given, we may safely assume the fortunes are underestimated and that some billionaires have provided no statistics. For the current figures, see *Népszabadság*, weekend supplement of 15 May 2010, pp. 2–3.
11. After the publication of this book in German (2010), and in particular after the appearance of the Hungarian edition (2011), I too became the target of vicious and personal attacks launched by the right-wing Fidesz media.

11. COLD WAR AT THE TOP—ORBÁN VERSUS GYURCSÁNY

1. A similar phenomenon may be observed in neighbouring Austria, where since the 1990s traditional working-class voters have defected en masse from the Austrian Socialist Party, a party often led by mediocre politicians and mired in corruption scandals and privilege, to the far-right FPÖ.
2. For a good summary of these events, see Gregor Mayer and Bernhard Odehnal, *Aufmarsch. Die rechte Gefahr in Osteuropa* ('On the march. The right-wing danger from Eastern Europe'), St Pölten/Salzburg 2010; see also Sebastian Garthoff, 'Szenen aus Budapest' ('Scenes from Budapest') in *Aus Politik und Zeitgeschichte, Beilage der Bonner Wochenzeitung Das Parlament*, 13 July 2009; for a sound political analysis, see Zoltán Ripp, 'Haza a mélyben' ('The Fatherland in decline') in *Mozgó Világ* 2007/1, pp. 5–23.
3. The red and white Árpád stripes first appeared in 1202 on a coat of arms used by King Emeric of Hungary, a member of the Árpád dynasty, though they are said to be older. They were used as symbols by Arrow Cross supporters, the Hungarian Nazis.
4. The legal scholar László Sólyom played an important role during the transition to democracy and was then elected president of the Constitutional Court. In 2005 the Liberals were not prepared to support the Socialist speaker of parliament Katalin Szili as the candidate for state president. In two rounds of voting and a series of humiliating intrigues, the opposition succeeded by a margin of just three votes in securing the post for Sólyom, who had originally been nominated by environmentalists and civil rights activists. It was a defeat with serious consequences for the left. It was also an unnecessary one due, as it was, to Szili's own stubborn insistence upon her hopeless candidature and to the inability of the two governing parties to find a compromise candidate acceptable to both sides. After the electoral victory of Fidesz, Szili publicly broke with the Socialists in 2010.

5. *Népszava*, 20 December 2006.
6. The rubber bullets used by the police caused open wounds in the chests and stomachs of demonstrators, whilst two of their number lost an eye each. Cf. Gregor Mayer and Bernhard Odehnal, *Aufmarsch. Die rechte Gefahr in Osteuropa* ('On the march. The right-wing danger from Eastern Europe'), St Pölten/Salzburg 2010, p. 47.
7. Cf. Gregor Mayer and Bernhard Odehnal, *Aufmarsch. Die rechte Gefahr in Osteuropa* ('On the march. The right-wing danger from Eastern Europe'), St Pölten/Salzburg 2010, p. 81.
8. György Dalos, *Der Vorhang geht auf. Das Ende der Diktaturen in Osteuropa* ('The curtain goes up. The end of the dictatorships in Eastern Europe'), Munich 2009, p. 196.
9. See *Frankfurter Allgemeine Zeitung*, 23 December 2008.
10. For the interview in full, see *Osteuropa*, Berlin 6/2010, pp. 19–30.
11. See Krisztián Ungváry, 'Belastete Orte der Erinnerung' ('Encumbered places of remembrance') in *Aus Politik und Zeitgeschichte, Beilage der Bonner Wochnezeitung Das Parlament*, 13 July 2010, pp. 26–44.

12. THE ROMA AND JEWS—TARGETS OF THE EXTREME RIGHT

1. Cf. *EU Agency for Fundamental Rights, Part I, The Roma*, Budapest 2009; cited by Melani Barlai and Florian Hartleb in 'Die Roma in Ungarn' ('The Roma in Hungary') in *Aus Politik und Zeitgeschichte, Beilage der Bonner Wochnezeitung Das Parlament*, 13 July 2009, pp. 33–9. For details on the situation of the Roma, see numerous articles in the weekly publications *Élet és Irodalom, Magyar Narancs, HGV* etc., especially those by János Kis and Szilvia Varró in 2009 and 2010, as well as the study by the political scientists Gergely Karácsony and Daniel Rona on the criminalisation of the Gypsy question and the associated rise of Jobbik in the magazine *Politikatudományi Szemle*, January 2010.

2. Since Bogdán's death in 2006, his work has been carried on by his wife. Today the school has 300 pupils and takes in boarders.
3. See Mária Vásárhelyi in *Mozgó Világ* August 2009; see also András Biró 'Az integráció ára' ('The price of integration') in *Élet és Irodalom*, 10 March 2010.
4. Cited by Stephan Ozsváth, 'Ungarns Anti-Roma-Hetzer' ('Hungary's anti-Roma rabble-rousers') in *Die Furche*, 2 October 2008.
5. Cited by János Kis, 'A cigánykérdés kriminalizálása' ('The criminalisation of the Gypsy question') in *HVG*, 21 February 2009.
6. The interview with Szilvia Varró took place in Budapest on 17 December 2009.
7. See footnote 5.
8. Cf. the lengthy reports in *Die Zeit* of 7 May ('Unter der Fahne der Faschisten' ('Under the flag of the fascists') by Christian Schmidt-Häuer), in the *Süddeutsche Zeitung* of 4 May ('Nein, nein, niemals!' ('No, no, never!') by Richard Swartz), in the *Neue Zürcher Zeitung* of 10 June ('Klima der Furcht und des Misstrauens bei ungarischen Roma' ('Climate of fear and mistrust among the Hungarian Roma') by Charles E. Ritterband) and in *Der Spiegel* No. 14/2010 ('Der Seiltänzer von Budapest' ('The tightrope walker of Budapest') by Walter Mayr), all published in the run-up to the European elections in June 2009.
9. For a detailed and reliable description of the activities of the Hungarian Guards and Jobbik, see Gregor Mayer and Bernhard Odehnal, *Aufmarsch. Die rechte Gefahr aus Osteuropa* ('On the march. The right-wing danger from Eastern Europe'), St Pölten/Salzburg 2010.
10. See footnote 1.
11. See footnote 1.
12. See Chapter 10.
13. Like the Árpád flag, the Turul bird, a mythical creature representing power, strength and nobility, became after 1933 a symbol of the pro-Nazi parties in Hungary, notably the Arrow Cross Party. Cf. Krisztián Ungváry, 'Belastete Orte der Erinnerung'

NOTES pp. [194–211]

('Encumbered places of remembrance') in *Aus Politik und Zeitgeschichte, Beilage der Bonner Wochenzeitung Das Parlament*, 13 July 2010, pp. 26–44.
14. Alexis de Tocqueville, *Souvenirs*, New York 1970, p. 12.

13. THE POLITICAL SUICIDE OF THE LEFT

1. A three-page description of this tussle appeared in the weekend edition of *Népszabadság*, 18 March 2010.
2. *Magyar Nemzet*, 6 February 2010.
3. Cf. the introduction to Chapter 11.
4. Michaela Seiser, *Frankfurter Allgemeine Zeitung*, 7 April 2010.

14. ORBÁN *ÜBER ALLES*—HUNGARY AT A DEAD END

1. See *The Economist*, 7 January 2012.
2. See Paul Krugman, 'Depression and democracy', *New York Times*, 11 December 2011; see also Kim Lane Scheppele, 'Hungary's constitutional revolution' in Krugman's blog on 19 December 2011.
3. See his excellent report 'Hungarian Rhapsodies' in *The American Interest*, January-February 2012 and his article in the *New York Times*, 13 December 2012.
4. Cf. Scheppele, op. cit.
5. József Debreczeni, 'Nyitány' ('Overture') in *Népszava*, 17 May 2010.
6. Charles Gati, 'Hungarian Rhapsodies', *The American Interest*, January-February 2012.
7. Lajos Bokros, 'A fékek és egyensúlyok elporladása—a populista autokrácia felé vezető csúszós úton' ('The demise of checks and balances—on the slippery slope to populist autocracy'), *Élet és Irodalom*, 21 January 2011.
8. The Szekler hymn (*Székely Himnusz*) is an unofficial national anthem of the Hungarian-speaking Szeklers, a large Hungarian sub-group living in Eastern Transylvania (today in Romania); it was originally written and composed in 1921–22 as a song. Its singing was banned by both the pre-war and the communist

247

regimes in Romania as it was regarded as a nostalgic nationalistic elegy for the loss of Transylvania at the Treaty of Trianon in 1920.
9. See *Neue Zürcher Zeitung*, 12 July 2010 and *Osteuropa*, Berlin, June 2010, pp. 3–12.
10. Gábor Halmai, 'Búcsú a jogállamtól' ('Good-bye to the constitutional state'), *Élet és Irodalom*, 23 July 2010; see also 'A jogállam leépülését nem kísérte civil ellenállás' ('The decline of the constitutional state has not been accompanied by popular resistance'), *Népszabadság*, 10 August 2010.
11. Cf. János Kis, 'Orbán számára nincs visszaút' ('There is no way back for Orbán'), *Népszabadság*, 24 January 2011.
12. The former Prime Minister and nine other Socialist MPs broke with the MSzP and on 22 October 2011 set up a new left-liberal party called the Democratic Coalition.
13. Helmut Schmidt, Fritz Stern, *Unser Jahrhundert* ('Our century'), Munich 2010.
14. József Debreczeni, *Arcmás* ('Image'), Budapest 2009.
15. See Gordon Bajnai, *Köztársaság, kiegyezés, kilábalás* ('Republic, Reconciliation, Recovery'), published by the *Haza és Haladás* ('Country and Progress') Foundation 9, January 2012.
16. János Kornai, 'Számvetés' ('Reckoning'), *Népszabadság*, 6 January 2011. He published a similarly devastating long piece in the same newspaper, 28 January 2012.
17. Cf. the comment of Miklós Haraszti: 'The five crucial legislative acts were passed in a hurry without any consultation with professional bodies. The main features that restrict freedom and pluralism of the media are all unprecedented'. www.eurozine.com/articles/2011-03-01-Haraszti-en.html. Cf. also the statement by Haraszti's successor Dunja Mijatovic: 'Hungary's media law continues to violate OSCE press freedom commitments' www.osce.org/fom/75990.
18. See his article in the *Vienna Review*, March 2011. The chair is Annamaria Szalai, 50, a former music teacher, reporter for a provincial paper and a professional functionary of Fidesz; since 1998 she has been a Fidesz MP and media spokesperson.

19. For the atmosphere see Charles Gati, op. cit.; for the consequences of the media law see *Süddeutsche Zeitung*, Munich, 27 December 2011; for the overwhelming control of the print media see *Magyar Narancs*, 4 August 2011.
20. For the events and methods see my book *The Bureaucracy of Truth*, London and Boulder, 1981.
21. See *The Economist*, 7 January 2010 for Clinton's letter to Prime Minister Orbán dated 23 December 2011. According to Hungarian press reports, the former US Ambassador Mark Palmer and Professor Charles Gati intend to launch an initiative resurrecting the Hungarian broadcasts of Radio Free Europe.
22. See fn. 15.
23. See fn. 2 and 4.
24. His statement to the MTI news agency was printed in the Budapest daily *Népszava*, 27 December 2011.
25. L.B. Namier, *Facing East*, London 1947.
26. Bajnai, op. cit.
27. For Csurka's political activities in the past see chapters 3 and 6. In one of his recent columns in his paper *Magyar Forum* ('Hungarian Forum') Csurka wrote that George Soros sought to promote the seizure of power by Hungarian Jewry and to strengthen the interests of the US Jewish community by helping the infiltration of Hungary by Israel. Csurka also claimed that by his pro-Fidesz stand and attacks against Jobbik he contributed 3 to 4 per cent to the Fidesz victory in April 2010 and that without his help Fidesz could not have won a two-thirds majority of seats. See *Népszabadsag*, 15 December 2011 and *Magyar Narancs*, 5 January 2012. Csurka died on 4 February 2012. The right-wing newspapers and TV channels carried fulsome obituaries, omitting any critical references to his anti-Semitic writings and speeches.
28. See K.P. Scheppele, op. cit.
29. Philip Stephens, 'A Hungarian coup worthy of Putin', *Financial Times*, London 6 January 2012.
30. For these and following figures see the article by former Finance

Minister Peter Oszko in 'Beyond the brick' blog of the *Financial Times*, 23 January 2012; see also Zita Mária Petschnig in *Népszava*, 26 November 2011.
31. See *New York Review of Books*, 28 April 2011.
32. See András Bozóki, 'A magyar demokrácia válsága' ('The crisis of Hungarian democracy') in *Élet és Irodalom*, 13 January 2011 and Péter Nádas 'Der Stand der Dinge' ('The state of affairs'), *Lettre Internationale*, Winter 2011; see also Ivan Krastev quoted in *Financial Times*, 6 January 2012.

INDEX

Aczél, Endre 36, 154
Alliance of Free Democrats, see SzDS
Antall, József 26, 29–51, 67, 69,
   91–2, 149, 161
anti-Semitism 45, 48–9, 53–65, 86,
   161, 170, 174, 175, 186–94, 225
Apró, Antal 104, 241–2
Apró, Piroska 104, 109, 134–5, 242
Arad 18
Árpád emblem 171, 176, 178, 191,
   244
Arrow Cross party 62, 65, 170, 176,
   178
Aspen Institute 30
Austria 12, 13, 34, 35, 70, 74, 89,
   127, 129–30, 139, 149, 179
Austrian People's Party (ÖVP) 35

Bajnai, Gordon 170, 201–5, 216–17,
   221, 226, 228
Baka, András 22–3
Balatonőszöd speech (Gyurcsány)
   141–5, 168, 195, 196
Balázs, Péter 127
Bauer, Tamás 82, 125, 128
Bayer, Zsolt 188, 190

Békesi, László 74–6, 79, 81, 92–3
Berlin, Sir Isaiah 114
Beszélő 15, 23
Bibó, István 58, 60, 115
Biró, Zoltán 38
Bogdán, János 181
Bokros, Lajos 77–8, 81, 87, 170, 210
border opening (1989) 70
Borókai, Gábor 156–7
Boross, Péter 41, 50, 149
Bracher, Karl-Dietrich 142
Bratislava (Pozsony) 119, 121, 240
Britain 35, 109, 134, 139, 205
Budapest passim esp. 1–2, 138, 153,
   156, 173, 176, 190, 192, 201, 225
Burke, Edmund 203–4
Bush, George W. 35, 95

Catholic Church 21, 82, 87, 151
Ceauşescu, Nicolae 18
Central European University 48, 183
Chirac, Jacques 35
Christian-Democratic People's Party,
   see KDNP
churches 87, 214
citizenship law 128–9, 211

INDEX

Clemenceau, Georges 117
Clinton, Hillary 221
Cluj (Kolozsvár) 119
Communist Party 3–6, 8, 9–14, 15–28, 46, 103, 133, 189, 193, 226
communist regime (1919) 57–8, 69; (1945–89) 1–14, 65, 99–101, 103, 133, 193
constitution 208
Constitutional Court 79, 152, 198, 218, 222, 244
corruption 46, 81–2, 87, 93–4, 110, 153, 169, 205
Croatia 121, 123, 129
Csányi, Sándor 78
Csillag, István 110
Csoóri, Sandor 23, 48
Csurka, István 23, 45, 46, 48, 86, 95, 97, 193, 225, 249
Czechoslovakia 20, 23, 24, 32, 57, 119, 120, 122, 126

D-109 affair 99–101
Dalos, György 175
Danube 24, 85, 107, 127, 190–1
Dávid, Ibolya 188–89
Davos World Economic Forum 20, 79
Deák, István 230
Debreczeni, József 33, 36, 38, 43, 88, 90, 91, 94, 97, 138, 162, 175, 197, 205, 209, 215
debt 14, 42, 76, 202, 225, 228
Declaration of National Cooperation 210, 214
Democratic Forum 153
Demszky, Gábor 190
Disraeli, Benjamin 205
Dobrev, Klára 104, 109, 134, 242
Donáth, Ferenc 173

Dunajská Streda 126
Dzurinda, Mikuláš 124

EBRD 96
economy (economic situation, economic meaures and policies) 11, 14–15, 42–3, 74–5, 77–9, 89, 94–5, 105–6, 140, 170, 202–5, 228–30
education 65, 75, 181, 191, 198
elections (parliamentary): (1994) 67; (1998) 82, 85–6; (2002) 97; (2006) 137–8, 140; (2010) 194, 207, 209–10
Élet és Irodalom 150, 152, 174
Elias, Norbert 196
Eörsi, István 23
Esterházy, Péter 143, 188
EU 73, 79, 89, 106, 108, 109, 113, 199, 200, 218, 228–30
European Central Bank 200, 228, 229, 230
European Parliament 109, 195, 223

Fellegi, Dr Tamás 157
Fenyő, János 155–6
Fico, Robert 125–6, 127
Fidesz (Fiatal Demokraták Svöversége, Alliance of Young Democrats), *see also* Orbán, Viktor 3–4, 24, 25, 27, 36, 67, 85–7, 91, 93, 95, 97, 122, 124, 141, 142, 148, 154, 157–63, 168–70, 172, 207, 209–28, 230
Financial Times 149, 227
Fischer, Heinz 79
Fodor, Gábor 88
Forum of Hungarian Representatives of the Carpathian Basin 123
France 35, 107, 117
Frankfurter Allgemeine Zeitung 147, 204

252

INDEX

Für, Lajos 177

Gabčíkovo power station project 24
Gati, Charles 80, 208–9
Genscher, Hans-Dietrich 79
Germany (pre-1945) 30, 59–63, 64, 65, 175
Germany (reunited) 70–1, 77, 115, 129, 139, 215
Germany, East 70
Germany, West 34, 70–1
Gogolák, Lajos 128
Göncz, Árpád 23, 38–9, 41, 43, 47
Gorbachev, Mikhail 15, 22
Görgey, Artur 155
Grósz, Károly 16–20, 26
Gyárfás, Tamás 156
Győr-Moson-Sopron 110, 132
Gypsies, *see* Roma
Gyurcsány, Ferenc 104, 109, 110–11, 115, 131–45, 161, 162, 165, 167–78, 195–201, 213, 216

Habsburg era 56, 58, 80, 155, 236
Habsburg, Otto 80
Hando, Tünde 223
Haraszti, Miklós 218
Havasi, Ferenc 14
Hazai, Baron Samu 56
Heller, Ágnes 224
Heltai, Ferenc 56
Helyi Thema 156
Heroes' Square 1–2, 18, 184
Heti Válasz 157, 159, 175, 187
Hitler, Adolf 59, 178
Holocaust 54–5, 60, 62–4, 115, 176, 178, 186–7, 189, 190–1
Horn, Gyula 20, 137, 139, 167, 169
Horthy, Miklós 49, 116
Hungarian Democratic Forum, *see* MDF

Hungarian Guard 148, 170, 176–8, 179, 184–6, 189, 210, 211
Hungarian Justice and Life Party, *see* MIÉP
Hungarian Permanent Conference 123
Hungarian Socialist Party, *see* MSzP
Hungarians in neighbouring countries 18, 19–20, 39–40, 59, 113–14, 115, 117–29, 238
Huns 116

Illyés, Gyula 12
IMF 14, 77, 100, 199, 228–30
inequality 11, 14, 138
Inotai, András 105
International Press Institute 47, 49, 148
Israel 179, 192

Jászi, Oszkár 58
Jews 45, 48, 53–65, 161, 174, 177, 186–94
Jobbik 9, 128, 148, 170, 171, 173, 181–6, 210–12, 214, 220
Johnston, William M. 116
judiciary 220, 222–3, 225

Kaczyński, Lech 203
Kádár, János 5–6, 12–21, 32, 48, 54, 68, 150, 155, 164, 169, 190, 193, 221
Kajdi, József 42
KDNP (Christian-Democratic People's Party) 24, 36, 67, 209
Kecskemét 19
Kenedi, János 150, 151
Kertész, Imre 48, 54–5
Kézai, Simon 116
Kis, János 24, 76, 102, 183, 197
Kiss, Péter 136, 161

253

INDEX

KISZ (Hungarian Communist Youth Federation) 133–4
Klubradio 220, 221
Koestler, Arthur 55
Kohl, Helmut 35, 70–1, 77, 79
Komarnó 127
Konrad, György 230
Kornai, János 217
Košice (Kassa) 119
Kosovo 129
Kossuth, Lajos 155
Kötcse 208
Kovács, László 83, 96, 103–4
Kövér, László 161
Kreisky, Bruno 12, 13, 139
Krüger, Horst 53
Krugman, Paul 208
Kryuchkov, Vladimir 16
Kun, Béla 57

Lakitelek 19, 32
League of Free Trade Unionists 25
Lec, Jerzy 153, 159
Lékai, Cardinal László 151
Lengyel, László 10, 42, 49, 73, 89
Liberals, *see* SzDSz
Lloyd George, David 118–19
LMP (Lehet Más a Politika) 213

Magyar Demokrata 159, 161, 162, 189
Magyar Fórum 193, 225
Magyar Hirlap 154–5, 159, 162, 183, 188, 191, 193
Magyar Narancs 153, 182–3
Magyar Nemzet 47–8, 99, 141, 154, 158, 159, 161, 162, 163, 176, 183, 201
Magyar, Bálint 72
Márai, Sándor 119
Matolcsy, György 228

MDF (Magyar Demokrata Fórum, Hungarian Democratic Forum), *see also* Antall, József 9, 20, 23, 26, 29, 33–9, 44–8, 50, 67, 85, 86, 109, 155, 162, 188, 213
Mečiar, Vladimír 83, 125
Mécs, Imre 23
Medgyessy, Péter 4–5, 75, 96–7, 99–111, 132, 135–6, 196, 201
media 46–8, 65, 92, 147–65, 175–6, 183, 188–9, 210, 217–21
Media Council 218, 221
medieval history 55–6, 116
Mellár, Tamás 229
Michnik, Adam 7, 208
MÍEP (Hungarian Justice and Life Party) 86, 95, 97, 193
Minc, Alain 113
Miskolc 72, 182
Mislivetz, Ferenc 7
Mock, Alois 35
Moldovans 129
Morvai, Krisztina 174
MSzP (Magyar Szocialista Párt, Hungarian Socialist Party) 8–9, 26–7, 36, 46, 67, 71–3, 85, 96, 97, 99–111, 132–45, 153, 167, 168–9, 194, 195–205, 213, 216

Nádas, Péter 143, 163–4, 179–80
Nagy, Imre 2–6, 12, 17, 20
Nagymaros hydroelectric plant 83
Napi Gazdaság 157
Năstase, Adrian 96, 108
National Bank 229
National Media and Telecommunication Agency 218–19
NATO 114
Németh, Miklós 4, 16, 18, 19, 20, 22, 26, 71, 96, 103
Népszabadság 189

INDEX

Neue Zürcher Zeitung 187
Nobilis, Kristóf 157
Nyers, Rezső 26

Olaszliszka 181–3
Orbán, Viktor 3–4, 8, 45, 67, 101, 104, 123, 128, 136, 138, 140–2, 145, 152, 154, 155, 157, 158, 164–5, 167–78, 203, 205; as Prime Minister 85–97, 105, 106, 114, 122, (since 2010) 115, 207–32
OSCE 217, 218
Oszkó, Péter 203

Pálinkás, József 224
Paskai, Cardinal László 151
Pásztor, Albert 182
Patriotic People's Front 12, 19
Pécs 133, 152, 180–1
Pető, Iván 101
Petőfi, Sándor 190
Petschnig, Zita Mária 95
Poland 24, 25, 153, 203
police 126, 172, 173, 182, 183
polls 43, 68, 101, 181–2, 200, 212, 213
Popper, Sir Karl 130
Postbank 81
Pozsgay, Imre 16, 19–21, 23, 26–8, 32, 38, 153, 193
Princz, Gábor 78
privatisation 73, 77–8
protests (demonstrations, etc.) 18, 32, 40–1, 171, 172–3, 204, 220

Rabár, Ferenc 44–5
Rádai, Eszter 44
radio 46–7, 149–50, 156, 157, 160
Radio Free Europe 24, 160
Radnóti, Sándor 54, 224

Rajk, László 12
Ránki, György 62
refugees 18, 30, 62, 70, 121
Ripp, Zoltán 21, 50, 140
Roma 63, 159, 160, 180–86
Romania 18, 20, 57, 96, 102, 108, 113–14, 117, 120, 121, 127–8, 129
Röpke, Wilhelm 34
Russia 82, 108

Scheppele, Kim Lane 222, 226
Schmid, Ulrich 187–8
Schmidt, Helmut 215
Schmitt, Pál 217
secret service/secret police 23, 32, 35–6, 45, 80–81, 99–101, 150–53, 162–3
Serbia 114, 119, 120–1, 123, 124, 127–8, 129
Simicska, Lajos 158
Simor, András 229
Slota, Ján 125
Slovak National Party 125–6
Slovakia 60, 83, 113–14, 115, 117, 119, 121, 122, 123, 124–7, 240–1
Slovenia 123
Smallholders' Party 24, 36–7, 39, 46, 67, 85, 93
Social Democratic Party 24, 170
Socialist Party, *see* MSzP
Sólyom, László 79, 126–8, 172, 176–8, 244
Soros, George 48
Soviet Union 9–13, 15–16, 20, 22–3, 39, 69, 115, 175, 193
Speder, Zoltán 157
Status Law (2001) 122–3
Stephen, King St 55–6, 116, 127, 214
Suchman, Tamás 73
Switzerland 163

255

INDEX

Szabó, István 152
Szabó, Iván 45, 46
Szarka, László 122
SzDSz (Szabad Demokraták Szövetsége, Alliance of Free Democrats) 9, 24, 25, 27, 35, 37–8, 67, 72–6, 82, 97, 101, 102, 109, 110, 169, 196, 197, 198, 200
Székesfehérvár 191
Szekler hymn 211, 247–8
Széles, Gábor 155, 156, 188
Szepesi, György 152, 243
Szigeti, László 121
Szigetvári, Viktor 197
Szili, Katalin 216, 244
Szögiu, Lajos 181
Szűrös, Mátyás 5, 193

Târgu Mureş (Marosvásárhely) 128
Tatárszentgyörgy 184–5
television 4, 46–7, 149, 153–4, 156, 172–3, 219–20
Thatcher, Margaret 35
theatre 225
Tocqueville, Alexis de 194, 200–1
Tocsik scandal 76, 81–2, 87
Tőkéczki, László 161
Tőkés, Rudolf L. 21, 27
Transylvania 18, 60, 102, 117, 118, 119, 128, 141
Trianon, Treaty of 57, 59, 80, 115, 116–20, 128, 211–12, 231, 238

Ukraine 20, 119, 121, 123
Ungváry, Krisztián 150, 151
Ungváry, Rudolf 189
uprising of 1956 2–6, 8, 12, 20, 22, 69, 172
USA 30, 73, 95, 162, 221

Vajda, Mihály 224
Városliget 1
Varró, Szilvia 182–3
Várszegi, Asztrik 152
Vásárhelyi, Mária 62–4, 116, 158, 163, 164
Vázsonyi, Vilmos 56
Veres, János 137
Veszprém 182–3
Vienna 35
Vienna Awards 120, 234, 240–1
Vitézy, Tamás 156
Vojvodina 60, 119, 120–21
Vona, Gábor 173, 177, 186, 211
Vranitzky, Franz 79

welfare and health 78, 89, 198, 199, 204, 209
Wiesel, Elie 190
World Bank 77, 199
World Federation of Hungarians 124
World War I 57
World War II 30, 57, 176, 178, 189

Yugoslavia 20, 57, 60, 70, 113, 115, 120–1